The Springer Series
on Death and Suicide

ROBERT KASTENBAUM, Ph.D., Series Editor

Dennis Klass, Ph.D., is a professor at Webster University in St. Louis, Missouri. He received his doctorate in the Psychology of Religion from the University of Chicago, and has written over 25 scholarly articles and book chapters on issues in bereavement, self-help groups, and the psychology of religious leadership. With Audrey Gordon, he co-authored *They Need to Know: How to Teach Children about Death* (1979). He has also written many articles for the lay public and is on the editorial board of *Omega, Journal of Death and Dying*.

Dr. Klass is a licensed psychologist in private practice with Resources for Crisis and Change, a group specializing in complex loss and life transition. He has been a consultant for hospitals, hospices, and school systems. Since its inception in 1979, Dr. Klass has been the professional advisor to a local chapter of The Compassionate Friends, a self-help group of bereaved parents. He has conducted workshops for bereaved parents at regional and national Compassionate Friends meetings.

PARENTAL GRIEF

SOLACE AND RESOLUTION

Dennis Klass, Ph.D.

SPRINGER PUBLISHING COMPANY
New York

Springer Publishing Company, Inc.
536 Broadway
New York, NY 10012

88 89 90 91 92 / 5 4 3 2 1

LIBRARY OF CONGRESS
Library of Congress Cataloging-in-Publication Data

Klass, Dennis.
    Parental grief: solace and resolution/Dennis Klass.
      p. cm.—(The Springer series on death and suicide; 9)
    Bibliography: p.
    Includes index.
ISBN 0-8261-5930-3
    1. Grief. 2. Bereavement—Psychological aspects. 3. Parents—
Psychology. 4. Children—Death—Psychological aspects. 5. Parent
and child. I. Title. II. Series.
    [DNLM: 1. Attitude to Death. 2. Grief. 3. Parent–Child
Relations. W1 SP685p v. 9 / BF 575 . G7 K63p]
BF575 . G7K55 1988
155 . 9'37—dc19
DNLM/DLC
for Library of Congress   88-4889
                                                   CIP

Printed in the United States of America

To
The St. Louis Compassionate Friends

Contents

APPENDIXES

Acknowledgments

Many people have helped me try to understand the dynamics of parental bereavement. The St. Louis chapter of The Compassionate Friends allowed me to listen as the members struggled to find words adequate to their sorrow and as they found ways of helping each other toward resolution. Conversations with Beth Shinners, Marie Hoeppner, Janalee Tomaseski-Heinemann, Mary Peach, and Dee Berman helped to formulate and then to reformulate the questions. Three papers, later reworked into this book, were presented in the St. Louis Study Group in Applied Psychoanalysis. The members of the group, William Caspary, Nadia Ramsey, Gerald Isenberg, David Hadas, Jane Loevinger, Paul Roth, Steven Post, Marilyn Wechter, George Shulman, and Joseph Loewenstein, were kindly critical in ways that allowed me to let the ideas grow and develop. Robert Wilke and Beth Shinners read successive revisions of the book. Their criticism and questions were invaluable. Long case discussions with Samuel Marwit and Kenneth Russ opened me to many of the less obvious dynamics of bereavement. My wife Carol read and critiqued the first attempts in a way that helped give direction to the book. As the project progressed, she encouraged me during the dry spells and helped me keep the focus. Saturday breakfasts were often book-talk time.

A great deal of the illustrative material is from Compassionate Friends newsletters around the country. Most of them were signed by the authors. I have taken small parts in a way that conforms to fair use but, except where the authors asked that their names be used, I did not include them because I did not want to attach my own labels to specific individuals in print, and I also wanted to be responsible for any misreading I might have done. I do want, however, to thank publicly national board members Thomas O'Hare and Art Peterson for their encouragement, and St. Louis chapter leaders Margaret Gerner, Judy Hanley, Dean Young, Phyllis and Hyman Eisenberg, Pat Donelon, Dorothy Gerner, Claire McGaughey, Warren and Lois Altman, Betty Meyerpeter, Mary Decker, Vera Babb, Harry and Tahm Reed, Jacque Stockhausen, Sue Shelley, and the newer leaders who have followed them. Their imprint is on every word of the book, and it is to them that the book is dedicated.

Introduction

A baby is born. As the child is placed on the mother's stomach, a new phase of her life begins. She is different. She is a mother. In the delivery room, the father too knows he has changed. Is it a boy? Is it a girl? The answer to this first question will set the tone of the parents' new life, for the child is born into a world of hopes and expectations. A daughter, a new woman in the father's life; a love to be melded into the love he has for his wife and for his mother. A daughter, the continuation of the bond the mother has with her own mother. A boy, a new addition to the men in the family and dreams of companionship and accomplishment.

The house changes. Dressing table and crib take their place, as do the diaper pail and formula. The rhythm changes too. Feedings and naps mark the hours. Later the hours will be set by bedtime stories and snacks, still later by school, sports, and lessons, and later still by dates and jobs. The child is now a consideration in every decision the parents make.

There is a new bond between the parents. They share the excitement of a new tooth, a bicycle mastered, a book read, a school honor, a college scholarship. And they share the frustrations and fears of a high fever, a temper tantrum, a failure at school, a late-night coming home.

Sometimes the child brings conflicts between parents. A mother at home with three small children blurts out: "If it weren't for you I could be free." A father finds more comfortable companionship with his friends. Parents' expectations of each other clash. Sometimes the child is the only thing holding them together.

There are joys and disappointments. She practiced all summer to be a cheerleader but does not make the first cut. His teeth grew crooked and he is self-conscious about his braces. She and her mother fought as they shopped for the right prom dress. She is beautiful as she poses for pictures with her date in the back yard. He grew sullen when he got to high school and often withdrew to his room to listen to music. He was arrested for drug possession but is making progress in his treatment program.

The phone rings. There has been a car accident. Please come to the hospital. The receptionist ushers the parents into a small room and says the doctor will be in to see them. Somehow, the parents already know. The resident is nervous. He says the spinal cord was too damaged. There was nothing to be done. He would like to take the kidneys and eyes for transplant.

The parents have begun a new journey. It will take several years. At the end of it, they will be as changed from their former selves as they were after the birth of the child. This book is an attempt to describe that journey.

BACKGROUND

The work upon which this book is based began in 1979 when I was asked to help in a short-term support group for bereaved parents. That group led to the founding of the St. Louis chapter of The Compassionate Friends. I was asked to be the professional advisor. I had worked with dying and bereaved people since 1968 when, as a graduate student, I assisted in the Death and Dying seminar led by Elisabeth Kubler-Ross and Carl Nighswonger at the University of Chicago Hospitals. Audrey Gordon and I had done videotape-based research on the ways people transcend in their religious encounter with death (Klass & Gordon, 1978), and we had written a book for parents and teachers on teaching children about death (Gordon & Klass, 1979). But I was unprepared for what I experienced with groups of bereaved parents. Clearly, here was a grief that had a different quality from what I had seen before.

The first lesson was that I could not truly share their experience, for theirs was a world I could not imagine for myself. I could at moments think of my own death—a sometimes frightening and sometimes welcome prospect—but my mind kept me from contemplating for very long the death of one of my sons. It was their lives that even in my most depressed moments gave meaning to mine. When I allowed myself to think about the possibility of their deaths, it interfered with my parenting. I did not want to give the children freedom to face the dangers that are a normal part of growing up.

I attended the Compassionate Friends meetings each month. As other chapters were formed in different parts of the city, and for particular kinds of death—parents of infants, parents of murdered children—I attended two and sometimes three meetings a month. But I was an outsider. They were members of a club I hope never to join. I could be useful to them with group process skills, as a contact with community resources, and as a sounding board for the leaders as they learned by trial and error. I could, as an outsider, also reflect their thoughts. For several years I wrote a monthly column for the local newsletter in which I tried to speak to their condition. I called the column "Reflections," for I was trying to mirror their lives in a way that would be helpful to them. The feedback from those "Reflections" allowed me to begin to understand their grief—not as a grieving parent, but as one who wanted to help.

Early on, I realized that the role of professional advisor was the insider/outsider position of ethnographic research (Becker, 1970; Glaser & Strauss, 1967; Powdermaker, 1966; Wax, 1971; Whyte, 1973). I was a trusted confidant, one who they felt would understand as they shared their lives. But I had to translate their experiential knowledge into my outsider's knowledge. I made research part of my relationship to the group. I was aided early in that task by social work graduate students Beth Shinners, Marie Hoeppner, and Janalee Tomaseski-Heinemann. Beth and Jan became pediatric social workers, Beth with neonates and Jan with cancer patients. Each has long since moved from being a student to being a colleague. Later we were joined by Mary Peach, a hospice social worker, and by Dee Berman, a bereaved parent and psychoanalytically trained social worker.

The data collected from the meetings of The Compassionate Friends is full and rich. Each meeting lasted 2 hours, during which the parents poured out their sorrow and tried to share consolation and help. After the meetings, parents stayed an hour or more talking in pairs or small clusters about shared problems and solutions. If I needed clarification about something, I could ask in the postmeeting coffee time. At social occasions and special meetings I met the surviving children and the families. The trust I had earned with the parents seemed to extend to the larger community, enabling me to understand more.

We began doing interviews with parents soon after the group formed. First it was with parents who had attended one or two meetings and had not returned. Then we did systematic interviews with those who attended regularly. Later we did interviews with parents who had not used The Compassionate Friends. Over the years, we were able to follow many people, from right after the child's death, through the acute times, and into the resolution. Many parents became old friends, whose lives were to be caught up on when they returned for a holiday candlelight memorial or came for an interview.

In the newsletters, parents wrote for each other about their grief and about their resolutions. For many, writing was a part of resolution, as they found putting their thoughts on paper clarified their thinking and made the emotions less frightening. Those newsletter poems and articles have been invaluable data, for they were conscious efforts to describe the authors' inner worlds.

A final strand of data has emerged from a limited private practice of psychotherapy. The individual complexity of the grief could be more fully explored in that setting, and my observations from meetings, newsletters, and interviews could be checked with those of the bereaved parents in the consulting room.

I have tried to maintain a coherent theoretical framework in this book. In ethnographic research the data is the primary basis for the development of *grounded theory* (Glaser & Strauss, 1967). The theoretical framework of this book is not pure grounded theory, for I have benefited greatly from spirited inner dialogue with authors whom I have cited throughout the text. At the same time, however, the theoretical framework is grounded theory in the sense that I have tried to let the full range and depth of the data be criteria for interpretation.

Before I started listening to bereaved parents, I knew most of the current theoretical models of grief. During the time I was doing this study, several important books about particular models of grief were published. But often my data did not fit the explanations based on those models. I found, for example, that the symptomatic descriptions of grief put forward by Lindemann (1979) and his successors were true. Most of the parents to whom I have listened should have been classified as among Lindemann's most severe cases. However, Lindemann's symptomatic analysis did not help me understand the long term changes in the self that I observed. Models that find resolution in integration of the loss (for example, Weizman & Kamm, 1985) seemed right, but did not help me understand the intricate workings of that resolution within the social-support network, the complex life history of each individual, and the many symbol systems by which the life history of the individual is integrated with the social environment. The model put forward by scholars following John Bowlby (1980) shows changes in the social self, but excludes identification from the process of healthy grief; yet I found identification to be a part of most resolutions of parental bereavement that I observed. The modern psychoanalytic model of grief (Volkan, 1981) helped me to see the inner processes in grief that the Bowlby group excludes. Horton's book on solace (1981) helped me expand the psychoanalytic model in a way that made it better fit the data.

The most consistent criticism of the early drafts of the book was that I became too involved in discussions of theoretical issues. The criticism was well taken, for I wanted to write a book on parental grief, not on grief theory. Where I thought it might help the reader, I have included discussion of the theoretical literature, especially in Chapters 2, 3, and 8. As a way of indicating some of the problems parental grief raises in contemporary models of grief, I have written Appendix II, delineating John Bowlby's model of grief and the problem of identification.

I put off writing this book for a long time because I did not think I understood parental grief well enough. Over the last 2 years, however, some helpful ideas have solidified, and now it is time for this book. I am still an outsider, and I am still not sure I can really understand what it must be like to have one's child die. But I have tried. If the book helps others to understand better, I will have succeeded.

I

The Process and Resolution of Parental Grief

Introduction to Part I

Part I is a systematic description of parental grief. Parental grief is different from other griefs because the bond of an individual to her or his child is unique. Chapter 1 explores the nature of parenting and parental grief. The themes of identification, differentiation, and competence help us understand both the dynamics of parenting and of parental grief. The resolution of parental grief may be best understood as the achievement of a new social equilibrium and a new psychic equilibrium. Chapter 2 describes the means by which parents achieve an equilibrium in their social world. The chapter relies heavily on the grief model developed by John Bowlby and his followers. Chapter 3 describes the means by which parents achieve an inner equilibrium. The concept of solace provides the core around which the chapter is constructed. The chapter relies heavily on the psychoanalytic model of grief, especially as developed by Vamik Volkan. Chapter 4 portrays the lives of four of the parents we interviewed. The dynamics described in the first three chapters can be seen as they interplay in individual lives.

1

Parenting and Parental Grief

PARENTING

The quality of parental grief is unique because the bond the parent has with the child is unique. The sense of selfhood involved in parenting is a central part of our being. The bond with the child is intertwined with many other important bonds in the parent's life. The obligations to which parents commit themselves are grounded in the defining ideals of the society. When the child dies, there is a break in a very intricate web of connections. As an introduction to parental grief, we will examine some elements of parenting. Three terms can orient us: *identification, differentiation,* and *competence.* Then we will look briefly at parenting turned pathological—in child abuse and neglect, where the issues of identification, differentiation, and competence can be clearly seen.

Identification

Parenthood is a developmental process. The experience of becoming a parent activates two sets of largely unconscious memories: (1) the memory of how one was parented, and (2) the memory of what it was like to be a small child. To the parent, the child represents both the parent as a child and the parent's parent (Benedek, 1959, 1970, 1975; Miller, 1981). Bearing a child may mark one's transition into adulthood; thus the parts of the self that were associated with childhood may be put on the child. Within all that individual complexity, there is also the intermingling of the dynamics of both father and mother.

In the early weeks of parenthood, "it is the narcissistic investment of the loving parent in the child which represents a demand on the projected self-expectations" (Benedek, 1970, p.68). The investment in the helpless infant gives the parent a sense of omnipotence,

4

which the infant also feels. In the day to day relationship with the child, however, the parent's feeling of omnipotence is challenged, for "at the same time that they are fostering the intrapsychic child as a hope of their self-realization. . . . the negativistic behavior of the child separates him from the self-system of the parents" thus forcing the parent "to see what he or she does not like within himself (or in significant objects of his present or past)" (Benedek, 1970, p.125). The unconscious, however, guards against too much recognition on the parents' part as "the self assurance of the parent in his motivations toward his child seems to justify his authority (which) helps the parent to repress and deny his fears and anticipations, his unconscious feelings toward the child" (p.126).

Parents retain elements of their early identification with the child throughout the child's life. For better or worse, the child is a reproduction of the parent. The child's success becomes the parents' success and the child's failure the parents' failure.

Identification with the child creates an opportunity for the parent to relive his or her own life through the child's developmental stages. The child's life can be the occasion for the parent to regress.

> [In the regression,] the reworking of childhood conflicts leads to resolving them, i.e., to intrapsychic changes within the parents. It would be difficult to generalize in a meaningful way about the multitudinal psychic resources which support the parents' egos in their functioning. One is rooted in past experience, in the fact that adults can counteract their fears by reliance on their achievements, in their conviction that they were able to overcome their conflicts. The other is the love for the child which maintains the hope that the child will become a better man than his father was. Each parent has to deal in his own way with the positive as well as the negative revelations of himself in the child. (Benedek, 1970, p. 131)

The identification with the child also creates the possibility for the ambivalence within the parent's self to become an ambivalence within the relationship to the child. If, for example, the child is the parent's parent, then difficulties in the relationship between the parent and the parent's parent become difficulties within the relationship of parent to child. If the child is both the parent's best self and the parent's less-than-good self, then unresolved conflicts in the parent's psyche play themselves out in the bond with the child. We can see ambivalences early in parenting. Studies of the bonding process between parents and infants have noted differences in mothers' ability to respond to the child's signals (Ainsworth & Bell, 1970; Stayton & Ainsworth, 1973). The differences appear to be related to the ambivalence in the mother's bond with the child. As early as age 12 months, ambivalences in the parent–child attachment can be seen.

Differentiation

One of the psychological tasks of parenting is to counter indentification, to separate the child from the self, and to hold the child as an individual distinct from the self. When the child is experienced as being distinct, then the parent empathizes with the child and tries to meet the child's needs and desires on the child's terms rather than responding to the needs of and desires of the child as if they were the needs and desires of the parent. Miriam Elson (1984), in an analysis of Kohut's development of narcissism, describes the task of parenthood as a progressive movement away from projection and toward empathy.

> Parents who are able to function in empathic merger with the forming self of the child, allow the use of their psychic organization as the child's own, and at the same time, phase specifically in tune with the child's changing needs, accept the child's separateness, a center of perception and initiative. Thus, support of the forming and firming narcissism in the child is the developmental *task* of parenthood. The continuing transformation of their own narcissism is the developmental *process* of parenthood. (p. 299)

She notes, however, that many parents are not able to complete the process:

> History is strewn with the locked combat of parents and children in this arena when the immaturity and rigidity of the parents' narcissism exacts behavior from the child which will exactly mirror the parents' needs. Unable to be free of a noxious merger, the child cannot elaborate skills and talents which will permit the expression of ambitions to realizable goals which stem from centrally perceived initiative. (p. 303)

Competence

From the beginning, parents strive for a sense of competence in their relationship with the child. Competence is difficult in the early days and weeks of parenting, for the needs of the infant are indistinct to the parent and the infant's crying can be experienced as a reproach for incompetence, just as the child's sleeping contentedly can seem a reward. Susan Goldberg (1979), reviewing the research on bonding, notes that the conceptual model that seems to account best for the data is an interactive model in which the "parent-infant interaction system appears to be one of finely-tuned reciprocal behaviors that are mutually complementary and appear to be preadapted to facilitate social interaction" (p. 214). The motivation on the part of both infant and parent, Goldberg says, seems to be a sense of competence, defined as a need to cope effectively with the environment. In infants, competence is seen as play, exploration, and curiosity. After all, why else should an infant learn to walk when the only early reward is the pain from falling? Part of the adult's sense of competence may be the ability to live up to the obligations of parenting bonds, which are different from the contractual obligations with the spouse. If adults do not feel competent in the parental role, they feel a sense of failure. They feel helpless and in panic. Children help the parent feel competent by being readable (giving clear signals), predictable (responding in similar situations in similar manner), and responsive (being able to react to external stimuli).

Social Support

Both the ability to hold the child as distinct from the self and the ability to feel competent in the parental role are in large measure dependent on the parents having an adequate social support system. Anisfeld and Lipper (1983) measured the quality of the bond between mother and child by measuring the mother's attempts to interact with the child (looking at infant in face, smiling at infant, vocalizing to infant, touching, kissing, stroking, rocking, inspecting, and attempting to elicit response from infant). Mothers with weak social support had the lowest affective contact scores, whereas mothers with strong social support had the highest scores. Anisfeld and Lipper note that the sense of competence can be raised by compensating for the lack of social support.

We can observe such social support in the common ritual by which a new baby is introduced into a family, a work group, or a neighborhood. The child is passed around from person to person as each tries to establish a positive interaction with the baby. The parent's bond to the baby is strengthened as the baby creates a lesser bond with each member of the group. Then, as the baby tires from the effort to respond to the other adults, the baby is handed back to the parent, and parent's role as primary bond and competent caretaker is affirmed.

Pathological Parenting

Pathology often teaches us a great deal about normalcy. We see in the literature describing child abuse and neglect the multiple investment of the parent in the child and the problems of experiencing the child as same as the self and as apart from the self. The issue of competence also plays a central role in abuse and neglect, for the parent is identified with the parent's own parents, and the new baby is experienced, through reverse identification, as having the attributes of the parent as a small child (Miller, 1983). Steele's (1980) description of the interactions that lead to the moment of abuse puts in bold relief the issues of identification, differentiation, and competence.

> On a deeper psychological level, the events begin with the parent's identification of the cared for infant as a need-gratifying object equivalent to the parent who will replace the lack in the abusive parent's own being-parented experience. Since the parent's past tells him that those to whom he looked for love were also the ones who attacked him, the infant is also perceived as a critical parental figure. . . . The perception of being criticized stirs up the parent's feelings of being inferior. It also increases the frustration of his need for love, and anger mounts. At this time there seems to be a strong sense of guilt, a feeling of helplessness and panic becomes overwhelming, and the haziness is most marked. Suddenly a shift in identification occurs. The superego identification with the parent's own punitive parent takes over. The infant is perceived as the parent's own bad childhood itself. The built-up aggression is redirected outward, and the infant is hit with full superego approval. (p. 59)

In the case of neglect, in which the child "fails to thrive," there is a similar pattern, but the mother is working from depression rather than aggression; that is, she is almost without a sense of competence.

> There is a tendency, however, for failure-to-thrive mothers to show a higher degree of depression, a lower self-esteem, and poorer coping ability in general. Not rarely do they take very poor care of themselves physically and neglect their personal appearance. . . . Their response to the infant is that the situation is hopeless, that the baby is not really worth caring for and is, therefore, significantly neglected and underfed. This misperception of the infant is related unconsciously to the mother's own perception of herself as a worthless human being. (p. 65)

Videotaped interviews with these mothers show them unable to understand the child apart from themselves. In one tape, the child is hungry and reaching for a bottle, which the mother holds in her hand. The interviewer asks why the child is crying. The mother replies that she does not know, but that probably the baby does not like her because she is a bad person.

The child is thus both self and other. Parenting is at once a great personal achievement and a strong threat to self-esteem. The child is a recapitulation of long-standing character and conflicts, and at the same time the child is a new opportunity to fulfill the character and resolve the conflicts. The child is born into and lives out a world of hopes, dreams, and expectations. When a child dies, the whole intricate bond between parent and child must be resolved.

CHARACTERISTICS OF PARENTAL BEREAVEMENT

Parental bereavement is complex and may be described from many different perspectives. The viewpoint of this book is the long-range resolution. Although there is a good deal of variation, parental bereavement often takes 3 or more years to resolve, although the first year is characterized by more dramatic symptomatic expression of the grief. We will first look at the symptoms of the early period of grief, and then we will look at two longer lasting characteristics of parental grief: (1) the loss of a part of the self and (2) the loss of a sense of competence and power.

Symptomatic Expressions of Grief

The death of a child represents the loss of a significant everyday interaction in the parent's world, and thus the death involves a significant loss of psychobiological regulation. As Lindemann (1979) noted in his 1944 study, the early months of grief are characterized by disorientation and emotional numbness, volatile emotional swings, loss of appetite, inability to sleep, and loss of short-term memory. For many bereaved parents, these symptoms of the early months are an added burden. One of the first questions parents ask in self-help groups and counseling is: "Is this normal or am I going crazy?" One of the easier tasks in working with bereaved parents is to assure them that what they are experiencing is normal and that they need not waste energy on the fear of craziness.

Recent biological research on grief has shown a range of physiological changes in the endocrine, immune, autonomic nervous, and cardiovascular systems. There is good evidence that those changes lower the body's defenses against many diseases (Osterweis, Solomon, & Green, 1984). In his presidential address to the American Psychosomatic Society, Myron Hofer (1984) offered an explanation for the changed biology in grief:

> We know that in adult animals and humans, homeostatic regulatory systems remain under environmental control to a certain degree. . . . Thus, it

may not be too far-fetched to ask whether it is possible that some of the changes following human bereavement might result from withdrawal of specific sensorimotor regulators hidden within the many complex interactions of the relationship that has ended. (p. 188)

In other words, the death may occasion physiological changes in the parent simply because interaction with the child was one means by which the parent's hormonal balance was maintained.

For many parents the bond with the child is the most significant interactive relationship they have. Further, the death of the child creates problems within the social environment. All the family members were linked to the child in a matrix of interlocking roles. Each element in that matrix must now be redefined in terms of the missing child (Herz, 1980; Turner, 1970). Some of those interactive relationships are simply a part of day-to-day life. If a dead child had been the practical joker in the family, an important aspect is now missing from the conversation. Some of the interactions have more long term significance for parents (Edelstein, 1984). One woman we interviewed had a difficult time finding a sense of identity as an adolescent. When she had a baby, she could build a social self on the role of mother. She reported that when the child died, "I started dressing different. When J. was alive, I chose things that a mother should wear. When she died, that wasn't there any more."

In their larger community, the death of a child changes the parents' daily interaction patterns. The bereaved parent in this culture is in a taboo or marginal social role. One parent remembered:

I was in the grocery store a few days after my daughter's first birthday after her death. I ran into a friend who used to help with the girl scout troop my daughter was in. She said, "How are you?" I said, "I'm doing better today." She said, "I didn't know you had been sick."

It is not surprising that we find parental bereavement involves extended symptomatic expression, for loss of the attachment is the loss of a major interactive regulator within an environment in which many other interactions have significantly changed. Sanders (1980) and Clayton, Desmarais, and Winokur (1968) found bereaved parents show more intense symptoms than did individuals bereaved by other kinds of loss. Owen, Fulton, and Markusen (1982–1983) found the death of a child to be more debilitating than the death of a spouse or parent. A mother whose child was hit by a car recalled that for the first year:

Every day I cried. Every day it hurt. I remember really being weak and sick. It feels like somebody punched you in the stomach. The pain would just well up and I would let it be there. Then I'd cry and try to force it down so that I could go on. It also helped to drink wine. But I didn't do that to any excess. I never got drunk or needed any sedatives.

Another remembered:

When I would drive I would say, "Maybe I can have an accident so I can be with V." I would stand in the shower with the water running and just moan with tears pouring down my face. I was just that way for a while—up and down, up and down. I got angry with people. The anger was, like, if I'd only had more help, some more support, then I could have had more time with V. I resented every time I had to work while she was sick because I was fixing seven meals a day, and she was on steroids and starving. I resented the fact that I was so tired because I stayed up day and night. People thought I was real together—but if they only knew what was going on in my head!

Although there has been some research on widows that shows fewer symptoms after anticipated deaths than after unanticipated deaths (Glick, Weiss, & Parkes, 1974), our observations support Miles (1985), who found that although there were radical differences between bereaved parents and a control group of nonbereaved parents, there were no differences between parents whose children had died of chronic diseases and parents whose children had died in accidents.

The loss of regulators in a stressful world is concretely expressed in problems that seem very practical to others, but which are reported by parents to be of great existential difficulty. Among the problems are how to celebrate holidays and birthdays, what to say when asked how many children do you have, what to do with the child's belongings, and how to respond in interactions with the spouse. A father whose daughter's first birthday since her death was the next week reported:

We had this custom of giving lots of presents to kids on their birthday and for the other one, we would buy an unbirthday present so they wouldn't feel left out. The grandparents always sent a box and there was an unbirthday present in that, too. So a few days ago Beth, O.'s little sister, asked if there were going to be any presents on O.'s birthday this year. I said, "No." She asked why not, and suddenly I just felt this welling up in me and I screamed, "Because dead kids don't get presents." That was uncalled for and I apologized. She is right; we need to do something to remember the day, but I don't know what to do.

Loss of Part of the Self: The Amputation Metaphor

The child is a part of the parent's self, in that the child is the projection of the parent's best image of the self, and the child threatens to be the parent's worst image of the self. The child also represents the ideals of the society that the parent has internalized. Having a child also gives the parent new social value and status in the role of parent. When a child dies, the part of the self that had been given over to the child is lost. Freud gave scant attention to the meaning of parenthood, but when his daughter died, he wrote to a friend:

> For years I was prepared for the loss of my sons (in war); and now comes that of my daughter. Since I am profoundly irreligious there is no one I can accuse, and I know there is nowhere to which any complaint could be addressed. "The unvarying circle of a soldier's duties" and the "sweet habit of existence" will see to it that things go on as before. Quite deep down I can trace the feelings of a deep narcissistic hurt that is not to be healed. (Jones, 1957, Vol. 3, p. 20)

That sense of deep narcissistic hurt appears to be the basis of the metaphor of amputation that we find so often in working with bereaved parents. All grief contains the sense that a piece of the self has been cut out, but it appears that this sense is longer lasting in parents after the death of a child. One father in The Compassionate Friends expressed it as, "It is like I lost my right arm, but I am learning to live as a one-armed man." The analogy of amputation offers an interesting insight into the difference between parental grief and other forms of grief. Parkes compared the grief responses of widows and amputees. He found that although widows showed more distress in the first year, the distress tended to diminish after a year. The equivalent distress reported by amputees remained unchanged in the follow-up year (Parkes, 1975). Bereaved parents seem more like amputees than widows, yet most literature on the duration of grief is derived from studies with widows.

A parent who seems to have had experience with amputees wrote an extended newsletter article on the parallels between amputation and parental bereavement:

> After the initial bereavement, the parent just like the amputee, must begin the long, arduous task of accepting his loss, and begin therapy he/she needs to become a useful person again. . . . Of course, life will never be the same ever again . . . but with time and work your life will take on a new, much different quality. For example, the amputee knows he can't run up steps two at a time but takes his satisfaction in knowing that he CAN make it to the top in his own way, even if it takes longer. . . .

> For the amputee, the raw bleeding stump heals and the physical pain does go away. But he lives with the pain in his heart knowing his limb will not grow back. He has to learn to live without it. He rebuilds his life around his loss. We bereaved parents must do the same.

Parental bereavement is a permanent condition. It is not something to be gotten over, for it is an enduring change in the self. In their study of grief symptoms in mothers who lost neonates, Peppers and Knapp (Knapp, 1986; Peppers & Knapp, 1980) found that they could not report a reestablishment of previous functioning. They could define the end of grief as lower levels of some symptoms:

> . . . reminders of the loss, such as the nursery and the baby's things, can be confronted without emotions bubbling to the surface. The misery and despair begin to fade. The self-doubt, guilt, the anger, the bitterness fade. Appetite returns, sleeping problems are overcome, strength returns, irritability diminishes. . . . Depression subsides. . . . they can once again fondle babies . . . and . . . they can have discussions of the loss without the worry they may be "upsetting." (Peppers & Knapp, 1980, pp. 45-46)

But there is more to the resolution of grief than the relief from symptoms. Peppers and Knapp (1980) found what they called the *shadow grief*, which is a sense of loss that the parents will carry for the rest of their lives. This grief beyond symptoms, they said:

> does not manifest itself overtly; it does not debilitate the individual. No effort is required to cope with it. In fact, a fairly established normal existence is usually resumed. On the surface, most observers would say that the grief has been resolved and the individual has resumed a normal life. (p. 47)

Except for their comment that no effort is required to cope with the longer lasting changes brought on by the death of a child, Peppers and Knapp could be describing any parental grief, not just the neonatal loss they studied. Grief is not over when the symptoms subside, for a part of the self is missing and it remains missing all their days.

A sense of the missing part of the self remains as an empty historical track, which we find life-long in most bereaved parents. It is as if, when the child was born, the entire life of the child was programed into the parent's ongoing life. Parents report that they think thoughts like, "He would be 18 years old and graduating from high school this year." The empty historical track is most painful at

times that would have had significance in the life of a child. Nancy
Brubaker wrote a newsletter poem about her child's birthday

> Walking, talking and asking "why? . . .
> You would've been three today.
> Running, jumping and trying to fly . . .
> you would've been three today.
> Saying hello and waving goodbye . . .
> You would've been three today.
> Playing house and baking mud pies . . .
> You would've been three today.

An examination of renewed discomfort in bereaved parents often
reveals that the trigger is a child of the age the deceased child would
have been, or developmental events in which the deceased child
would have been participating at the time of the discomfort.

Bereaved parents often remind themselves, "When your parent
dies you lose your past. When your child dies, you lose your future."
A child is one of the kinds of immortality a person finds in the world.
In ancient times, to die childless was the worst fate, for the meaning
of the individual life was within the continuation of the lineage. That
old feeling remains. A mother whose only son was killed five years
after her husband died of cancer reported that her husband's father,
on first hearing the news of his grandson, said, "Well, there goes the
family name."

In the modern world, the future is more individualized, but the
child remains the center of a constellation of meanings to which other
constellations of meanings are subordinated. Some people find fulfillment in a career or in a position in the community. But often a part of
that fulfillment is providing status and opportunity for their child.
When the child dies, that part of the self is lost. A single woman
whose only child died reported:

> I was proud of the job I had. I did it well, and got good feedback from my
> boss. But when K. died, it didn't seem to make any difference any more. I
> remember when I got a promotion I thought, "I can hardly wait to tell K."
> And she was great. She baked a cake the next day after school and we
> celebrated. I got another promotion after she died, and it just didn't mean
> anything. I thought a long time about quitting.

Loss of Competence and Power: Guilt

The sense of parental competence and sacred obligation is seriously
challenged by the death of a child. "You are supposed to be able to

protect your child," one father said. "But I couldn't protect him from doing one foolish thing and that one act cost him his life. Still, I feel like a failure as a father. I feel so helpless." Father's Day brought on this thought in a newsletter about the role of the father and the difference between intellectual and emotional understanding.

> One of the many mixed feelings a father will have on Father's Day will be one of failure—failure as a protector of his child who has died. The roles of protector and father are synonymous. The father's duty is both to love and to protect that child from harm. A man may intellectually know he did his best; but the child, his charge, is still balefully absent on this Father's Day.

Competence is such a major issue in parental bereavement because it was a major issue in parenting. A newsletter editorial reflected on "the myth of perfect parenthood" as it contributes to the pain of parental bereavement:

> The feeling of worthlessness is strong in many bereaved parents. I believe that the myth of Perfect Parenthood that is deeply set in us is one of the main causes. We expect that we will raise perfect children, provide them with the very best we can afford, and most of all, see that they are safe and secure in their lives. Then when the unspeakable happens and our child dies, we feel we have failed totally and completely. . . .
> Not one of us has ever said, "I expect to be the perfect parent," but on all sides of us, it is implied that we should be. The television and advertising media are big contributors to this myth. . . . We ourselves expect to do a better job of rearing our children than our parents did. All around us, other parents seem to be doing a better job with their children than we are. . . . Even before our child died, many of us felt inadequate as parents at times, but when our child died, we saw ourselves as total failures. Our unconscious minds told us we were not perfect parents, so therefore our child was dead. We failed. We were worthless.

The sense of the loss of power and competence is often experienced as guilt. It is not, however, the guilt from the sin of commission. That is, it is not guilt at having violated a prohibition. Rather it is guilt at not having lived up to the expectations of the sacred obligations of parenthood. "Guilt feelings in bereaved parents arise from a deep sense of helplessness in not having been able to prevent the child's suffering and death and from a sense of personal responsibility for the child's well-being" (Miles & Demi, 1986, p. 100). They were supposed to protect their child, to provide the child with a long life, to give the child happiness, to give the society a person worthy of the highest ideals of the society, and to complete in the child that which they had been unable to complete in themselves. When the child dies, they are shown to be powerless.

Guilt can be experienced as a general feeling of failure, or it can be particularized into a specific search for "What did I do wrong?" that brought on the child's death. In some cases, the care of the child during a long illness can provide the material by which the sense of competence can be extended after the death (Mulhern, Lauer, & Hoffman, 1983). But that sense of competence is not reasserted easily; even in those cases where the care is exemplary, after the children's deaths the parents question whether they were good enough. In one case, in which the social worker described the parents as "absolutely heroic in the way they treated that child," the father had quit his job to be with the child full time along with the mother. They spent day and night at the hospital. Yet a few weeks after the child died, the mother remembered a time when:

> I was taking a nap when she was given a shot. I must have been too tired to wake up, so I was not holding her when they gave the injection. I woke up when she was crying. I was not there when she needed me. I know it is not rational, but somehow I feel I let her down, and that if I had really given it all I had, we could have saved her.

In cases of sudden deaths the question of preventability of the death is often a major topic in work with bereaved parents. Larry Bugan (1979) has noted that the duration and intensity of grief is a function of the degree of perceived preventability. Often parents find themselves recreating an accident with miniature cars, pacing off the distances at the accident site, or going over and over the events leading up to the death. The sense of competence has been challenged, and parents seem to need to resolve the specifics of that challenge early in the grief.

An interesting variation of competence and guilt is found in those parents of children who die of genetic disorders. They may believe, for instance, that if either the father and mother had conceived a child with another person, the baby would have been fine. But the couple's particular genetic combination created the condition that led to their child's death. Their love for each other therefore seems ill-starred.

The guilt of helplessness can merge with other guilt in the parent's psyche. The child's death might be a punishment for the parent's sins. There are few parents who do not regress to childlike thoughts of retributive punishment (Piaget, 1965) as they wonder why evil has come upon them. When a child dies, it is as though it is a punishment, but for what? There is at least an answer to the question of "why?" when the death was caused by the parent's moral offenses. One woman we interviewed sometimes thought that the boy who died was not her husband's child, for she had been unfaithful once in her marriage, around the time of the conception. She had also been sexually active with her husband at that time. The thought that the child was not her husband's had created great ambivalence in her parenting. The guilt now extended the ambivalence into the grief.

CONCLUSION

How does a person find resolution to a loss so central in the human psyche and so intertwined with other bonds within the parent's life? After the death of a child, the parent faces two tasks. First, the parent must learn to live again in a world made poorer by the death of the child. That means not simply severing the tie with the child, but growing and changing the way one is in the world. The second task is retaining the bond with the child by internalizing the inner representation of the child in a way that brings solace. The next two chapters will explore those two tasks. Chapter 2 will explore how parents learn to live in the changed world. Chapter 3 will explore the internalization of the child in the ongoing life of the parent.

2

Achieving Social Equilibrium

The death of a child creates two disequilibria. First, there is a disequilibrium between the self and the social world, for the death of a child radically changes the social environment in which the parent lives. Second, there is a disequilibrium in the inner life of the parent, for the child who died was part of the parent's self. The resolution of parental bereavement is achieved when bereaved parents reach new equilibria in these two areas. This chapter addresses the means by which bereaved parents adapt to their changed social environment. Chapter 3 discusses parents' transformation of the inner representation of the child in order to gain solace.

SOCIAL EQUILIBRIUM

To find a positive resolution to parental grief is not simply to return to *status quo ante*. Parental bereavement is a permanent condition. One of the consistent themes we have heard from bereaved parents is that the resolution of their grief is not simply cutting the attachment to the child and going on with new attachments in their lives. Rather, they speak strongly of something about themselves that is changed. They are not the same person they were before the child died. As they reconstruct their model of the self, so too they reconstruct their way of interacting within the social environment.

Parents do not "get over" the death of a child, but they do go on living. A parent whose child had been dead for 5 years said at the end of our interview:

> I guess it's that same old question in my head: "Have I really resolved anything?" I have learned to live with it. But sometimes I wonder if I have really progressed anywhere. Sometimes I feel I'm back at step one, except

the shock value and the intensity is not there. But the feelings are. The anger and the pain are still there.

Q: I hear you saying that you can go on with your life, that you don't think about it all day, every day, and yet it is so real.

Right. If you look at it as yes, I'm working, yes, I'm functioning, yes, I can go out and have a good time, then I think it is really great because I realize how quick life can end. And every once in a while I get those feelings that life is great.

Q: Is that a good enough resolution for you, or do you want more?

The first thought that came to me is, "That's enough if there is no more." If there's more, then I want it. If there's not another stage, I will be content. I don't ever want to get to the point where I've got no feelings about it.

The resolution of grief as a resolution of an equilibrium between the self and the social environment is the focus of a large body of scholarly work based on John Bowlby's attachment theory (Bowlby, 1969–1980; Parkes, 1972; Parkes & Weiss, 1983; Raphael, 1983; Worden, 1982). In this literature, individuals "recover" from grief "in the sense that they replan their lives and achieve a new and independent level of functioning" (Parkes & Weiss, 1983, p. 5). The resolution of grief, for these writers, is giving up old roles, patterns of interaction, and sources of gratification and finding new ones.

> The longer term adjustments to the loss may involve many processes. The bereaved person may need to grieve, and mourn, and finally relinquish old roles, patterns of interaction, and sources of gratification that were once fulfilled by the person who has died. Only when these are relinquished may new and satisfying roles, interactions, and sources of gratification evolve. (Raphael, 1983, p. 57)

The process by which the new social equilibrium is achieved is multifaceted. It involves intellectual recognition of the death, emotional acceptance of the loss, and a reorganization of the individual's model of the self and the individual's social interactions to match the changed reality (Parkes & Weiss, 1983). Each facet holds special difficulties for bereaved parents.

SOCIAL SUPPORT

The most consistent finding of research on grief is that social support is central to the quality of the resolution. Most of the research has been done with widows (Arling, 1976; Bowling & Cartwright, 1982; Cary, 1979–1980; Lopata, 1973, 1979; Maddison & Walker, 1967;

Parkes, 1972; Parkes & Brown, 1972; Parkes & Weiss, 1983; Raphael, 1983; Sanders, 1980–1981; Silverman, 1986; Vachon et al., 1982). A number of studies on bereaved parents have shown similar results, though the studies are far less extensive (Bourne, 1968; Carr & Knupp, 1985; Forrest, Standish, & Baum, 1982; Kowalski, 1984; Rando, 1986; Spinetta, Swarner, & Sheposh, 1981). One study (Schreimer, Gresham & Green, 1979) showed that so simple a social support as a caring and concerned phone call to the mother from the physician after a stillbirth led to decreased problems in an intervention group, as compared with mothers in the group who had not been called. In another study, Forrest, Standish, and Baum (1982) found that those in a support group did better than those not in a group. It appears that, just as the quality of parenting is enhanced when the new bond is shared within other social bonds, the quality of parental bereavement is enhanced by the same sharing (Kirkley-Best & Kellner, 1982).

There are some needs in the immediate crisis of grief that widows and bereaved parents share. Maddison and Walker (1967), for example, found that widows felt they needed other people who would allow them to vent emotions and to talk, especially about the negative inner representation of the dead husband and the emotional states such as guilt and anger within the inner representations. They found that when widows perceived others as blocking their expressions of negative emotions by minimizing their grief with platitudes or by advising them to forget the grief and get on to their future, the widows reacted angrily. They found that when the widow perceived herself as receiving empathic friendship, she was more likely and more quickly to find positive resolution to her grief. Lehman, Ellard, and Wortman's study (1986), which included both widows and bereaved parents, found that the most helpful social supports were contact with others who had a similar loss, expressions of concern, providing an opportunity to ventilate, and "being there." The most unhelpful attempts at social support were giving advice, encouraging recovery, enforced cheerfulness, and misplaced identification, such as the expression "I know how you feel."

Bereaved parents share with all grievers the need of an empathic, supportive community, but often the social support they find is inadequate. While the parents strive to comprehend the reality of the loss, they find themselves within a social system that refuses to assimilate the truth that the child has died and that the parent has been wounded to the core of the self. The parents need to express feelings in order to understand and then to resolve the emotions that accompany the death of the child. But they search through their world to find a few people with whom they can share the love they have for the dead child and with whom they can share the anger, guilt, and frustrations of their loss.

The resolution of parental bereavement is not simply replacing the investment in the child with other investments. Rather, the resolution of parental grief is a reorganization of the self and the self's interactions within the environment (Edelstein, 1984). Parents need to master the practical issues of the role of bereaved parent. They must, for example, learn to laugh in a world that now includes abiding sadness. The parents must learn to live in a world in which their control and competence have been radically challenged.

Each element of the reorganized self puts the parent in a new relationship with those around them, for as they resolve their grief, they are not who they used to be. In the best of cases, significant people in the social environment will affirm the new self; but just as often, others demand that the parent remain the same as before. The ability of the parents to resolve the grief and find a new equilibrium in the social world may depend on the degree of flexibility they find in the social world as much as it depends on the degree of flexibility the parent can find in the self.

The social environment includes the child's other parent. Although the resolution of grief depends on social support, each parent is radically alone in grief. The reorganization of the self within the resolution of grief may open the parents to a new depth in the marriage. On the other hand, it is possible that the marriage will be inadequate for the new self the parent has discovered while resolving the grief. The new equilibrium in a changed world brings a new equilibrium in the relationship with the child's other parent.

COMPREHENDING THE REALITY

In the months right after the death, the parents have difficulty assimilating the reality of the child's death. Each new situation that would have included the child must be processed with the understanding that the child is not there. One of our interviewees reflected on the question of the hardest part of her grief.

> The hardest part—I think reality, realizing the finality of it. Realizing that it is real, it's true. Living day to day without her. Holidays.
> Q: How does that sense of reality come to you?
> One place is in my career planning. When I'm planning to do things I

might stop to think, maybe I can't do that, but then I say, "Oh, I can do that, I don't have to worry about how doing things like traveling will affect K. anymore." I moved into an apartment. It had two bedrooms, and I thought, "This bedroom should be hers." I kept thinking, "She should really be a part of this." Do you know what I mean? Immediately when I make plans for things, especially happy things, I always think she should have been part of them. It certainly is not as painful as it was in the beginning, but yet it still is a little cloudy.

Special days that would have included the child are difficult, for each of the days comes with the message that the child is dead. "I didn't know a year had so many holidays," said one bereaved mother, "Thanksgiving, Christmas, Valentine's Day, Easter, Mother's Day, Father's Day, and his birthday and my birthday. Every time I think that he is not here and it hurts all over again."

If the parent does not see the body, the question of whether the death really happened may remain nagging. One woman reported:

She died of a highly communicable disease. They didn't know that's what she had when she died, so I could have gone to see her in the emergency room after she died, but I didn't. I now regret that decision, because they didn't embalm her when they found out what she had. They just sealed her in a plastic bag in the casket. So I never saw her dead. Sometimes I still think that's not really her in there. I go to the grave and wonder if she is really there. I called the undertaker and asked if he was sure it was B. that he put in the casket. He said she was the only teenage girl to die at St. Francis Hospital that week, and the only body they picked up at St. Francis that week, so it had to be her. I know it is her, but it took me a long time. I think it would have been better if I had seen her.

In the first few weeks, and for many parents the first six months, the shock is so great that their system shuts down. Unless the funeral has special meaning because of their religious background, we have found that many of our interviewees have no memory of the funeral a year later. The whole time immediately after the death is hazy for them, though they remember with astonishing clarity the details of the accident or final illness. This is especially true if there are poor communications in the home or in the immediate family. One of our interviewees said:

It was a period of time that I didn't go anywhere. I didn't really do much of anything. I don't remember a lot. I just kind of existed. Inside it was like, "You are to blame for all this," and I couldn't get it out. I didn't have anybody to talk to. Then about October, one of the doctors told my husband that he had to get me out and away from it. I was in a total depression. That's when they sent me to my mother's in New York and I stayed there a month. It was just kind of like one day, then, I just woke up and I realized that I had a family and a life that I had to start putting back together if it was going to work. So I told my parents that I wanted to go home.

Because symptoms of grief resemble those of clinical depression, we find too often that physicians, whose powers to cure have been challenged by the death of the child, prescribe drugs. Other parents, who have previously found alcohol as a way to escape pain, often use it again. An interviewee reported:

The drinking got more and more. Not only that I drank more, but it was all being trebled because I was taking antidepressants. The blackouts were really bad. Fortunately, I only drank in the evening. I always kidded about being a night time alcoholic because I wouldn't drink in the daytime because I had the responsibility of the kids. But come eight o'clock, that was it. That gave me some relief. During the drinking bouts I would get violently angry. I would rant and rave and carry on. I would feel better for a few days. I look back now and see that I didn't make the connection between my drinking and carrying on and the fact my child had died.

In less dramatic cases, we find that there is an extended period of time when what Bowlby calls searching continues. A newsletter poem by Don Fiegel reads:

I looked for you today; I thought I might gaze, stare, enjoy your beauty; blue-green eyes and golden blonde hair.
But you were nowhere to be found. . . .
I searched for you today, to put my arms around you, hold you, kiss you, and tell you how much I love you.
But you were nowhere to be found.

One of the ways of accepting the reality of the death is to learn the full facts. A few months after the death we often find parents going to great lengths to learn the details about the deaths. At this point, the larger community provides the socially validated reality that the parent seeks. Autopsy reports, medical examiners' reports, and, where they exist, police reports are read over and over. Sometimes there are differences within the family about how much each individual wants to know. One father wanted the full account of the torture and rape of his daughter before the murder, but his wife did not. At a Compassionate Friends meeting, an operating room nurse talked of wanting to ask the surgeon all the details of the operation during which her daughter had died. Another responded:

> They let us see the tape they had made of the operation. We had studied so much about her problem that I had become a medical expert. I felt weird watching her heart beat, but I wanted to see it. I even thought about getting a copy of the tape. If that was all I have of her, then I wanted it.

We asked parents of murdered children who wanted full details why they wanted them. One father said:

> I've just got to settle my mind. I kept imagining different things, and I was afraid of what might have been. Now I know and it is horrible. But I know and I can deal with the horror. It hurts, but at least I know.

The problem of intellectually recognizing the death is not simply a problem within the minds of the parents. Bereaved parents have a difficult time accepting the reality of their child's death, in part because the reality is not accepted by the social system. Reality is, after all, a social construct. That is, we define our world in terms of our membership in a social system (Berger & Luckman, 1966; Mannheim, 1936). The socially given reality includes the individual's sense of the self as well as of external reality. As R.D. Laing has written:

> Self-identity is a synthesis of my looking at me with my view of others' view of me. These views by others of me need not be passively accepted, but they cannot be ignored in my development of a sense of who I am, for even if a view by another of me is rejected it still becomes incorporated in its rejected form as part of my self-identity. (Laing, Phillipson, & Lee, 1966, p. 6)

When bereaved parents can recognize themselves as being one who has lost a child and who is grieving, the reality of the loss can become real. Most literature and research on grief assigns to the bereaved the primary responsibility for recognizing reality. Among bereaved parents, however, the majority of reports are that the community has difficulty recognizing the reality in everyday interactions. When the parents are within a social system in which the child's death is not recognized within the everyday reality, then the parents may have to spend a great deal of energy rejecting the others' view of them and yet, as Laing said, incorporating that view in its rejected form as part of their own self-identities.

In the social systems of bereaved parents we often find the interaction pattern that Glaser and Strauss (1965) called *mutual pretense*. In mutual pretense all the members of the group know the reality, but each acts as if it were not true. In the early months of grief, bereaved parents often find that their natural support system experiences the reality of the death and of the parent's pain as so difficult to assimilate that the topic becomes forbidden. One parent reported:

> There we were at my mother's house for Christmas three months after F. was killed, and not one person, not one of my brothers or my parents, mentioned his name all day. I just sat there boiling. It was like they didn't care and they wanted to go on as if nothing had happened. The next time I saw my mother I told her how much that had hurt me. She said, "Well, we didn't want to make you sad by bringing it up." What else do they think I am thinking about?

Very often, social interactions which the parent thinks he or she can expect from the community are not forthcoming. An interviewee said:

> The minister never came to see me once after J. died. His wife who is a close friend never came and she waited 3 months before she even called to talk. Church songs were horrible . . . and sermons on faith would kill me because that usually means you didn't have enough. I wanted to scream at the people who were giving it.
> Q: Well, that's how you were feeling.
> Oh, yeah, but when you get down the road you realize that these people were having as hard a time as I was. This poor young fellow who'd never had a parish before had to handle a very hard situation, and he had no training for it.

One of the ways others use to protect themselves from the full reality of the pain the parent feels is to convince themselves that the parent is "strong" or "handling it so well."

> That always came back to me, that, "You handled it so well." Well, I didn't handle it well. I didn't want people to tell me that anymore. I was so sick of hearing it.
> Q: You were hurt on the inside and people were telling you on the outside, "Gee, aren't you strong."
> But yet they couldn't talk about it. The hurt was there, but I couldn't show it and I didn't know how to handle the loss. I was like a zombie and they took that to mean that I was strong.

Another frequent method others use to protect themselves from the parent's pain are statements of compensatory consolation, such as: "You are lucky you have other children." Parents whose newborn dies hear: "It is good you don't have many memories to be sad about." And parents whose older children die hear: "Well, at least you had her for a few years."

We find that many parents go to great lengths to have others to share the overwhelming inner reality they carry. The woman whose pastor did not come to see her remembered:

> I did some real strange things. I wanted strangers to know that my child had died. I wanted to let them know that they could feel sorry for me if they wanted. Really in bizarre, manipulating ways, being sure I found ways to tell them. It's really strange. And I'd think about how strange I was behaving. I remember a man coming to repair something in the house and I weaseled my way around to getting him to ask about all the things that were going on in my life.

Because the reality is so strong inside, but not integrated into the social reality, some parents are confused about how they appear to others. That is, they have trouble establishing others' views of themselves that correspond with their own views of themselves. Conversely, they have trouble in their views of others because the social reality in which others are acting is so different from the parents' inner reality. In a newsletter another parent wrote:

> One of my most interesting problems, now that I look back on it, was that of feeling self-conscious all the time. Whenever I was out in public, at the grocery store, the mall, or wherever, I felt that everyone was looking at me and that they knew that my son had died. . . . The other side of the coin was in walking through the mall and wondering how everyone could be acting so normal, even happy, when I felt so rotten. I wanted to shout, "Don't you know my son is dead?"

One of the problems faced by many bereaved parents is finding others with whom the reality of the child's death can be fully a social reality and thus shared and explored. As we will see in the study of self-help groups, when we speak of a community where the loss is a social reality, we are talking about more than the facts of the death being acknowledged. Word of a child's death spreads quickly through information networks. The reality that the parent seeks to share is the loss of the child, not the mere factual information. When a child is born, the social support means sharing the bond with the child as well as affirming the mother and father in their new social role of parents. When a child dies, it is not simply the fact of the death that the parent wants to be socially real, it is the loss itself that the parent needs to share. When the loss is shared, the particular elements within the bond to the child become clarified, so that the grief, like the bonding in early parenting, can be less ambivalent.

OWNING EMOTIONS

For bereaved parents the symptoms of grief can be extreme. Parents often have no energy for several months after the child's death, a problem thus characterized by one parent in an interview: "I just tried to make it through the hour; never mind trying to think about making it through a day." They feel listless, tired, and unable to concentrate. This is especially difficult for those parents who must return to work a few days after the death. Bereaved parents report that they are unable to perform routine mental tasks such as checking lists of numbers or typing. There is a loss of short-term memory, so they often find themselves driving but not knowing where they set out to go, or having put something down and not being able to find it. One man reported, "One of the most frustrating things is this mental thing. It's not enough that I lost my child; I'm losing my mind too." Several men in one support group shared that they had all been given about 2 months of below-par performance on the job, and then they had been expected to be back up to their old standard. In that group, three of the eleven had been laid off or fired.

The emotions seem out of control. At any moment the parent might begin to cry. At other times when the parent expects to cry, the feeling is apathy. Relationships between spouses often become strained. If surviving children are young, parents often report they have limited patience and find themselves out of control when they begin to respond to slight misbehavior. An interviewee reported:

> I found myself yelling at the kids all the time, but then I wouldn't follow up on the punishment I threatened. When they tried to reason with me, I fell apart, because I knew it wasn't them; it was me. So I was either yelling or crying. I know I was being a lousy mother. Here I was grieving for a child who had died, and not being a good mother to the kids I still have.

Parents' ideation is often strange. They think gruesome thoughts trying to recreate the accident or to picture the body in the grave. They blame themselves for sins or imperfections that could have caused the death. They may contemplate suicide as a way to join the child.

Part of the process of coming to terms with the reality is assessing the possibilities that the death could have been prevented. Each news report of a medical breakthrough brings the thought that it might have been the one that could have saved the child. Events leading to the death are examined for possibilities of error. Should the child have been taken to the physician earlier? Should the child have been told to get the car fixed before driving it? One father whose son was killed in a fire in the house he lived in at college remembered thinking when he took his son to the house that an old wooden building needed smoke detectors, but he never acted on it.

For some, magic thinking takes over. One mother read Hemingway's novel, *A Farewell to Arms*, in which a baby is stillborn. Then her child died the day after it was born.

> I kept thinking I had caused it. I know it is irrational, but it's the irrational part of me that is in this whole grief thing. I don't read or see anything now where bad things happen to kids, because I'm afraid it will happen again.

One mother lost her husband in an accident the year before her child died in another accident. She had always had low self-esteem, and the son who died had been closer to the father than to her. She vacillated between several thoughts, but each time she tried to focus on one thought, her mind would turn to the other. She was angry at the husband for not being alive, now that she so needed him. She thought the child in dying had rejected her in favor of the father. She wondered if the child had committed suicide, though there was no evidence except for her feeling that in dying the child had rejected her. These thoughts are real to the parent, but not part of the socially validated reality. It is in sharing the thoughts that parents can listen to themselves and come to terms with both the irrational ideas and with the fact they are thinking them. One of the functions of self-help and support groups is to assure the newly bereaved that such thoughts and feelings are normal and that the parent is not going crazy.

There is very little consistency of symptoms among bereaved parents as they go between attempts to act normal and wide swings of emotion. One of our interviewees reported:

People kept telling me how strong I was, how fortunate I was to have three other children. I remember that feeling of just gut level resentment. It wasn't as bad when we visited family in Columbia, but when we got home to Springfield it was this jolt all over again. The house screamed, "P.'s not here." . . . I went from screaming at the kids —violent temper tantrums— one minute, to the next minute when I'm telling them how sorry I am and feeling this terrible guilt. I just felt awful, because when I walked into a room it was a big decision whether I should sit in this chair or that one. It was this kind of slowed down thinking. At other times it would be race thinking. My head was crazy, just absolutely crazy.

For some bereaved parents, the entire effort is spent trying to control the pain. In those cases, there is usually a tacit agreement within the household not to talk about the dead child or about the circumstances of the death. Evaluations about the self are expressed in terms of hurting or not hurting. Early in our work with The Compassionate Friends, we called several people who had attended one or two meetings, but who had not returned thereafter. We found that the majority had good natural support systems and did not think they needed the group, though a few years later some of those people did begin attending. A few parents we called, however, found that sharing painful memories and experiences with others was very stressful. One mother, for example, reported that her family was making every effort to get back to normal and that when they talked about the child everyone simply became upset, so they had put away all reminders of the child and things seemed fine now. After about eight minutes, she said that the conversation with us was difficult and she terminated the interview.

When there is good social support, the pain is shared and the emotions within the inner representation and within the experience of loss can be expressed. The parents can thereby allow themselves to experience the pain of the loss. In a newsletter poem, Cynthia Kelley said:

> I crash on rocks of anger —
> My faith seems faint indeed —
> But there are other swimmers
> Who know that what I need
> Are loving hands to hold me
> When the waters are too swift,
> And someone kind to listen
> When I just seem to drift.

For some parents, several years may pass before they find a community in which they can find their way through grief. One newsletter report told of eleven years the family spent trying to control the pain from the death of an infant son. When a second child, their daughter, died, the couple tried the same style of coping but found that it was not effective.

> I felt in my grief that it was a choice of being over-controlled or out of control, so I decided to choose the former. From my present perspective, I think this was a mistake. Our family, I think, would have worked through our grief in a better way had we been more open with each other about the grief we felt. I think that many of the problems we faced after our daughter died were really due to our grief, which was unrecognized and unresolved because it was unexpressed. It was compounded by the earlier grief of our infant son, who had been born prematurely and for whom we had not been encouraged to grieve fully when he died.

Letting go of control is very difficult for some people, and therefore expressing the pain they feel seems dangerous to them. A parent for whom, "feelings are strange creatures we don't really know what to do with, or worse yet, what they will do with us," reported in a newsletter that once she tried, with the encouragement of a support group, to let go, she experienced something new.

> After I've let myself experience the unwanted feelings, I realize a few things: (1) These feelings didn't consume or destroy me, as I thought they would; (2) I feel more aware of who I am and of what has happened to me; (3) when I see other people express their anger, frustration, despair, I am able to accept these expressions because I understand. In the past, I would have been confused and would have walked away.

For others, sharing has always been a part of their way of being themselves, and they continue that pattern after the child dies. One of our interviewees told us of an old friend:

> We would sometimes just go out for a beer together after work or spend the whole evening talking. We have done that since we were boys. When he went through his divorce, it was my time to listen. This was much harder, but he was still the friend he had always been. I sometimes worried about telling the same things over and over, but he just stuck with me.

Both the quality and quantity of time together are important in the sharing that bereaved parents need. Even within the focused groups, such as Compassionate Friends, we find that the members look for further contacts with each other. People call one another on the phone; small groups gather for coffee; and some attend more than one meeting a month. As Bowling and Cartwright (1982) found with widows, the availability of a large number of kin is not an indicator of the availability of the kind of sharing that bereaved parents need. Often in our interviews we found that one or two people were the central social support of the bereaved parent even when there was a wider community to which the parent was connected. A single parent whose only child died moved back into her parents' home and reestablished a close relationship with her mother, who had lost a child several years earlier. For her mother, the loss of the grandchild reawakened the feelings from long ago.

> In the beginning I just ran all the time. I was busy; I was always gone, just running from the hurt and running from reality, just running from grief. And mom hurt so bad and I couldn't be there for her. Yet she needed me, and I think me not being there was bad for the whole situation. Another child had died, someone she had invested in, and the thought of what I would go through almost did her in. Then she moved; and about 6 months later she got better, and I leaned on her and she leaned on me. I would say from about 6 months and after she did everything she could to help me get through. We had dinner every night together and we would talk at least 2 hours after dinner. I don't care what was going on, she made the time to talk to me—in the middle of the night, on weekends, whenever—she was there to talk to me.
> Q: What would you talk about?
> We talked about V., over and over again. The time in the hospital. The pain. How do you get back into this life? Why does it look so difficult? Why do I feel so different? Why can't I adjust? I really felt so angry at people. I felt hurt, lost. I really felt like I was dead it hurt so much. We talked about suicide and about my need to stay here.

Another interviewee reported that she had a good friend whom she did not know had lost a child until after her own child died. She also had a therapist for a short time. The qualification she found most important in the therapist was that he was personally acquainted with grief.

> The support system I had was a friend. I guess several friends, but one friend in particular was always there. She had suffered the loss of an infant. We had been friends before that, but I didn't know she'd lost an infant until I lost G. She was very supportive.
> Q: What kind of things did she do?
> She would listen. She would come over and bring her kids and we'd go out. We'd take the kids out and go the the park and we'd just talk.

She's the one who encouraged me to get counseling. I think I was really using her to fulfill that need and I think she was feeling a little burdened by it. She had the facility to do it, but I don't think she wanted to get involved because that wouldn't really have helped the friendship. So she urged me to see the psychiatrist. He had an interest in grief. He had lost his wife and the woman he was engaged to had terminal cancer. He was very helpful.

A single parent whom we interviewed found that the relationship with her surviving child was more as a peer than as a parent. Her daughter had died after six years of cancer, and during that time the sibling had assumed a good part of the care, especially when the mother was working.

Susan and I just spent a lot of time together. We really clung to each other. Where most women would cling to their husbands I clung to Susan and Susan to me. We talked about L. an awful lot.

SELF AND SOCIAL INTERACTIONS TO MATCH THE NEW REALITY

How does a parent learn to live in a world that includes the fact that their child is dead? As one mother we interviewed said:

It's not over after a year or 2 years. It's an ongoing thing. Your life has changed. Its like moving from one town to another. You can't go back. Even if you did go back, it's not going to be the same.

The parent must build a new life with a diminished self in a poorer world. A newsletter article reflected on the comment from a friend that the parent was "picking up the pieces and going on."

Well, I am picking up the pieces all right—but what she doesn't know is that they are almost a whole set of new pieces! I haven't been able to go on as though nothing about me has changed since my child died. I'm a different me and I am still learning about how the new me reacts to old situations. . . . Some of the old pieces are still hanging in there, but they don't quite mesh with some of the new pieces. I am in the process of grinding off the rough edges now, hoping eventually for a better fit.

Experiential Learning

The parent is confronted with a series of practical problems that have existential implications. For example, what should the parent say when asked the common question, "How many children do you have?" The question reaches deep into the bereaved parent's life—for what does it mean to "have" a child? We are seldom asked if we "have" a parent. When a woman delivers, she "has" a child and the parents "have" the child thereafter. But how does the parent still have the child after the child has died? The question raises the problematic social role of the bereaved parent, for others are often uncomfortable with the reality the bereaved parent carries. So the question raises the degree of intimacy the parent has with the person asking the question. We can see the difficulty by the complexity of the answers parents must figure out. One parent reported:

> Now, when I am asked how many children I have, I answer, "I had two children." The criteria I used in determining if I go any further is whether the person asking is going to be a continuing part of my life . . . . Better, I think, to have it out in the open. It then loses its ability to interfere with the relationship. . . . If, on the other hand, the person asking is simply passing through my life, then I feel no need to go any further than I "had" two children. Seldom does anyone catch the "had" instead of "have" and pursue it. If they do . . . I tell them first that my . . . son was killed in an accident. Then I tell them about my daughter who is alive and doing well, which gives them a choice. They can either acknowledge my son's death and ask questions, or they can ignore that and ask about my daughter.

Other experiential issues include how to celebrate holidays and birthdays, what to do with the child's belongings, and how to deal with siblings and spouses.

For parents of infants, for whom the death of a child is closely linked to their experience of pregnancy and birth, special issues are connected with having more children. We find among this group a strong desire to have another child after the infant has died. In part that seems to come from the need to demonstrate to themselves and others that they are competent in childbearing. But now pregnancy, birth, and early child care are linked with the experience of loss. The parents now know the possibilities that previously they could convince themselves "only happen to other people."

Many have difficulty bonding to the new child. One woman who was seven months pregnant in the second year after her child had died said:

> I can't bond to this baby. By this time with N., I was bonded. I would talk to him. I knew he was mine. But I don't feel connected. I know it is inside me, but I am afraid to get attached. By this time with N. we had the baby's room fixed up. Last week my husband said, "Let's go look at baby beds."

Well, when he says he wants to go shopping I know I better take advantage of it. So we went to Toyland and all the cribs were beautiful, but I just couldn't buy one. When we walked out of the store, I felt just awful. I felt like there was something wrong with me that I can't love this baby.

A young mother whose son was killed in an accident when she was 8 months pregnant with another child nearly delivered her child prematurely during the week of the funeral, but was stabilized and delivered full term. We asked how the death of her child affected her relationship with the new baby.

I couldn't bond to the baby for 6 weeks. I took care of her. I breast-fed her, but it was a problem because I was upset—and when that happens you lose your milk. But I didn't feel close to her. A friend said, "She is your baby and she needs you." One afternoon I was nursing and I looked at her and she was beautiful, and I said, "You are mine and I love you."

The solutions to experiential problems are not simple. In a support group of bereaved parents, as the solutions are shared the parents listen to the various solutions others have adopted. When the solution that seems right is offered, there is often a relaxed smile of recognition, for the solution implies a way of being in the world that is understood as a whole.

The experiential problem of the role of happiness and laughter can move parents toward a fuller engagement with the social world. The loss of a child brings a pervasive sadness and painfulness to every aspect of life. Often, when parents find that others are not sharing in their loss, the parent feels a responsibility to be sad, for otherwise the child will be forgotten. "All I have left of my child is my sadness," said one person we interviewed early in her grief. "If I give that up, I feel like I have to give up my child." As we will explore in the next chapter, parents find ways of keeping the child without the constant sadness. As they do so, they learn that they can find pleasure and not violate the memory of the child. They do find happiness and laughter, although it is happiness tempered with a knowledge of the ephemeral and laughter with a tinge of the tragic. Still, the first time parents know they can laugh is often the first time they know they can survive in the world that is now changed by the child's death. In a newsletter meditation on spring and rebirth one parent wrote:

There are those of us who have gone through several springs without being aware of them. It was not even possible for us to smile, let alone laugh—and we were positive that we would never be able to do so. Does anyone remember the first time he laughed, as I do? It was at least 6 months after the death of my son, and I was visiting a very close friend who made some comment which must have struck just the right chord with me—and I actually reeled back in my chair and I asked, unbelievingly, "Did I do that?" For me, that was the first small burst of spring coming back into my life! But, of course, I still had a long way to go.

The New Self

The bereaved parent has moved to a whole new world. In that new world, they find new ways of being the self. In those cases where they had been easily hurt by others, they protect themselves from that hurt. The sense of the tentativeness of life brings reordered priorities. As they have felt the hurt and known the social estrangement that comes with the death of a child, they have become acutely conscious of themselves and have made some decisions about the stance they take in their world. In our interviews we asked people how the death of the child had changed them. We found some rather consistent themes.

Weakness and Control

Issues of strength and weakness often come up in our interviews and are linked to issues of power and control over life and other relationships. Control and security seem linked to the concept of self-protection within their social network. One person answered the question, "Do you feel you have changed since the death?"

> Before, people could walk all over me and I would have never said anything back to them. I don't think I've become a real cold or hard person, but I don't allow myself to be as easily hurt. I realize I've been hurt as bad as I can be hurt and had no control over that hurt. Other hurts I do have control over. When someone does something to hurt me, I let them know how I feel.
>
> After you lose your child, you begin to look at life differently. You realize you never really know how long you have, and life is too short to live doing things you don't want to do. I realize more what is important to me. Also as a person I realize I have needs too and sometimes I have to put me first.

For some the loss of security leads to a tentativeness about other security points, such as religious teachings. One of our interviewees said:

I guess I don't have the same sense of security. You realize that life is fragile, that everything can change so drastically so easily. Everything in our family was so right, then suddenly everything was so wrong.

I have not found the answer to "Why?" I do read quite a bit and listen to anything related. I have found that books on life after death are helpful. You have to keep faith that there is something beyond this earth, so you can't just back off from religion entirely or it's all been for nothing.

If there is estrangement and insecurity about the lack of ability to control the external world, a sense of security can be found in that very estrangement. For some people, the insecurity brought on by the death and the separation from the natural support systems have allowed them to find within themselves the strength and courage to live in a bigger, albeit less secure world. A woman who had become a leader in a support group reported:

I've become much stronger. I'm now able to consider moving away from the family. Before, it was so important to be close to them, but that's not actually where most of my support came from. I have found a lot of my support system outside the family. I have been working on being more honest with my family on how I feel, and it has helped them become more supportive.

Indeed, there is a certain sense of security and control in the complete insecurity brought on by the child's death. Four years after her son died, one of the parents we interviewed said:

I think I've become a stronger person. Nothing will ever hurt me more than that. I felt like I was as low as I could get at the time of O.'s death. That was rock bottom. There is some comfort in knowing that it can't get any worse. So, if you take that as a starting point, you can work your way up a little at a time from there.

Distance and Sensitivity

Although there is a distance between the bereaved parent and the external world, there is also, paradoxically, a new sensitivity to the world. One man, for example, could say that instead of distancing himself, he had found the experience of losing a child had made him more vulnerable, more open to others.

One of the things that occurred before E. died and was due to the trauma of my divorce, was that I became considerably more sensitive. Certainly the trauma of E.'s death made me more sensitive. How much more sensitive I don't know. Perhaps not as much. Perhaps it's been dulled some-what. But certainly I'm a far more sensitive person than I was 3 or 4 years ago. I'm much more in tune with other people's feelings. In our group I'm especially sensitive to those that have suffered through sudden deaths.

Many parents make a conscious choice to face their situation directly. They often do not know what that choice means, for they do not have a plan to follow when they decide that they do not want to remain as they are; but they decide to do something. A man whose son died said:

> In 6 months you could be nowhere if you aren't working at it. You have to make a concerted effort, even if you don't know where you are going, or how you are going to get there, or what the conclusion will be. You have to be purposely working toward some change, trying to move along—maybe not to move beyond it, but just to move along.
>
> Q: So you are saying that where you will be at the end of six months depends a lot on if you work at it?
>
> Yes, even if you don't know for sure what you are working at. You have to decide, "I really do want to survive this," and say to yourself, "I am going to try to get through today. Then, if I get through today, I'm going to start on tomorrow."

For some, the decision to do something about their condition was a decision to live and to remain living. One of our interviewees reported:

> Up until that time I didn't want to live. I went to the cemetery every day and thought about suicide all the time. . . . I couldn't bring myself to think ahead enough to cook or clean the house. . . . If I did plan something I would seldom follow through. One day, when I was upset at Gary and Judy, I took off and walked miles to the cemetery. As I walked a weight was lifted off me and I realized at that point that I could have been easily like the thousands of mothers who walk away from their families and never come back.

She joined The Compassionate Friends shortly after she walked back from the cemetery.

Competence

Many of the changes in the self which we find in the resolution of parental bereavement are aimed at a restoration of the sense of competence, which was damaged by the death of the child. Many

parents find ways of demonstrating competence within the community. Some find an adequate memorial for the child. This is especially
helpful to the parent if the memorial is a way for the community to
share in the loss. Scholarships named for dead children are part of
most high school graduation awards and college financial aid monies.
One of our interviewees was active in early childhood education
when her toddler died.

> We didn't want any flowers. We put that in the newspaper and that we
> would accept memorials. We had five hundred dollars after the expenses
> were paid and I wanted to do something that would be special and child
> like. So we developed a toy lending library in the public library. It's called
> J.'s Toy Box.
> Q: What does it make you feel to know that it is there?
> That does so much for me because the memory of J. remains childlike.
> It remains in something that he liked to do, play with toys. He had just left
> the early childhood age and I wanted him to leave them something that
> they'd remember him by. His name will be remembered over time. They
> will remember that a child died; his name was J. and this is what he did.
> Q: It's an immortality that can be shared with the community and it
> feels good to have him shared that way.
> It does because I really think he was a beautiful and unique child. I
> also wanted something that was more living, more than a cold statue that
> stood somewhere that people couldn't get involved in. I was also pleased
> to be able to be involved in setting it up.

In cases of wrongful deaths, parents often work tirelessly to
ensure that the police and court systems bring justice to the death.
These parents are particularly challenged in their competence because the human psyche still seems to be governed by the ancient law
that demands that the family redress the insult to honor brought by
the killing of the child. Yet they are powerless, for the state has taken
over the responsibility of revenge. Thus they must marshal whatever
power they can to overcome the helplessness they feel. They hound
the police to make sure the case stays active until apprehension. They
pressure the prosecuting attorney until conviction. Where law per-
mits, they follow the case in parole hearings. The mother who had
developed the memorial at the library had also testified at the trial of
the driver of the other car in the accident.

> I was the witness in the trial, so I had to be able to stand up in front of a
> court and be able to say that he was dead. I think the people who came and
> watched the trial were in more agony than I was by that point, and that

was 10 months later. They were suffering from hearing me, but I was able to speak what happened. I think there was also something very helpful for me to do in resolving. I agreed with the idea that I'd lost the right of protection for my child. One of our roles as a parent is to protect our child, and that right was taken away from me. So I felt I needed to follow through as far as I could in the criminal resolution of what had happened.

Q: In testifying at the trial, that was a resolution—protecting what was left of the child.

That's right. I felt I owed it to him. I didn't have any hesitations. My mother's only fear was that I was going to be subjected to this one more thing. It wasn't a difficult thing for me to do. I was motivated.

Q: It was almost an act of love.

That's right. I was also interested in seeing that we took that as far as we could. I was really concerned that here was this schizophrenic who was possibly going to be riding around and doing it to me again or doing it to someone else. I never thought for a moment that this person had deliberately sought us out. We were in the way. We just happened to be in the right place at the right time. I just thought we had to get him off the streets. We lost the trial, in that he was found not guilty by reason of insanity. He was certified schizophrenic.

Q: How did that make you feel.

Very numb. Very resentful of the judge. I just felt that the judge had somehow made a mistake. It's not that I resented the fact that the man was really mentally ill. It's kind of a two-pronged conflict that I have. If the man was mentally ill, he should have the help he needs and he shouldn't be treated as a criminal. However, the way the laws were written at the time, his mental illness prevented him from being tried for anything. One thing that we did, though, was to attend some earlier hearings about his driver's license. Someone leaked the word back to the Secretary of State that this man was so heavily sedated on his medication for schizophrenia that it would not be appropriate for him to drive a car.

Q: So they lifted his license?

Yes, but I don't know for how many years. Maybe three. Maybe he's driving now. I think we took that as far as we were able to and he just got off free. So that made me more angry at the system and more resentful of the attorneys, especially the defense attorney. He's still high on my list of people that I'm angry at.

Parents of murdered children often find that the criminal justice system does not do an adequate job, and they move to political activism in victim rights organizations. In other wrongful deaths, the killer can be transformed into a generalized group, such as drunk drivers, and political pressure brought to bear for harsher treatment of those who drive under the influence. A few parents are able to carry on that fight alone, but most form or join groups, which become the immediate social support for them. But the support of the larger society is important. Parents look eagerly for legislators and government officials who advance their cause. The news media, which was often seen as insensitive right after the death, is regarded as supportive if coverage of their plight is good.

Many of the phenomena observed in parental bereavement can be understood best as assertions of power and competence. Some parents feel a strong drive to respond to the death of the child in a public way. We find a whole genre of literature by parents who write about their dead children. In addition to the grief work done in writing, the publication of those works can be seen as an assertion of competence on the parents' parts as they make sure the child's memory remains alive. We also often see in some bereaved parents strong desires to found or to manage organizations. Organizations founded by bereaved parents include those devoted to supporting research on the diseases that killed the children, those promoting legislation against drunk driving or for victim services, and those that serve other bereaved parents. These public responses to the death can be understood as an assertion of competence in one's parenthood and as a reclamation of power within one's world.

Finding a sense of competence is not an easy task for some parents. One of our interviewees said she had not lived up to her parents' expectations and had married early as a way of getting out of the house. She found her sense of selfhood when she had a child. The child died in a home accident she thought she should have prevented. For several years, she was unable to face the death effectively. She and her husband rapidly developed a distance between them and were "married in name only" when we interviewed her eleven years after the death. Eight years after the death, she developed an intimate friendship with a teacher in a college course. Within a new social support she could find a new self.

> He took my writing seriously. He said it was good when it was good and showed me how to make the rest better. But he also really read my work. He understood what I was trying to write about. We would have long talks after class. He encouraged me to go on for more education. He told me I really have talent. Nobody in my family had ever said I was worthwhile just as me.

With that realization, she said, she could begin to rethink her role in her daughter's death and to remember the child in a comforting way.

Marriage and Divorce

For bereaved parents, the relationship to the child's other parent often presents special difficulty in the disequilibrium between the self and the social environment. As parents build a new self and as they move through the grief process, they do so in relationship to the child's other parent. As we listen to bereaved parents recount their journeys, we often find that intertwined with their personal account is the account of their relationship to their spouse or former spouse. Our cultural ideal is that marriage should be the greatest social support available to the parent. But reality seldom matches the ideal; so, often added to the burden of the child's death is the burden of a problematic marital relationship. The resolution of parental bereavement in the building of the new self is often also a resolution to problems in the marriage, though such a resolution may sometimes mean the end of the marriage.

Marriage and divorce among bereaved parents is among the most discussed and least studied aspects of parental bereavement. Studies have reported divorce rates among bereaved parents from 24% to 70% (Kaplan, Grobstein, & Smith, 1976; Strauss, 1975); however, no studies to date have a sample large and diverse enough to draw adequate conclusions. Still, it is clear that maritial tension is one of the hazards of parental bereavement.

Mother's Grief; Father's Grief

There are some studies of differences in fathers' and mothers' grieving styles (Cook, 1983; Fish, 1986). Men tend to feel the loss as a void and seek solitude. Men often describe their grieving as a private matter. Women tend to feel the loss as isolation and may therefore be extra sensitive to distance between the spouses—precisely at the time the man is seeking solitude. Mothers tend to describe their grief as more public. Fish (1986) did an innovative analysis of the categories on Sanders's (1980) Grief Experience Inventory to find differences between the grief of fathers and mothers over 5 years and differences between fathers and mothers depending on the sex and age of the child. But his sample is too small and self-selected to draw wider conclusions.

In self-help groups, it appears that the fathers are more likely to be active attenders if there is something they can do. Whereas some fathers attend without their wives, mothers are more likely to attend without their husbands. In the group of parents whose children died of cancer and in the Parents of Murdered Children, there are a greater percentage of men attending than at groups of general populations, suicide survivors, or parents of neonates. The reason seems to be that there are concrete actions that the men could perform within the group. In the cancer group, the men were involved while the child was still living and were necessary for activities such as lifting children on and off the bus during trips. In that activity they built up a camaraderie that carried over within the group after the children died. In the Parents of Murdered Children, learning to operate within the legal system seems to the men like something they can still do for their children.

Peppers and Knapp (1980) found in their study of parents after the death of neonates that the degree of bonding the father had done to the child determined the degree to which he grieved. The degree of bonding can be quite different at that early stage of parenting, for the mother's physical relationship to the unborn child is very direct and the father's is indirect. It is difficult, however, to make generalizations about differential bonding as parenting becomes more grounded in the history of interactions with the child.

Although the great majority of research on parent/child bonding has been done with mothers, Main and Weston (1981) used both fathers and mothers in the Ainsworth Strange Situation. They found that as a group, children responded in the same way to the absence and return of the fathers as they did to the mothers. That is, some were securely attached, some ambivalent, and some resistant. They also found that individual children were differently attached to father and mother and that it might be the mother to whom the child was ambivalently attached or resistant. Thus, in trying to understand marriage and divorce among bereaved parents, we should not adopt stereotyped images of fathers and mothers as they grieve until better data is at hand.

The Paradox

The bereaved parents we interviewed indicated that the death of a child has a paradoxical effect on the relationship between the parents. The shared loss creates a new and very profound tie between them at the same time the individual loss that each of them feels creates an estrangement in the relationship that is very deep. The paradox is expressed differently in couples with different relationships prior to the death. The paradox plays itself out in different forms as the parents individually and as a couple come to terms with the emotional and spiritual dilemmas presented to them by the death of their child. But the paradox of a new bond amidst estrangement is a central theme in the marital relationships among bereaved parents.

The parents we have listened to say there is not a simple relationship between parental bereavement and divorce. Our interviewees indicate that marriages don't die with the death of a child, but often they receive an overdue burial. If there is a causal relationship between parental bereavement and divorce, we probably should look at it in a positive way. As bereaved parents build a new self within the social environment, the self who was in the marriage may not be adequate to the changed reality. Parents have had to stand the pain of the loss of the rich and full relationship to the child, so the pain of losing the withered marriage is not so threatening.

Continuing Marriages

Many parents who lose a child remain married, and for some the experience is a difficult but, in the end, a positive factor in the marriage. For those bereaved parents with relatively stress-free marriages before the death, the different grief patterns of each partner seem to present some problems to the relationship. We have found that many of these parents discovered self-help groups and marriage counseling have helped them through the stress in the marriage brought on by the grief at the death of the child. A man reported:

> We had been unable to express our anger at each other, and I felt I was continuously walking a tightrope trying not to set her off. Meanwhile, I had to keep functioning at work. Then we found that at the TCF meetings, we could express ourselves freer within the "safety zone" of others around.

When all of life is called into question by the death of a child, there are very few bereaved parents who do not at least consider separation or divorce. Especially in the early months of grief, when the couple are establishing their patterns of support and communication within their grief, there can be some very difficult times between the marriage partners. Each parent is looking for ways to lighten the load they carry, so they wonder if the pain of communications between them is worth enduring. That question is usually solved as they learn to share and communicate within their grief. A woman reported:

> For Walt and myself, when everything was falling apart, the marriage had its doubts. I had to ask, "Do we really want to stay together?" . . . We were

separate in our grief. Walt became absorbed in his work. The kids and I were blocked out of his world. He had never brought work home before, yet he started to bring to work home every night. Now, though, we are closer—even more than before V.'s death, because we learned how to talk things out. Before we never discussed our problems. . . . It's funny though, he wouldn't go to the meetings, but always wanted to hear about them afterwards. Then he went willingly. . . . He doesn't share a lot during the meeting, but shares afterwards. I realize now that he did love V. as much as I did, but is just reacting in a different way. Now we share a lot more openly.

Even marriages that are rock-solid are challenged by the death of a child. A woman who had built a family business with her husband while raising four children told us:

I felt for a while there that I could have left Sam. I thought he didn't care about me. I thought he didn't understand my feelings. You know how you expect a husband to help a wife. Well, he couldn't help me because he couldn't help himself. Sam was more down than I was. . . . Some days he wouldn't come home after work, but would go down to the river [where the accident happened] and just look and look. He would ask anyone around questions on what happened, looking for an answer. But you don't get any answers. I finally said to him, "Listen, Sam, I'm sitting here waiting for you while you are sitting down there by the water. What am I going to do while I'm here waiting for you? I've been waiting for thirty-some years. Our marriage was here before the girls or the family or this tragedy. I'm still here. Still waiting. I haven't changed, have you? If you don't want to come home, fine. Go get yourself a pad somewhere. But if you do, I'm here."

When she could understand how her husband was coping with his grief, she could find support in the marriage.

One night we were at a TCF meeting and a man who lost his son in a fire told us of his experiences. Afterwards Sam went up to him and said, "How can you experience these things about your son and write about him? My wife does such and such, but I can't." When I walked up on them and heard this it was a turning point for me. I didn't realize Sam was struggling to make these communications with the girls. I said to myself, "I've got to stop thinking about myself so much and do a little bit more for him."

Just as parents as individuals grow beyond the person they were before the child died, the marriage may grow beyond what it was before the death of the child. In the intensity of parental grief, the focus of the marriage becomes the working out of problems associated with the grief. For many couples, this is a new level of intimacy and sharing. They have talked before, but often not in these terms about their innermost being. Yet, as they each find a resolution of the grief, they must move beyond the grief in their relationship. This often presents a problem, especially when there has been a prolonged illness before the death, for the care of the dying child and then the grief for the child formed the basis of much of the bond the couple had with each other. Four years after the death, one father reported:

> It is a very strange relationship we have right now. It is as if we are dating again. We spent so much of our time dealing with the problems of A.'s cancer, and then with the problems each of us had with the grief and the problems we had between us within our grief. That became what we shared. But whatever is the end of a parent's grief we have reached it. We don't have to talk about that much, though A. comes up in our conversation when it is appropriate—like when we have something that she liked to eat. And both of us are very different than we were before. When we met, we were both kids. We didn't know what we were doing. Everybody was getting married, so we got married. I think I loved her, but then again, I am not sure I knew what love was then. I know I lusted for her, and in those days you waited until you were married. But we are not kids. This whole thing has changed us. So now it is like we are getting to know each other again. It's strange and really kind of fun. I guess I'm just glad that I like this new woman as much as I liked the girl she used to be. I wonder what would happen if we had grown in such different directions that we were not right for each other anymore.

It would appear, then, that these couples use positively the paradoxical dynamic of estrangement and a newly forged bond. They are able to get outside themselves and to identify with the grief of the spouse. Where there is a way to solve the problems within the marriage, by being more understanding and taking the other's point of view, by realizing the other person's needs, or by providing an occasion for sharing, it appears that marriages can grow and thrive after the death of a child.

Divorced Before Bereavement

Some bereaved parents were divorced when the child died. Among those people, the new tie between the couple may be a simple truce between them during the dying process; but more often it is a sympathetic understanding that transcends the recent interpersonal strife. The griefs which each of them feels, however, makes their estrangement terribly clear. A woman who had been divorced several years when her child got cancer reported:

> I dreaded the next day, when I had to meet my ex-husband at the funeral home for arrangements. Prior to O.'s death we had a "truce" to be nice to each other in order to make O.'s last days as easy as possible. But when O. died, that was the end of the truce. I had my daughter and her husband go with me to the funeral home as a support, and to speak for me if necessary.

The death can make individuals reflect on the current status of their estrangment, and in that reflection see the distance and at the same time see the issues within the divorce. A man who had been divorced a year when his daughter was killed in an accident said:

> Our relationship was very strained prior to this point [the death]. One of the reasons for the divorce was the inability to communicate. It forced her to become more communicative. Paula realized she couldn't continue the isolation that she was attempting.

On the other hand, he said:

> One of the things I'm able to reflect on is that my ability to love someone and my ability to share are still severely impaired. I was in the process of rebuilding my life after the divorce when this happened . . . . I believe what they say about the devastating effects on a marriage after a child's death. If we hadn't been divorced, we would have been after this.

Divorce After Bereavement

Some couples get divorced within a few years after the death of the child. But those who get divorced after the death do not seem to feel that the death was a central factor in the divorce itself. After accepting the reality of the loss of the child, accepting the reality of the prior death of the marriage is a small step. A woman who filed for divorce 2 years after her youngest child was hit by a car said:

> This may seem strange, but it really didn't affect our relationship. The marriage was good the first 10 years, so-so the next 10 years, and dead the last 10 years. More than one counselor told us it was hard to believe that two people so totally different and incompatible had managed to stay together so long. The only difference that C.'s death made was after that I knew nothing could hurt me as bad and the pain of a divorce wasn't as frightening. Besides, after surviving the ultimate loss and attempting to get

on your feet again, it's hard to find the sense of staying in such a bad situation

When a child dies, both parents must grieve in their own way, for the death of a child is a matter of the self in its solitude. When the grief of the spouses does not synchronize, previous issues in the relationship are exaggerated. For example, the inability of one spouse to share and the renewed drinking of the other make separation seem inevitable. Yet even in these cases, the paradox of a new tie in the pain of loss amidst the estrangement is present when they can see the pain in the other even though they cannot reach out to help. A woman reported:

> We just moved farther and farther apart. A lot of it was me, not just him. To this day I can't talk to my husband about it. He can talk to me, but I can't share my feelings with him. He would want to sit and talk about it and cry, but I couldn't. I ran. I was afraid if I started crying I couldn't stop. . . . He started drinking again. I couldn't handle the drinking problem, which began long before A.'s death. He took it out on me. . . . It tears us all up to see the shape he's in. For a long time I hid the fact that my husband is an alcoholic and that he left me.
>
> You can't blame the death for the breakup of the marriage. But many, like ours, were shaky and this was the last straw. You've got enough trying to hold yourself together and are almost helpless in helping your mate.

CONCLUSION

When a child dies, the parent's social environment is changed. The parent is faced with the task of redefining the self within that changed social reality. The parent must find new ways of interacting with the social environment. In doing so, the parent must recognize the reality of the loss, accept the pain, and learn the possibilities and pitfalls of the new world of bereaved parenthood. In the process of restoring equilibrium between themselves and their world, parents can be aided by adequate social support. But social support is often a problem for bereaved parents, for the loss they feel is not shared with others and the parent's normal experiences of grief only serve to distance them from their natural support system. One of the unique factors in parental bereavement is that the loss is shared by the child's other parent, but the shared loss may not lead to adequate social support within a marriage.

The resolution of parental bereavement is not simply the cessation of the early symptoms of grief. The resolution of the disequilibrium between the parent's self and the social environment is the establishment of a new self within a changed world.

There is more to the new self, however, than simply changed interaction patterns and new sources of gratification in the world. There is a more private and intrapsychic aspect to the new self, for the relationship with the child is not severed. The world of the bereaved parent is a far poorer place than it was before the death of the child. To live in a diminished world requires solace. We find that, as part of the resolution of parental bereavement, the inner representation of the child is transformed in a way that gives solace. The restoration of psychic equilibrium in the emergence of solace is the subject of Chapter 3.

3

Achieving Psychic Equilibrium

The child is part of the psychic structure of the parent. At the same time it is the task of mature parenting to maintain the child as a person distinct from the self in such a way that it is possible to empathize with the child's needs and desires separately from the needs and desires of the self. Separation is seldom complete. To the parent the child continues to represent both the parent's good self and the parent's less-than-good self. The joy of parenting is the ability to provide a world in which the child is fulfilling the parent's hopes. The disappointment of parenting is the inability to provide a world that invites the child's fulfillment—or else it is the child's acting out the less-than-good self.

We saw in Chapter 1 that amputation is a metaphor that many parents use to describe the death of a child. They feel as if a part of the self has been cut off. The sense of a missing part of the self is an ongoing aspect of parental bereavement. As an amputee learns to live without the missing limb, so the parent learns to live "as a one-armed man," as a bereaved parent.

This chapter addresses two interrelated questions: First, what happens to the inner representation of the child after the child dies? Second, how does a parent find solace after a wound so deep as the death of a child? The answer to both is in the process of internalization of the inner representation of the child. The inner representation is made part of the ongoing self in such a way that it provides consolation to the parent, even as the parent learns to function within the world made poorer by the death of the child.

Death is not the end of a relationship, but it is a significant change in the role the relationship plays in the life of the survivor. As Robert Cantor (1978) wrote,

The emotional pain caused by loss suffered does not move toward forgetfulness. It moves, rather, in the direction of enriched remembrance; the memory becomes an integral part of the mourner's personality. The work of mourning has been completed when the dead person no longer appears as an absence in a barren world, but has come to reside securely within one's heart. . . . no longer an idealized hero or maligned villain, but a presence with human dimensions. Lost irreversibly in objective time, the person is present in a new form within one's mind and heart, tenderly present in inner time without the pain and bitterness of death. And once the loved one has been accepted in this way, he or she can never again be forcefully removed. (pp. 66–67)

This intrapsychic aspect of the recovery from grief has been the focus of most recent grief theory offered from the psychoanalytic perspective, though only recently have theorists begun to include the concept of solace within their work. In many ways this chapter can be understood as an expansion of Vamik Volkan's (1981) work. For Volkan, the basic task of grief is to internalize the inner representation of the dead person. There are three elements to an inner representation: (1) those aspects of the self that existed before the child was born and are identified with the child; (2) characterizations or thematic memories of the child; and (3) emotional states connected with those characterizations and memories (Fairbairn, 1952). Following Schafer's (1968) model of internalization, Volkan finds two kinds of internalizations of inner representations: identification and introjection. Identification is the integration of the inner representation into the self in such a way that the two are indistinguishable and the ego is enriched. Introjection is the process of maintaining the inner representation as a frozen entity in the psyche, one that is separate from the ego.

Volkan finds identification to be the healthiest resolution of grief. He defines pathology in grief as when introjection outweighs identification. If Volkan's definition of pathology is right, then the great majority of bereaved parents find a pathological resolution, for it is clear that a great many of them introject the inner representation of the dead child. But when we listen closely to bereaved parents talking about the role the dead child plays in their continuing lives, we find that the child brings solace to them. Their solace does not seem to be a matter of pathology.

The defining characteristic of solace is the sense of soothing. The word *solace* means to comfort, to alleviate sorrow or distress. It is that which brings pleasure, enjoyment, or delight in the face of hopelessness and despair. Solace brings cheer to sadness. We find solace after loss.

Solace emerges within irreducible meaninglessness in our lives. It is that which we need when we reach what Paul Tillich called *meonic non-being* (1967, Vol. I), that place in human life where chaos seems to outweigh order, where the absurd abyss opens before us, where the purpose for our living seems overwhelmed by purposelessness.

Solace is a social matter, for we interpret our world within the meanings given to us by our community. The search for meaning is done in relationship to others, whether they be others in our natural support system, or others as we know them from their books or in the mass media (such as television). The solace that another person finds can become our solace when we adopt the belief or experience as our own. When we know that others have found solace, we have hope and that hope becomes our solace.

Paul Horton (1981) finds that the majority of people have a history of solace that they nurture. He finds that the earliest solace is what Winnicott (1953, 1971) called the *transitional object*. That is, an object in a psychic space that is neither self nor not self. It is a continuation of the internalized mother figure. Solace has three characteristics: (1) It is experienced as blended inner and outer reality; that is, it feels as if it is both inside the self and outside the self. (2) It is derived from, but not reducible to, the internalized mother figure. (3) The comfort of solace is not challengeable, for the experience of solace is self-validating (Horton, 1981, p. 26).

A familiar transitional object of Winnicott's sort is the security blanket of the character Linus in the Peanuts comic strip. The security such an object provides helps children explore new situations and adjust to unfamiliar environments (Passman, 1976; Passman & Weisberg, 1975). Many people continue to use physical objects into adulthood. For example, I was consulted by a woman who had an inner sense of terror when she learned that the family farm on which she grew up was being sold. Her terror was that a special secret place with a big tree—where as a child she had communed with the animals—would be destroyed. The knowledge that the place was still there had sustained her through many difficult times, and now that the solace object was to be taken away, she was panicked.

The transitional object, Horton says, can be transformed as we move into maturity. Art and religion have the quality of solace objects for many people, as do recurrent fantasies or dreams. The calming effects of music would seem to be solace to many. These adult objects are no longer transitional, for they are an ongoing part of the adult's life. Horton finds that solace is necessary for the individual who can live in a society. Psychopathic criminals, he says, have no solace in their lives.

Volkan took Winnicott's concept of transitional object and developed it in the idea of linking objects in grief. The mourner holds an object, a physical object, a memory, a fantasy, and uses it magically to evoke the presence of the deceased person. But Volkan does not incorporate solace in his understanding of the linking object; rather the introjection is understood as a refuge from the world of reality, and is therefore seen as pathological. It is pathological in the psychoanalytic tradition because psychoanalysis sees health as rooted in the *reality principle*. Freud's concept of grief work is holding each element of an attachment up to the bitter truth of reality and letting it go (1917). As Karl Abraham (1927) has written:

> The person reacts to a real object loss by effecting a temporary introjection of the loved person. Its main purpose is to preserve the person's relation to the lost object. "My love object is not gone, for now I carry it within myself and can never lose it." (p. 254)

The introjection is understood to be a temporary matter. The real resolution of grief in the psychoanalytic view is giving up the lost object.

Volkan goes to great lengths in his therapy to make sure the bereaved person recognizes the reality of death. In the case of an adolescent girl whose mother had committed suicide, he reports that "her mother was referred to as an inanimate object consisting of degenerating anatomic structures such as skin, muscle, and bone" (Volkan & Showalter, 1968, p. 370). Most of us, however, cannot maintain such Freudian stoicism (Rieff, 1959) in the face of major loss. Our children are "bone of my bone and flesh of my flesh," not degenerating anatomic structures. Health, for most of us, as Horton (1981) says, needs a sense of solace.

An examination of the lives of bereaved parents shows that introjection of the dead child is a common feature of the resolution of parental bereavement, that those introjections bring solace, and that such solace is a healthy part of the ongoing life of the parent. The introjection changes over time, especially in the first two or three years after the death. But for many parents, the introjection is the permanent residue of their loss. Some inner representations may move toward identification, but even in those parents who meld an inner representation of the child into their ego, other inner representations of the child remain as solace giving introjections.

SEPARATING INNER REPRESENTATIONS

Before solace is possible, many parents must spend time separating the inner representations of their child from their self-representations or separating conflicting inner representations of the child from each other. We will examine the process of separating the varied inner representations of the child, and then we will discuss the ways these inner representations can serve as solace.

Separating Inner Representations from Self-Representations

A parent does not internalize the inner representation easily. The first elements of identification are often with the pain of grief and the pain the child knew. One mother we interviewed had a two year old daughter who died after several months in the hospital. The child had blood drawn many times and feared the procedure, for it always hurt her. A few months after the death, the mother went to the clinic to have blood drawn.

> As I went in, I found myself saying over and over, maybe even out loud, "Look at mommy, she can have them take blood, and she will be a big girl so it will not hurt. See, J., mommy is going to be a big girl." When they stuck me it really hurt. I have given blood a lot and it never hurt like that—I mean, it never hurt before, but this time it really did. When I told my mother about it she said, "This may seem strange, but I think that was J. who was hurt." I think she is right. I cried all the way back to work and I knew what she had suffered. The next time I had blood drawn it was like always, just a little prick.

Two meditations by the same bereaved mother can help us to see this early identification as she makes the connection between her problems with separation and the child's earlier problem with separation.

> I was blessed with the ability to nurse my babies, and he was no exception. The exception was that when he was of an age to be weaned from his mother, it was a very frustrating time. . . . By the hour I held him close as he cried softly. Finally he accepted the fact that he had to let go. . . . He was my child and only my child from the day he was born. A tiny replica of myself, and the cord at birth was never cut. . . .
> One day he found a little pink stuffed rabbit. . . . He tried hard to be a little man so he substituted the rabbit for his mother. . . . The time came when he entered kindergarten and it was a very traumatic experience. He

not only had to be away from his mother, but his beloved rabbit also. . . .
By the time he entered first grade he began to realize that big boys don't
suck their thumbs and sleep with rabbits. He tried so hard to give them up.
Night after night he struggled but the rabbit always won. . . . Then came
the night he decided to let go. He called me into his room and handed me
his security, the rabbit. . . .

Now I live with the memory of a young boy who was taken from me
suddenly. I couldn't be with him, and he had to go alone and without me,
his mother. Now his mother can't let go.

Perhaps her identification with the child is so clear because, at least as
she reports it, she never achieved the experience of the child as
distinct from the self. In a meditation on the message "hang in there,"
we can see the child is still part of her.

They live within me—the child and the mother. Today, I am a child, so
small and alone, with arms reaching out and tears in my eyes. I beg "Hold
me." But the world only sees a grown up, a mother, and all I get is "Hang
in there. . . ."

Today is not a good day. I hurt. As I was trying to "hang in there" and
felt my fingers slowly loosing their grip, I looked down and saw no one
under me to break my fall. . . . Now the child in me is lying bruised and
battered but still crying, "Hold me. Kiss my hurts away." I'm sorry my
child. I just couldn't hang in there today.

There is literature on *replacement children* occurring in circumstances in which the inner representations of the dead child are not
separated out, but are kept intact and made part of the bond to
another child. Clinical studies have been done of the children, but not
of their parents. It is clear that trying to live up to the hopes, expectations, and standards of an idealized dead child takes its toll on
these replacement children (Cain & Cain, 1964; Johnson, 1984; Legg &
Sherick, 1976; Poznanski, 1972). The phenomenon manifests itself
years afterwards in the children's problems and is known through
their perception of their family history, so it is difficult to know how
often this happens. Among our interviewees, the only case in which
the parent thought such a factor was a problem concerned the surviving twin of the dead child, and that parent reported that the sibling's
identification with the dead child was self-chosen. Several of the
parents we interviewed, however, were aware of the tendency, but
reported that they guarded against it.

One of the things we try to be conscious about with Fred is whether he feels extra pressure. Jane quit school and got married, and H. died and never graduated. Out of three kids, he's the only one that is going to go to college, the only one that graduated high school. . . . When the kids were young, we always talked about whether we could buy this or that, but we decided to save our money for when the kids went to school. And out of all that, one kid graduated from high school and is going to college. We have asked him whether he feels pressure like he has to carry on for everybody else. He says that there is a little pressure. So we tell him that we don't mean to do that. I'm sure he carries with him that he will fill those dreams and expectations for us.

Several of our interviewees reported that grandchildren to some extent feel like a replacement for the dead child if the grandchildren are born within a few years of the child's death. The psychodynamics of grandparenting, however, seem to be different enough from the psychodynamics of parenting that the literature on replacement children does not apply. Those bereaved parents who find solace in grandchildren seem to be able to hold the child as separate from the self, and as separate from the dead child in a way that the parents using replacement children could not.

Separating Conflicting Inner Representations

If there are conflicting inner representations of the child, the parent faces the difficult task of separating the inner representations from each other. Separating inner representations can be simply a matter of purging the representation of stressful memories and holding the child in an idealized way. Such idealization of the dead occurs in most grief. Most parents do this to some extent, for we typically find them describing the dead child in glowing terms. The common advice to "forget the bad and remember the good" is an attempt to help grieving parents to purge stressful inner representations.

Purging uncomfortable memories can take the form of coming to terms with guilt stemming from what the parent now sees as less than adequate parenting. For example, one father regretted the time he spent on his career, which was taken from time he felt he should have spent with his child. The guilt present in multiple inner representations is somewhat different from the *survivor guilt* experienced earlier in parental bereavement. That early guilt is from the massive experience of the loss of power and competence. The guilt in the ambivalence of *multiple inner representations of the child* seems more grounded in the real lived experiences with the child that were less than the parent wished they had been.

Guilt, if it is too great, may be an occasion for psychological turmoil as the parent seeks forgiveness, which may be difficult to obtain. In one case, the family went to a community picnic where activities for children were separate from those of adults. The wife wanted to go home, but the husband wanted to wait for a drawing, "Because I was sure I was going to win and you had to be there to get the prize." He did win fifty dollars and, as he came off the platform, he was informed that his daughter had fallen off a playground swing and broken her neck. She died 2 days later. He could not forgive what he now saw as his selfishness. His wife blamed him for the child's death. Five years after the death, he remained in the same emotional place he had been in the first week.

When there are conflicts within the parent's relationship to the child, the grief may be prolonged until inner representations are sorted out. Hofer (1984) suggests that mourning may not be a single process, but may be multiple processes.

> Thus, evidence from the psychology of grief supports the idea that multiple representations of the lost person exist, and in grief, unlike normal states, they tend to fragment and are dealt with separately by the bereaved individual. It is possible that each of these individual units of representation may be related to particular biologic responses much the way certain memories make us blush. (p. 193)

Orbach (1959) demonstrated the complexity of parental grief nearly three decades ago in his article "The Multiple Meanings of the Loss of a Child." He gave one detailed case of the death of a woman whose son by her second marriage died. The child's death was part of a string of deaths experienced as repetitions of a grandmother's death when the mother was young. It was also associated with the death of a close supportive brother who died during the pregnancy, after whom the child was named, and of whom she believed the child to be a "carbon copy." There was a strong intimacy between the mother and the child, and an estrangement between the mother and the father, partly because of the husband's feelings of masculine inadequacy and failure to meet his wife's needs for male strength and support. The mother had hoped something bad might happen that would make the husband closer to her. Her neighbors stopped quarreling when their child became sick. So the woman prayed that her own child would become sick. Thus at one point she thought her prayer caused the child's death, while at the same time she was unconsciously denying the child's death.

In such ambivalent grief, each of the inner representations of the dead child must be resolved, to some degree, independently of each other. The difficulty of the resolution varies with the complexity of the ambivalences in the attachment between parent and child. Those with more inner representations that are of the less-than-good self, or which are extensions of attachments to negative figures in the parent's history, produce more difficult griefs. One study (Shanfield & Swain, 1984) found that parents of children who died in traffic accidents showed greater psychiatric symptoms and health complaints if they had an ambivalent relationship with the child or if the child was perceived as having problems at the time of death. A similar pattern is found after children died of cancer when the parent-child relationship was characterized by negative feelings (Stanfield, Benjamin, & Swain, 1984). More positively, it seems that when parents have open communication and can wholeheartedly support a child through terminal cancer, they show stronger resolution than do parents with more ambivalent relationships (Spinetta, Swarner, & Sheposh, 1981).

In one psychotherapy case, a mother whose son was born with a deformed leg had spent most of his childhood protecting him from the taunts of other children. He was killed by a drunk driver. The man responsible was tried and convicted on criminal charges. The grief was difficult for both parents, because both carried conflicting images of the child. The special care he had needed made a great deal of the activity in the home center on him. The parents spoke of a distorted home life and of the situation that two other children were estranged from them. The handicap had given the mother a sense of needing to protect the child. The father had been strongly in favor of pushing the boy to be more independent, and the mother had resented the pressure on the boy. In therapy, the task was separating out those images; but it was difficult, for the anger at the child was directed by the mother toward the father, and by the father toward the court system that had, in his opinion, not done an adequate job punishing the person responsible for the death.

There can be many variations in the way inner representations are sorted out. One mother reported that she first needed to identify with a dominant thematic memory before she could purge parts of the memory. Her daughter was born with a chronic degenerative illness and was in great pain most of her life. The mother did not empathize with the pain, though she strongly empathized with the daughter's fight for a normal life. After the daughter committed suicide, the pain of the parent's grief was understood in terms of the child's pain.

They say suicide is a way to pass the pain. The person who does it feels great pain, and after the suicide the survivors know the pain. When my daughter was born, the best social workers and helpers at the hospital told us to try to lead a normal life and to help her be as normal as possible. We made the decision to do that. She was in pain every day of her life, but I could not allow myself to feel that, because my job was to try to provide a normal life for her. If I had felt the pain, I could not have done what I did; I just couldn't have carried on. So she suffered and she told us, but I really didn't share it. Well, now I know pain. If you will, that is her legacy to me.

So long as there are conflicting inner representations, it is difficult for the parent to transform the representations that will be used in the long-term resolution of the grief. When the negative representations have been purged or resolved, then inner representations that seem good to the parent can be transformed by introjecting them into that space where they go in their lives to find solace. Still, for many, purging or resolving the negative inner representations is never complete. When we asked those we interviewed where they find solace or how they find comfort, many began the answer with a limiting phrase. "I find some comfort," they said, or, "I don't feel it all the time, but sometimes." Solace is never complete, for solace comes within our loss, within our perplexity, within our meaninglessness, within our defeat. Solace is a light in the darkness and the extent to which it overcomes the darkness depends on how bright it shines and how close we can hold it.

SOLACE THROUGH INTROJECTION

Linking Objects

Linking objects are objects connected with the child's life that link the bereaved to the dead; and in so doing, they evoke the presence of the dead. We find that many parents use linking objects that are physical artifacts for extended periods after the death of their child. We can see how linking objects function in a simple way in a letter written to a dead child at the end of the day the family brought out Christmas decorations.

The nice thing about today was that in getting everything unpacked, I got a part of you back for a while. It was comforting to get all those things out that family and friends had given you. All those ornaments to put on the tree with your name on them. There's also that blonde little boy on the rocking horse figurine that will always be with me. And last, but not least, your stocking. . . . It's hanging proudly along with the rest of the family's. . . . As I sit here writing this and looking at the tree and stockings, it hurts to know you are gone. I miss you more than I could ever say, but you'll be with us in spirit this Christmas, just as you are every other day of the year.

We find in the use of linking objects a development through the early months and years of grief. That development, when clinically examined, appears quite idiosyncratic, for the symbolism of the object is deeply rooted in the relationship with the child. The general movement, however, seems at first to be close and immediate physical contact with the object, then having the object in close proximity, and finally having the object out of view, but taking solace knowing the object is safely stored. We can see that movement in a report on a child's stuffed orange dog:

When he died . . . that orange dog became a special symbol to me. When I looked at it I remembered how D.'s face brightened so when he saw it. . . . It even smelled like D to me. . . .

That dog was like a crutch for me. I felt that as long as it was near me as I went to sleep each night, so I could reach out and touch it or smell it, that D.'s death was not so final. And this went on for a while, I'm not sure just how long, but as the smell of my son faded from the dog, so did the worst of the pain I was feeling. . . .

Slowly, then I realized that I didn't notice the dog as much. . . . A day or two would go by without me being ever-conscious of its presence. . . . One day as I cleaned, I put the dog in another room and found I didn't miss it. By then the memories of D. were ingrained into my mind so well I didn't need to look at a symbol of his life to remember him by. . . .

Now the orange dog sits on my dresser in a rather inconspicuous spot. It will never be just another stuffed toy to me, but it has served its purpose and now sits as a friendly reminder of its past owner.

Sometimes the linking object is held in proximity more permanently, but the object still appears to have taken on a soothing function in the parent's life. In a birthday letter to his child 6 years after her death a father reported:

I haven't been able to part with the bicycle cart that I bought for you and your sister a few weeks before you died. It's never used anymore but I keep it in my study at home. . . . I still see your smile as you sat there holding your puppy. . . . Your little wind-up toy, the one of Donald Duck sitting in a shoe, sits on top of the file cabinet in my study. I feel close to you when I'm close to your favorite things.

The biggest linking object we found in our study was a truck. When we asked a father whose daughter had died 5 years earlier if he had an object that helped him feel her presence, he replied:

> It's that old pick-up truck. She used to ride around in it with me. She would lean against me on the seat. It has almost 200,000 miles on it, but I am not going to sell it. By now I probably couldn't get anything for it anyway. I told the boys they could work on it and use it if they got it going. But I'll never sell the truck because I can sit in there and feel my daughter. It's great.

Some linking objects are not really physical objects in the environment, but are fictional characters that have been shared with the child. Compassionate Friends national board member Marcia Alig wrote a poem in which the solace of memory and religious affection are held concretely by dinosaurs as linking objects. The child's imagination had been carried by the dinosaurs to a time in the distant past. Now the dinosaurs carry the parent to a time of imagination shared not so very long ago.

> Dinosaurs once roamed our roost
> Lego blocks, and machines to boost
> Streaking cars 'round oval tracks
> And picture books with missing backs
> Used for obstacles and ramps
> To challenge the racer boosted amps.
>
> Now blocks, tracks, books—all are packed
> Away in neat boxes, carefully stacked,
> Not forgotten but out of sight
> Where none can see or remember fright
> Of sirens, telephones, friends who came
> To cradle us and whisper his name.
>
> We still remember the years of fun:
> Who could forget the way he'd run
> And jump upon a favorite friend,
> Or plead with teary eyes for me to mend
> His ragged blanket filled with love,
> Or greet his brothers with hug and shove?
>
> He's someplace else now, safe and warm,
> With dinosaurs and toys, far from harm,
> Held in memories and loving hearts

Where we can reach him from other parts
To talk and share what happens today.
He'll always be there, not far away.

But dinosaurs still roam our place
Tho' we never see them face to face.
They travel in another dimension
With our son's stories and imagination.
Until the time comes for us to be
A part of that great eternity.

Religious Solace

If the linking object is rich enough in its symbolism, it can serve as an enduring sign to the parent. For this to happen, the object must have a cultural meaning by which the parent can connect her or his personal solace to that provided within the social reality. The butterfly is the most common enduring solace symbol among bereaved parents. It has been adopted as a symbol within The Compassionate Friends. The metamorphosis within the cocoon from caterpillar to butterfly can represent the rebirth of the child from the confines of the grave and the rebirth of the parents from their grief. One of our interviewees found another personal linking object that has cultural symbolism. She and her husband share its meaning. When we asked the question, "Do you ever sense that C. is still around?" she answered:

Every time I see a mourning dove. Mourning doves are magnificent. The day after C. died, Cliff and I were sitting in the den looking out the window and there was a mourning dove on the porch. I didn't know what it was at the time, so I got out my bird book and looked it up. It is m-o-u-r-n-i-n-g dove, not m-o-r-n-i-n-g. It was so ironic because here I'd just lost a daughter and I'm getting out my bird book to look for mourning doves. It was phenomenal that we would see a mourning dove when we were mourning. It's got to mean something, right? So the two of us took this as, "This is C. C. is with the dove." Then, a few days later, there were two doves there. Cliff decided that it was C. telling him that she had a friend with her. It's really fascinating because I'll find myself thinking about her and I'll look around and see the mourning dove. That has become a symbol of C.

It was on the year anniversary when we were going to the cemetery and Cliff said, "I wish I could see a mourning dove." So I said, "Come over here, there is usually a mourning dove over here." And I'll be damned if there wasn't a mourning dove on the wire. He said, "That's a sign. Now I can go to the cemetery."

The culture has many symbols that have been developed from the experience of generations. Most parents have used at least some of these symbols as solace before their child died. After the death of the child, some of the thematic memories of the child and the emotional states connected with the memories are integrated into the religious faith that the parent had previously held. To the extent that religious devotion occurs in the psychic space that is both inner and outer reality, it has the character of a transitional object (Bollas, 1978; Eigen, 1981; Gay, 1983). Because religious devotion has that character, it has a sense of security similar to that first experienced with the mother, and has within it truths that are self-validating to the believer.

For those parents with a well-developed sense of the sacred within a stable religious tradition, the dead child can be integrated into the ritual experience of the sacred. After the death of the child, parents are not likely to adopt a tradition in which they can find solace in introjection (Cook, 1983b). But if the parent is grounded in the tradition before the death, the child may be made a part of the parent's experience in the tradition. One woman, who had lost two children in the same auto accident, gives the role of parent to God in a way that brings her peace. The ritual of the Catholic Mass, which makes the presence of the Son of God real, makes the presence of her children real. Yet the solace she has is not shared by her other children, and she feels uncomfortable speaking of her experience in front of them. She wrote a letter to her dead daughters:

> When I think of you in Heaven I feel peaceful. I think of all the angels and saints and even relatives you are with. . . . Every time I attend the sacrifice of the Mass, at the part where our Blessed Lord comes into our hearts, I feel so close to your angelic presence. What a divine experience! The only problem is that it doesn't last long enough. If only the others could share these feelings. I am afraid to say much about these feelings to your brothers and sisters-in-law. I don't want to widen their hurt. Please try to send some peace from God to them and all of us who miss you so much.

In Christian devotion, the Christ child at Christmas is every child. The wise men bringing gifts to the manger is reenacted in the giving of gifts to each child. At Easter, the resurrection of the Christ is the resurrection of each person who participates religiously in the event. One mother in a support group reported that for the first years of her grief, she had a special sense during Christmas morning worship. She said she was caught up in praise of a God who would send His son and that she felt a sense of unity with Mary, especially with the image of Mary standing at the foot of the cross.

A similar sense of Christmas as a time of anticipated sorrow and identification with Mary is found in a holiday meditation:

No more "Merry Christmas" for us, as we try and concentrate on a "Blessed Christmas." December 25th, the birthday of the baby Jesus who is destined to die at an early age as his grief-stricken mother kneels helplessly at His feet. Even our religious celebration of Christmas can bring a tear of sadness to our eyes. We've lived the sorrow this day of joy will bring to His Mother. . . . Christmas will always come and go. The pain of losing a child will come and go. Christmas trees can be discarded, the pain of losing a child cannot. When I smile with tears in my eyes at your "Merry Christmas," remember mine is a poinsettia, a drop of blood from a broken heart.

An unusual variation of a mother's identification with Mary is seen in the solace of a mother of a retarded child who died. Rather than taking the human story of Mary the mother of the human Jesus, she found solace in the doctrine of Mary the mother of God.

Since it was God's will for me to have a retarded child, the greatest thing I can say about it is that I thank God He chose me to be B's mother. I feel almost as privileged as Mary must have felt to be chosen as the mother of God.

For many parents, the solace they think they might find in their religious tradition is not there. It is difficult for some to reconcile the death of their child with their belief in God as an omnipotent protector. Doubts that might have been intellectual before are existential for the bereaved parent. One woman who had a baby die the night she brought it home from the hospital, and later had a stillborn, reported:

There's lots of people who go around thinking if they are good then bad things can't happen to them. I just tell them, "It has to happen to somebody." I don't pray in church anymore. I go because you are supposed to. How can I tell the children to go to church if I don't? But I don't pray. I just do my grocery list. I think I used to pray and feel close to God. But not anymore. I don't feel anything there.

For others, the simple faith they knew before has been challenged by the tragedy of the their child's death. One man in a support-group meeting talked of the months of praying during his daughter's illness.

Some of the children would get better and some would not. One night as she was going to sleep N. asked me, "Daddy, how does God decide who gets the miracles?" I didn't know what to answer her. I still don't. I guess I still believe in miracles. How else do you account for the kids I saw get better with no explanation. But we didn't get one. So where am I now?

The sense that the child is in heaven is a widely held belief among bereaved parents, even those for whom other aspects of their former faith have been unhelpful. Knapp (1986) found that his interviewees could not sustain a belief that there is no afterlife. A mother reflected in a newsletter:

> A. will always be my six-year-old "baby boy." The other kids will grow up and change, he never will. The other ones will have their own lives to live, their own interests, and their own families that will pull them farther away from me. A. never will leave me. . . . Silly as it may sound, I have this mental picture of A., free now to run and play and be happy in Heaven. No longer does he have to worry about taking care of me. I can visualize him running off to play, glancing over his shoulder saying in an off hand way, "Thanks mom, see ya!"

Though it is very difficult to know how often it occurs, and it is difficult to separate the parent's memory from the actual happenings, in a significant number of cases where the child has had a long illness and many hospitalizations, in the last few days or hours, the child often has nonordinary experiences that help the parent with the belief that the child is in heaven. One mother reported that her eight-year-old child had been distant from her and her husband the week preceeding his death. In a partial coma his last morning, he talked to an unseen figure, and said, "No, I don't want to go with you. I want to stay with my mama." The social worker on the case said she called the house to see how things were going that day and heard the child saying it in the background. On the social worker's advice, the mother lay with the child, and hugged him and said that it was all right to go, that she and his father would miss him very much and that they would remember and love him always. About half an hour later the child awoke from the coma, looked at his mother and said, "I love you, mama." Then he fell asleep in her arms. He did not awake. Though the mother is not actively religious, that experience is for her a self-validating proof that her child is in some kind of heaven and that she will see him again.

Not all parents have religious deathbed experiences to call upon.

When one father reported an experience in a support group, two parents shared similar experiences, but the other five present said they wished they could have had such an experience on which to hang their faith. For those who did not have such an experience, the experience of parents who did was not adequate to apply to them or to their child. They could only envy the solace the dying children's nonordinary experience brought those children's parents.

The sense of divine providence is also widespread in the culture. That God has a plan beyond the comprehension of humans means that life is not random, a condition of chaos, though the nature of the order cannot be specified. For some parents, the sense of divine providence brings solace. Solace is found in a sense of divine providence not when the grand plan is understood; but rather, solace is found when the individual death, absurd and meaningless on its face, is experienced as a part of God's plan. A mother struggling with the question "Why?" said:

> I just cannot accept that there is no reason for this. There has got to be some purpose. R. was a beautiful girl. She didn't deserve to die. I am a good mother. I cannot accept that God just lets things happen. I feel these changes in me. I see good things happening, like the way the kids at the school responded and the pages in the year book. There is a reason for this and good will come out of it.

Many bereaved parents use institutional religious symbols in their solace. Other people experience meaning through symbols not connected to institutional religion. Yet these symbols offer solace. An engineer/manager had risen to a high managerial position using the power of positive thinking. In psychotherapy after the death of his child, he felt guilty because he thought he should have been able to use positive thinking to prevent the death of his child. I introduced the concept of a random universe and he immediately said, "Yes, I know random theory. It is just numbers. It's probability." At that point his entire body relaxed and he looked quietly into space. Few of us who live in the humanities can appreciate the solace that can come in the elegant order of mathematics that is experienced as both inner and outer reality. The solace of probability theory in a random universe is philosophically the opposite of the religious sense of divine providence—but as solace, they function in the same ways in the life of the bereaved parent.

A sense of the religious as found in nature also is widespread in the culture. When bereaved parents have a naturalistic mystical experience (Hood, 1977), they can feel the presence of the child within that experience. One mother reported that on her daily walks she could quietly feel a sense of communion with her son who had been dead for 10 years.

> I'm a walker. I remember I used to take long walks with T. We would go at any time to the year. In the winter he would roll in the snow and make angels. In the fall he would gather leaves. In spring and summer he would watch birds and pick wildflowers. Sometimes I remember those times when I walk, but sometimes it is just the beauty. Like the other day, I was out early and as the sun rose, I was at peace and T. was a part of that.

Soren Kierkegaard (1938) described in his journal of 1835 the experience of nature which brings the presence of the dead:

> And as I stood there one quiet evening, as the sea struck up its song with a deep and calm solemnity, whilst my eye met not a single sail on the vast expanse of water, and the sea set bounds to the heavens, and the heavens to the sea whilst on the other side the busy noise of life subsided and the birds sang their evening prayer; the few that are dear to me came forth from their graves, or rather it seemed to me as though they had not died. I felt so content in their midst, I rested in their embrace, and it was as though I were out of the body, wafted with them into the ether above— and the hoarse screech of the gulls reminded me that I stood alone, and everything vanished before my eyes and I turned back with a heavy heart to mix in the busy world, yet without forgetting such blessed moments. (p. 12)

The nation also can be experienced in a religious sense and all cultures encourage the sense of the unity of the dead soldier with the abstracted nation. Lincoln's address at Gettysburg offers solace to the parents of those buried there, and at the same time it bonds the citizens to their country and to the war dead. Such solace can, of course, be used destructively. It matters not in the irrationality of the psyche whether the cause be just or unjust. The emotions do not know when they are being manipulated for cynical political ends. When the narcissistic wound is to be healed by revenge, blood must be answered by blood. In the name of those fallen for the cause, people on the other side may be killed with impunity, regardless of whether as individuals they were responsible for the death. A cycle of violence based in grief may be difficult to stop. On the other hand, when parents merge the inner representation of the child with larger principles of justice in the society, as did the mothers of children who disappeared during the dictatorship in Argentina in the 1970s, they further the possibilities for a more humane society.

Memories

Bereaved parents can find the space that is between the self and the other in memory that is cherished and nurtured in the bereaved parent's aloneness. Unconflicted and peaceful memory is often at the endpoint of a difficult process within parental bereavement. Memories are at first very painful, for they are reminders of the loss. To remember is to cry. Indeed, a common phenomenon among bereaved parents is guilt at that point in their grief when they no longer feel sad all the time. A day of relative normality may occasion guilt because, as one person said, "All I have left of my child is my sadness. If I give that up, then I really have to let go of my child." One mother reflected on the discovery that letting go of the pain did not also mean letting go of the child.

> You know, I remember being afraid that someday I would wake up and my feeling of being bonded to K. wouldn't be there. I thought that when the pain left, she would be gone too. But now I find that I hope the memories will come. The times in the hospital are not what I remember. I remember the good times, when she was well. Sometimes I just look at her pictures and remember when we took them. I never know when I will look at the pictures, but I feel better afterwards.

For some parents, the ability to remember the child in dreams in a pleasurable way is a dramatic breakthrough in the grieving process. One parent reported in a newsletter article on dreams:

> When we first lost our son, I couldn't get over the fact that I didn't dream about him. . . . In fact, in those days, I really didn't want to wake up, as every morning was like waking up to a bad dream. . . . Finally I did start dreaming but they were hard to remember the next day, as they seemed to be only brief glimpses of a child forever lost to me. They left a deep depression, because I could never see the front of him, nor could I talk to him. . . . Thoughts of suicide entered my mind and it was a battle not to give in. . . . Just when it seemed as though I could no longer hold on to my sanity, I had a sequence of dreams that gave me back some of my strength. I had a night of beautiful dreams of my son. They were the kind of dreams that seemed so real that each time I woke, it was with tears of happiness and not of sadness. The dream that was the most vivid and that I derived the most comfort from was the first one. He was laughing and playing and

when he saw me, he walked up to me and we both were so happy to see each other that we burst out laughing. I knew that I couldn't touch him, and I also knew he couldn't come back to me, but to be able to see so plainly in his face and eyes, and to see the love and happiness that was there just for me was all I needed. The day following the dreams was a very happy day for me. I have since had my ups and down, but when things are bad, I try to recall the happiness I saw on his face.

In work with bereaved parents, we may find them located any-where along the spectrum from pain to solace with their memories. It appears, however, that many know that the process through which they are going ends with the memories being solace even before they find the solace for themselves. A newsletter article reflected:

> It is too soon and the hurt too raw, but I pray for the day I can dig past the clippings and the cards without hurting and find peaceful memories as I look at the hand-drawn valentine that M. sent from Vietnam, and perhaps I'll even laugh at some candid snaps, like the one taken after he played barber. . . . and I'll know the healing process has begun.

For some parents, the quiet times with the memory of the dead child seem stolen and have about them a somewhat forbidden quali-ty, but the memory time becomes a personal ritual around which to build a day.

> Sometimes I pretend, when no one's around,
> that you are still home,
> creating your own special sound—
> the car, the stereo, singing in the shower.

Once the memory comes, the solace time is often ritualized. The yearly memorial in the Jewish ritual regularizes the memory to appro-priate times in the mourners' ongoing life. When the ritual is made part of the community, the bond with the child may become part of the bonds with the community. For their yearly holiday candlelight memorial service, many Compassionate Friends chapters have adopted a liturgy from *Gates of Prayer* (1975), a Reform Judaism prayerbook.

> In the rising of the sun and in its going down,
> WE REMEMBER THEM;
> In the blowing of the wind and in the chill of winter,
> WE REMEMBER THEM;

In the opening of buds and in the warmth of summer,
WE REMEMBER THEM;
In the rustling of leaves and the beauty of autumn,
WE REMEMBER THEM;
In the beginning of the year and when it ends,
WE REMEMBER THEM;
When we are weary and in need of strength,
WE REMEMBER THEM;
When we are lost and sick at heart,
WE REMEMBER THEM;
When we have joys we yearn to share,
WE REMEMBER THEM;
So long as we live, they too shall live, for they are now a part
of us as
WE REMEMBER THEM.*

However, we live in a time when the memory of dead children is seldom done in a communal setting. The candlelight memorial service is the largest gathering of the local Compassionate Friends chapter. When a memorial mass was offered by a local Catholic church, flowers that parents bought and then could take home filled the front of the church. But for the most part, we find that the child is not remembered in public for long after the death, and parents find quiet moments in their day and week during which they retreat from the world of now and, for a few moments, return to a time when the world was better.

The inner representation becomes a memory held in that space in the psyche that is neither completely self nor completely other, and which has been developed throughout a lifetime—beginning with the internalized experience of nurturant mothering. When we listen to bereaved parents for whom solace is this individual memory, we find thematic memories, that is, memories that for the parent catch the essence of the individual child.

I can still envision the surprised, happy look on his face that Christmas when he opened a gift and found a silver vest and pants to wear when he played his bass guitar with his beloved band. . . . I remember when he took me out to eat one Mother's Day, just he and I. . . . how handsome he was

---

in his tux and top hat and how he introduced his date for the prom . . . how
proud we all were at his graduation when he gave the welcome address.
. . . Wonderful memories are something that no one can take away. Some
memories just won't die.

As we listen to these reports of memories, the emotional states
attached to the thematic memories seem to be the aspect of the inner
representation that carry the quality of solace. Writing nearly 20 years
after the death of her daughter, a mother reflected on her memory of
a beginners' ballet recital.

I can't remember the details of that afternoon. . . , But I remember the
feeling, somewhere between laughter and tears. I remember loving that
small, beautiful person, my child. I remember my sense of admiration for
her, and a fittingly stifled flood of pride. . . . I have forgotten so many
things, but I remember the feeling. Always the feeling.

IDENTIFICATION

Linking objects, religious solace, and memory are all introjections in
Volkan's understanding of the resolution of grief, for all keep the
child as a frozen entity in the psyche. The majority of the solace we
find in bereaved parents comes from those introjections. We also find
the other kind of internalization, identification (Miller, Pollock, &
Bernstein, 1968). In identification, the inner representation of the
child is integrated into the self in such a way that it is difficult to
distinguish the two. Because the inner representation of the child is
maintained less as a separate entity, solace has a somewhat different
character. There is solace in identification. It is found in a sense of
reinvigorated life, in renewed feelings of competence. This solace is
less clearly defined, but it is solace, for it provides comfort in the face
of potential meaninglessness.
    Identification has its social aspect. Freud noted that membership
in a group and falling in love are both based in identification, for the
individual's ego is merged with the inflated ego of the leader or the
ego of the beloved (Freud, 1960). With adequate social support, pain
is shared and in that sharing, the relationship with the child is shared
within the supportive relationship. Thus, the identification with the
child is made a part of wider identifications. In that wider context, the
life of the child can be integrated into the whole self. This is the
process Volkan called the enrichment of the ego.

> Are we left with just memories
> Of a loved one we knew?
> Let us share all our feelings
> I am part of you too—

One parent described the self-help process in a Compassionate Friends meeting as a circle of weavers in which the bonds that were with the child now become attached and interwoven with other bereaved parents in the group. Thus, rather than having the child as a frozen entity in the psyche, the inner representation of the child becomes a part of the ongoing social relationship within the group. The sense of oneness with other bereaved parents is an enlargement of the self—or in Volkan's terms, an enrichment of the ego.

> I want to thank The Compassionate Friends for helping to bridge the span between "who I was" and "who I am." I will never be the same person; I can be a better, stronger person. Being a part of The Compassionate Friends has given me a sense of community and a feeling of belonging. It has given me an opportunity to turn a tragedy into something positive. The alienation I felt, and the desperate anxiety, have been replaced by an ability to care for and receive care from TCF.

Often identification is found in a decision to live fully in spite of the death. One parent wrote about positive ways of remembering the child by supporting public memorials to him, but more importantly by finding fullness and meaning in her own life.

> I came to the decision that I was going to try to use my gift of life to the utmost as J. had used his. . . . There is joy in my life now. . . We have sought positive ways to remember J. Members of our family continue to give books to a memorial shelf of books [at the library]. . . started by friends of J. Members of our family periodically give blood to the Red Cross, hoping to help others who may need that gift in their struggle for life. . . . Life will never be the same. I will always be disappointed that J. did not have a longer life, but I will always be proud of him and love him. I continue to search for ways to bring love, hope and meaning in my life as I try to make use of my one gift of life.

Sometimes the enriched ego is felt simply as a continuation of the expanded sense of self that comes with parenting, as well as the sense of strength at having survived the narcissistic wound of the death of a child. But we also find that the enriched ego is experienced as the parent realizes that the spirit of the child is their own spirit; in acting within that spirit, the parent finds a joyful solace. On the experiential problem of how to celebrate the birthday of a dead child, one parent reported:

> We celebrated his birthday by living like he would. He was a fighter who took all the joy and good times he could in his short life. So we celebrated his birthday by riding our bikes to go out for the pizza he loved. We went to one of those places with the clowns and the machines to play with. We laughed and loved each other because we knew what he had given us.

The enriched ego is for living in this world, not for dwelling in the past, and the child is carried symbolically into this new life of meaningfulness that the bereaved parent now lives. The child is a part of the new life, but the parents search for the right metaphor by which to describe the new relationship the parent now feels with the child, for the culture has few symbols that seem adequate. Poet Marcia Alig found the metaphor of prologue. It is as if the child's life and dreams were a prologue to the life she lives now.

Cut off in mid-sentence,
   your life remains
a mere prologue, thus . . .
I pick up your life's open volume
And wonder
   what might have been written.
Would your story have been
   straight and true
Or bent before the challenges you faced?
Would the promises of your prologue
   have been fulfilled
Or disappointment been your course?

Never to know
   the progress of your tale
I am suspended in doubt.
Must you remain forever a prologue
Or could I write the script,
And through my life
state your meaning?

Yes, I will present your messages.
Love, devotion, joy and knowledge:
These truths will speak
through my pages,
Making your prologue—
forever mine.

CONCLUSION

Parental bereavement is a permanent condition, for it is the amputation of a part of the self. The world of the bereaved parent is thus
forever poorer. In that poorer world they find solace, soothing comfort, in the internalized inner representation of the child. Before the
child can be internalized, the conflicting inner representations of the
child must be separated and the inner representation must be purged
of uncomfortable elements. For most parents, the inner representation is internalized by introjection. The child may be kept as a frozen
entity in the psyche by the use of linking objects. The child may be
merged into the parent's store of solace objects such as religious
symbols. The child may be maintained as special thematic memories,
which may be ritually recalled as a part of each day's routine. For
some parents, the child may be more fully integrated into their self
representation in identification, because the child's life gives meaning
to the parent's and the parent's ego is enriched.

The death of a child creates a disequilibrium in the social world of
the parent, and, as well, it creates a disequilibrium in the psychic
structure of the parent. Grief is the process by which the parent
moves toward new equilibria. It is clear that the relationship to the
child is one of the major constellations of meaning for the adult, a
constellation of meanings for which the adult often willingly sacrifices
other constellations of meanings. We should not, therefore, be surprised that the study of the death of a child takes us deep into the
social relationships and deep into the psychic structure of the parent.
And we should not be surprised that the death of a child calls forth
some rather complex reorganizations of the social self and of psychic
structures.

The same ambivalences and multiple representations that were
part of the living relationship with the child are part of the search for
equilibrium when the child dies. Neurotic parenting probably leads to
neurotic grieving and to neurotic resolutions. A mother whose child
is the image of her own problematic mother must wrestle again with
the feelings about her mother within her grief for her child, for the
child is not a distinct person, but rather a person invested with
energy from other relationships.

It is also possible that the resolution of parental grief can be less
conflicted than was the parenting. The past sets the limits of the
present, but the shape of the future need not be determined. Just as
the birth of the child can provide the occasion for reworking the
parent's own childhood, so parental grief provides yet another occasion. Identification and introjection are provisions for a new psychic

equilibrium, which can be a rich development of the self for the bereaved parent. One cannot work long with bereaved parents without realizing the strengths and depths of their lives. Reformed inner representations of a dead child provide the parent with personal qualities not available before. All ends are also new beginnings. Just as parenthood is a developmental process, so is parental bereavement.

4

Individual Lives

Each story of parental bereavement is unique, because the life history of each parent is different, and because each parent-child relationship is different. This chapter gives a fuller account of grief in the lives of four parents.

JOAN

Joan's 26-year-old daughter, Christa, was killed when a drunk driver hit the car in which she was a passenger. The accident occurred at 4:30 a.m. in an otherwise empty intersection. The passenger side of the car took the full force of the impact. Christa was dead on arrival at a hospital 5 minutes away. Neither the drunk driver nor the person with whom she was riding suffered serious injury.

Christa worked nights at a bakery. She was a clerk on the docks where trucks were loaded for early morning delivery to stores. After work, the young workers would socialize by going to an all-night pizza place where they would have their "supper" and wind down before a morning of sleep. Christa was on her way to the diner when she was killed. Joan and her husband, Ted, went to The Compassionate Friends meeting 2 months after Christa was killed and have become regular attendees. Joan sometimes arranges who will bring the cookies or cake for after the meeting. We interviewed her 3 years after the death. For Joan, motherhood was the fulfillment of selfhood. She said:

> To me, my child was my life. I guess everybody says that, but like the doctor told me, "You were born to have kids." My husband and I really wanted her. He and I went together since I was thirteen and he was fourteen. We started planning early. Even if we weren't going to get married, we started planning anyway. We even picked out names for our

kids before we had any kids, before we were even married. This doctor, one time, told me I was pregnant and I wasn't. That really threw me for a loop because I wanted to get pregnant. Christa was born not too long after that. I wanted two girls and two boys, but I didn't get the boys. I would still like to have more kids. The other day I told Sandra that I'd still like to have the two boys along with the four girls.

Joan has several sometimes-conflicting memories of Christa. She recalls her sitting on a rocking horse watching television in a cowboy outfit complete with holster and gun. Her favorite program was *Bonanza*. Christa would have her uncles and older cousins play the characters of Hoss, Adam, and Little Joe. As she grew older, Joan remembered Christa playing priest at an altar set up in a doorway. The boy next door was altar boy while the girl played the priest. As a high school student, Christa worked with handicapped children and for a long time dreamed of being a teacher in special education.

But there are also guilt-filled memories. Christa had been the first child. After Christa was 5 years old there were three other children born in as many years, and Joan did not have as much time for Christa. Joan felt that her mother-in-law used the occasion to "pull Christa away from me," by often taking Christa to stay the night at the mother-in-law's house.

When Christa was ten, Ted had a "nervous breakdown" after he lost a job. The family was living in another state and Joan had to go to work and leave Christa with people she did not know. Again the memories are of Christa's not being protected and of Joan's not able to provide proper care.

> They were not mean to her or anything, I don't think. But I just had to go to work and leave her, and when you've just moved to someplace, you don't know what people are like. I blocked out of my mind a lot of the stuff from then, so I don't remember. I don't really remember the people I left her with. It was about two or three different ones, so that wasn't good for her. That was hard on her.

Christa went away to college for a semester, but did not want to return for the second semester. She got the job working nights and lived at home until she died. During those last 7 years, Joan and Christa saw little of each other, for Joan worked days. Every few weeks, however, Christa would come and lay on Joan's bed, and the two would talk intimately about Christa's life and about the family. During that time, Christa was happy and felt she was living the kind of life she wanted.

One of the fears Joan felt about Christa during her last 7 years was that Christa had not married. For Joan, Christa and her other daughter who did not marry had "no one to take care of them after we are gone." The fear seems related to her concerns about the adequacy of the care she provided when they were young. Christa's assurances that she was happy being single, that she had a group of friends who enjoyed each other, and with whom she traveled on vacations, had to some extent quieted Joan's fears that there was no one to take care of her child; but the fears reemerged after Christa died, for now she was really beyond what Joan could do for her.

One of the ways Joan understands the experience of Christa's death is by reference to her husband's mental illness:

> When something is wrong with your body, you can understand it. But when it's your mind, you can't understand it. It's really weird. But it is something like this with Christa; you can never take care of it.

It seems a mystery to her, but Joan has accepted the mystery of life. For her, suffering seems just something to be endured. She knows that she suffers, but she wonders if ultimately God cares, though she cannot cast the question in so stark a term. The death of her daughter has brought Joan to a kind of plain-man's existentialism.

> You know, I don't think this feeling I have for Christa after her dying will ever go away. I know it will never go away completely. Some nights I just wonder. I sit and I think and I wonder. What do people do when they die?
>
> Q: You mean the people that die?
>
> Yeah, what do they do. Here, we've got to be doing something all the time or something's wrong with us. Even just a little work or doing something when you come home and go on vacation. But what do you do when you die? You're not supposed to suffer anymore. But you have to wonder if the people you love who have died wonder about you. If they don't have any worries or pain, why should they care about what's going on down here?

In her life as a bereaved parent, Joan has had difficulty finding living people who care about what is happening in her life. She has worked most of her life and the circle of friends she had were at work. Only two weeks before Christa was killed, she was transferred to a new department after being in her old job for 16 years.

> I hadn't had anybody to talk to because I'd go to work and the one friend I would have talked to had just changed jobs when this had all happened.

That was hard on me too because I worked with these people for sixteen years. I worked at Audhaus warehouse, but they tore that down and put up a mall there, so I got sent to the billing department. That tore me up too. Sixteen years is a long time to work with people. You know them inside and out. I didn't know any of these new people, and all of a sudden this happened. It was only like 2 weeks or so.

She has found a support group in The Compassionate Friends:

We started going about 3 weeks after she died. She died on the seventeenth of April and we started going to the first meeting in May. I went back to work about this time too. I was off 2 weeks before I had to go back. I went to the nurse at work and told her I needed some help. I just didn't know what to do. She told me about Compassionate Friends and gave me a name to call. I called and the person asked if my husband and I would like to go to the meeting. I asked him and he said that if I wanted to go, we should. I said that I thought we should try it because I needed something. But I couldn't talk about it then. I could barely tell them who I was. But we kept on going to the meetings. I think one time we missed about five or six months. It seems like it always comes up around that time. But we started going back. Sometimes I wonder why I'm going, but then when it gets to be time to go, I want to go.

I'm a big crybaby. I always was. A lot of times I'll go to bed at night and I'll just start thinking and crying, but nobody hears me. That's one thing I like about those meetings. You can cry and nobody thinks anything about it. I guess that's one reason I keep going back.

When we asked how the death had changed her life, it seemed to her as if everything had changed, though on the surface little had.

It just changes your life completely. The kids are always driving somewhere, and like when my daughter was going to Florida this weekend, that's something else for me to worry about because they are driving.

Q: How would you describe the changes in you?

That's hard to say. You just do the things that you did while she was here, anything and everything. And you can't have holidays. You go through holidays, but something there tells you that part of it is missing.

Q: So a lot of the joy and pleasure's gone?

Yeah. Thank God I have three children, but I don't really know how it is with them because they never talk about it. But you just can't help that.

Q: Has anything happened on the positive side of that? Not that there has to be a something positive, but is there?

I can't think of anything.

Joan is fighting what she sees as the injustice of Christa's death. She has filed a wrongful-death suit against the driver, but the case keeps being postponed. As with the parents of murdered children, each new court date is a reopening of the wound. But despite that pain, she keeps pressing the suit. She will make the drunk driver pay and she will not accept that her daughter's life was worth the light sentence the man received, nor the small sum she is now being offered to settle out of court.

> The guy's family want his name cleared, so they want to give me money. I'm not going to take it. I don't want the money. I don't want him cleared.
> Q: You want him prosecuted?
> He got like 5 years and they put him on 2 years' probation and that was it. That's over now. So he doesn't have to worry about that anymore.
> Q: So what's coming up?
> The lawyer filed a suit against him for wrongful death. But if I let them give us money, they can close the case and he won't have to worry about it anymore. So they are offering me money for Christa's life. They're saying that this $5000 is what she's worth. But I'm not going to let them do it. I've turned them down once and I'll turn them down again.
> Q: They want to put a dollar amount on your daughter's life.
> I'm not going to do it. I don't know what it will actually take to clean off the books. But I want to have it on the books, even if he's not getting punished for it, I want it known he is responsible.

Joan finds solace by developing ways of having Christa remembered within the family. When that happens, she feels supported and feels as if Christa is still part of the family. When we asked her where Christa is for her now, she said:

> I think she's just here. On the Sunday closest to the date, we have a Mass and we invite everyone who wants to come. And then we have a party downstairs. We have food and we sit around and talk. People can come in and leave when they want to. It's for her because she loved parties. She had a lot of friends in the neighborhood and somebody was always having a party. So we have a party for her every year.

HAL

Hal is an industrial chemist well known in his field. We interviewed Hal twice, once 18 months after the death of his son and again 4 years after the death. Shortly after our second interview, he married a woman he had been dating for 3 years. He and his first wife, the mother of the dead child, were divorced 6 months before the death.

Larry, the oldest of Hal's four sons, was killed at age 14, when a speedboat he was driving alone and without a life vest flipped in very high waves. He had skipped school for the day. Hal was out of town when Larry died. He was put on a plane and flew home immediately.

Hal was raised by an intellectual family. His parents believed in individual responsibility. He was given an allowance and freedom to spend it as he wished. He was to learn from the consequences of his actions. He tries to be the same toward his own children. "I try not to influence them," he said, "but I try to let them see the consequences. I try not to have expectations, but my main concern is having them come to terms with the world."

This philosophy made it difficult for Hal to come to terms with Larry's death, for it was a foolish act. Larry had driven the boat before, but had worn a life vest and had someone with him. Because what Larry did seemed so irresponsible, Hal has considered often that it was suicide, though nothing in the boy's previous behavior indicated that he harbored self-destructive thoughts. Hal also wonders if Larry had been smoking marijuana, for Hal thinks he had tried the drug before. For Hal, the essence of human life is the responsibility a person takes for the consequences of his or her actions. Larry acted irresponsibly and it killed him. Hal has difficulty deciding whether as a father he should have been able to protect his son from acting foolishly or whether the son was responsible for his own act.

One of Hal's memories is of Larry racing a friend in go-carts they had built. Larry had the slower car, but Larry made up for it in daring.

> He rushed him and rushed him. He was going as fast as he possibly could. The car was on two wheels. The next day I was talking to a friend and I said, "Larry is not going to live to a ripe old age." He had no sense of self-preservation at all. There was no margin there. His character was to take risks.

Six months before Larry died, Hal and his wife Anita were divorced. It was a difficult separation for him because he loved her and was very attached to the children. He got a house three blocks from Anita's and saw the children daily except when he was on a business trip. The children and he had vacationed together just before the death. For 4 years before the divorce, Hal had been attending Al-Anon. It was within that support group that he was able to understand the problems within his marriage and move toward the sad decision of divorce. In both interviews with us, he mentioned that he was still in close touch with her and felt bad about the hard time she was having.

Hal is an intellectual and a manager. He moved toward resolution of his grief using those skills. A fellow member of Al-Anon, whose son died 2 years before Larry, told Hal about The Compassionate Friends. Hal attended his first meeting 3 months after the death. He had planned to attend the second month, but was out on a business trip. Hal also reads a great deal. Schiff's *The Bereaved Parent* (1977) and Kushner's *When Bad Things Happen to Good People* (1981) spoke to him very personally. At the meetings and in his readings, he was advised to express his feelings and to allow himself to grieve as he needed. That advice was, for Hal, a program that made sense. A great deal of the material in both our interviews was an explanation of the grief process and an account of how he followed the program to resolve his grief.

> You know, what I think is important is allowing yourself to feel the hurt, allowing yourself to experience the grief. Initially, of course, it's so real and so raw you want to bottle it up. It takes an enormous amount of energy to keep it down. After about 3 months or so, you no longer break down in public and in your office. You tend to do it in those precious little moments at home or in a very private setting. One of the things Compassionate Friends says to do to release those tensions is to take a picture of the child while sitting at home, look at it and talk to the child. Of course it brings tears, but at the same time it becomes a release.

His son's death is an absurdity in Hal's life. It is, for him, the potential for losing control, for his being unable to manage his life. Hal went from a description of a man he knew who committed suicide to saying:

> It is so hard to know what he was thinking. I learned to deal with it, but it is like a big black hole that sucks you in. You lose total track of everything around you. You lose all perspective of your life or your family. You can't understand how it happened. How Larry could kill himself.

Hal's response to the issue of Larry's responsibility for his own death has been anger. He knows it is irrational, but he also knows it is a normal response, that he has it, and that he must not deny it.

> You know how frustrated you get in your daily life. It had its purpose. I had the urge to do something physical. It was frightening. I was probably angry at everything and everyone at that time. I certainly was very angry at

Larry, intense anger at my former wife. And you feel yourself an emotional invalid, but that was a temporary thing. I was angry at myself for having the boat and at my company for me being out of town, though I was the one who made decisions as to whether I would go out of town. Just angry. Highly irrational. None of this stands up under the light of examination, but that's the nature of anger.

The anger has the potential to be the black hole sucking him in, but he is determined that it will not overcome him. Hal has made a decision to survive.

When any child dies, I don't care what the reason—run over by a car or an illness—you can play "what ifs" until you go crazy. Part of regaining your life and your sanity is to stop playing "what ifs."

Q: You could have done that back and forth—did he or didn't he?— and spent a lot of time. It doesn't sound like it consumed you.

I never let it consume me. You know many of we parents crack under the horror of the loss, and lose the will to live. We even say, "I'd feel better if I committed suicide." I certainly felt those thoughts, but I didn't dwell on them for long. I guess I'm not that kind of a personality. I was bound and determined to survive it.

Q: It sounds like that might be one of the ways that helped you through it—the determination, the will to live in spite of it.

Yes, but I don't think that stands on its own. I think you have to sort of put that in the context of your whole life. As a parent, having other children, you need to care for those children and give commitment, responsibility, and love to those children, so you don't want to leave them. The fact that I have a profession which gives me a lot of satisfaction counts. Basically I'm a strong person who can survive misfortunes, and expect misfortunes in the future, and expect to survive them.

Survival for Hal does not mean simply hanging on, for he sees his life during last few years as growth and change. He sees Larry's death as one of a whole series of life-changing events. When we asked how he had changed as a result of Larry's death, he said:

I couldn't honestly say. The problem would be that it is almost impossible to determine because suddenly I'm going through all kinds of changes. In my case my divorce had become final only months before Larry died. That in itself was a major change and certainly there were a lot of changes that I've experienced which were related to that period of time. There was a lot of rebuilding, and now I have remarried and my career has changed. So many things have changed.

There is a direction in which, for Hal, all the changes point. He says they all lead him to being more sensitive. By that he seems to mean an openness to others' pain—but also attending to feelings as opposed to attending primarily to thinking.

> Your sensitivity changes from undergoing this kind of stress. I mean your sensitivity to divorce and to the problems others going through that are facing. And certainly my sensitivity to other parents who have lost children has changed. I have a second cousin who lost a little girl. That was 4 years before Larry died. I loved that child and visited her in the hospital 6 months before she died. I remember when I wrote a letter to her parents comforting them, saying that I felt bad that this had happened. I was not realizing what the parents had gone through; I was just seeing it in terms of me.

That new sensitivity has led Hal to more intimate sharing with others. He found a great deal of social support within Al-Anon and then in The Compassionate Friends. He has taken the experience of being supported by intimate sharing into his professional relationships. He reported conversations with three men around the country who lost children, one by suicide. Hal takes satisfaction in his ability to speak from his own experience and to empathize with theirs.

Hal still feels the missing piece that was Larry. When we asked what role Larry played in his life now, he said:

> In memories and good things and bad things. In a fairly realistic assessment of a child as someone who is not there. I think of him there periodically. It would be a thought like, right now he would be graduated from high school and he would be in college, if he had cleaned himself up enough to do that. He would have gone on to something else. But you really shake your head and wonder why, and you sort of think about those things.

Amidst all the ambivalent memories of Larry, there is one that Hal can at times bring back as solace:

> One of the things I clutch to as something really great happened between us a couple weeks before he died. The kids were at my uncle's place for a few weeks and when they came back, I had bought a boat. We were driving down the street and he was absolutely, incredibly thrilled that I would buy this boat. He thought it was the greatest thing. I took him riding one time and I let him drive and his eyes got big. We were cruising along and he said, "Dad, I really like you. I really love you as a person." It was quite a bond and at the same time it was a wonderful feeling.

The solace in the memory cannot quite be used in an unambiguous

way, for it was that same boat that Larry was racing without safety
equipment when he turned too tightly in rough seas.

TASHA

We interviewed Tasha 11 years after her child died. She had only
recently found some resolution to the death and requested to talk to
us when she heard about our project.

She had had a six-year-old and twin two-year-old daughters
when she had a hysterectomy because of uterine cancer. Two weeks
after she came home from the hospital, she was awakened by Ann,
one of the twins, who said the other twin, Louise, had not shared
"these." The child was carrying an empty bottle of prescription pain
medication. The bottle had been high on a mantel behind a plaque,
and the child had moved a table and climbed to reach it. Louise had
eaten about 30 tablets. Tasha and her husband rushed the child to the
hospital in their small town, but it was a Sunday and the physician
did not arrive to pump her stomach for 2 hours. They won a malprac-
tice suit for his delay. The child went into convulsions during the
night. About four in the morning Tasha was told to get some sleep.
She woke at six and "just had to go see her." When she came into the
room, the nurse had her back to the bed. The nurse did not know the
child was dead.

Tasha remembers hardly anything from the 4 months that followed, except that she could talk to no one about what happened and
that she would not let Ann out of her sight. A physician diagnosed
her as having severe depression and she was sent, with Ann, out of
state to her parents. After a month she woke one day and realized she
still had two children who needed her, and she made arrangements
to fly home.

Tasha's husband could not talk about the death nor about
Louise. In the 11 years since the death, they have not talked about it.
"It was rough on him," she said, "but he never talked about it. Right
now, I still really don't know how he feels." She was living in the
husband's hometown. None of his family was willing to communicate with Tasha about the death. About 3 years after Louise's
death, Tasha found she needed to talk, but no one else did. She spent
some time with her pastor who listened to her "and that helped," but
deep unresolved issues remained.

Having the twins had played an important role in Tasha's life,
and in Louise's death, Tasha felt the punishment of God for the pride
and self-esteem she felt at having them:

To me, having twins was accomplishing something that was kind of special. That was important to me. I didn't want to conform to the average. I remember once I was late with my period. My mother was worried to death. One day she asked me if I was worried about it and I said, "No, why should I be?" I think I so startled her that she never worried about me after that. Maybe I felt I'd been too good, but then I thought it was good to feel good about things that way. I began to really want to excel. I hadn't really gone to school, so I couldn't do it that way. So having the twins was a good way to do that. But then I found out that it didn't make the change that I thought it would with my husband.

I felt then that I was being punished. It was being taken away from me because I wanted twins so badly. It was like they meant too much to me. I don't know if it was like I couldn't share enough of that love with my husband or somebody else. I don't know. I just felt that God was punishing me by taking away what I so desperately wanted. Part of the reason, I thought, was that it didn't appear that I could give my husband a son, so instead I gave him twins, which was almost as good in his sight. I felt that he was disappointed. I had miscarried my first pregnancy, and immediately I got pregnant again. My eldest child was a girl and he wanted a son.

The remaining twin, Ann, suffered most of the symptoms of the family's unresolved grief. Tasha reports that the professional help Tasha and Ann received from two therapists focused on the child. At age seven, Ann was being called "Louise" by family members, and her being a twin was mentioned around her. She wanted to know what that meant, so Tasha and she would talk as they looked at pictures of the two babies. During puberty, Ann became obsessed that a part of her was missing. She got pregnant and, with Tasha's help, made the difficult decision to have an abortion. The counselor at the hospital where she had the abortion talked with Ann and said that Ann would need a good deal of support.

I said that her dad was not going to give it to her. So it was going to have to come from me. I told her I'd be there. So we started to work on it. We talked and I tried to find out why it happened. One of the things that kept coming back was that Ann needed something to love. When it finally got down to the end, it was that Louise wasn't there. There was part of her missing. We had talked about sex. She wasn't dumb on the subject. She loved children and for her, that baby was like a replacement for what she had lost by not having her sister.

After the abortion, mother and daughter could talk openly about Ann's sense of a missing part. They were able to find ways of symbolizing the integration of Louise into Ann's life. It does not seem, however, that it was only Ann who was integrating Louise, for one of the symbols is a set of pictures on Tasha's bedroom wall:

> In my bedroom I have a wall for each child. I have a place for Ann, one for Mona, and a place for the family. I have enlarged pictures up there. Ann told me she wanted a place for Louise up there. I asked if she was sure, and she said, "Sure, mom, she's family. I just don't have her anymore. I don't want to forget her." That's the first time that we really were able to go in and pull out pictures that were of her and Louise together.
>
> About a year ago, she started what she calls a hope chest. So she came to me and asked me if I had clothes and things from Louise and if she could have them. So we talked a little bit about whether she thought it would really bother her to see those things on a regular basis. And that was the first time she didn't cry when we talked about it.
>
> I had one set of dresses that they'd worn in the last pictures we'd taken of them dressed alike. There were a couple of sun suits. She wanted all of these. I put pictures of them up in my room like she wanted to. There are four areas, and one area is for the twins. She's very proud of that. When people come over, she wants them to see that. My bedroom has to stay clean because if anybody comes to visit, she has to show off those pictures.

Tasha has been growing on her own, too. She did not face the issue of religious guilt directly, but she did begin to feel differently about herself:

> You don't grow up until you're 30 years old or more. I remember so well waking up one morning when I was 30 or 31 and thinking "Where did it all go? Why do I feel like things were so good or so bad." I think I took a real interesting look at life.

She developed an important mentoring relationship with a man at work and shared with him her innermost thoughts. He was someone she had known for many years.

> The first time we really sat and talked was at a meeting. When you're away from your office with someone you tend to get closer and you talk more because you're with them every day for a week. He didn't realize that I had had cancer or that my daughter had died. At that time, I had decided to transfer to the Springdale office, and we were discussing that—and we just got into discussing everything.

He encouraged her to apply for a supervisory position.

He said, "I know your abilities. I know you can do it." No one had ever told me that. Not even my husband or my family had ever said, "You can do it. Go for it."

He encouraged her to return to school, where she completed an undergraduate degree she had been working toward slowly for several years. When we interviewed her, she was midway through a master's degree. As she changed her view of herself, her daughter changed too.

> It was just that I decided well, if one person cares enough, then maybe somebody else does too. Finally, I decided that the only someone else had to be me. I think that's when I began to realize that you've got to feel good inside about yourself. And you have to learn about yourself and understand what happened and how it affects you before you can help anyone else. And that's when I think Ann began to get better, because I was able to say to her, "I know how you feel." And she could pick it up. And she could come to me with anything.

She had not been able to feel totally close with her surviving children after the death:

> The hurt was there, I just couldn't show it and I didn't know how to handle the loss. So I just mothered my daughters and I kept that shut for a long time. I think it must have shown, because I loved my girls, but I couldn't be totally in love with my girls. I think I felt that if I did that they might be taken from me too.

But since the change in the way she feels about herself, she can get close; and in that closeness she can feel the self-sufficiency of her daughter.

> I'm sure that they knew that I wasn't as close as they wanted me. But in the last 3 or 4 years, I think that's changed. The girls are adjusting well. Ann is doing terrific. She is not thinking "if" I go to college. She says "when" I'm going to college. And Joyce is already going to college. Going to college was always important. Not so much that they work, but if they are ever in a situation where they have to, they can. They can take care of themselves. I guess that's part of what I felt. I thought earlier that I couldn't take care of myself. I felt that I had to have somebody taking care of me. And that's not true. I can take care of myself.

Within this new sense of self, Tasha feels some of the sense of a missing part that Ann felt so strongly. The dead child is internalized as a standard by which she can now judge herself. The standard can now be conscious, for she now feels she can measure up to it.

> I don't cry now. I cry tears a little bit, but it's not inside hurting so much. It's kind of like an "I really miss you." I wonder if in the back of my religious beliefs, if she can see all that we do. If she is ashamed of me as her mother. Would she want me to be her mother again. It's that kind of thing.

She now can find solace in a vision she had after her miscarriage of a grandmother with whom she identified:

> I had this dream. I think of it as a dream only because I don't think premonitions are ever like that. But I dreamed that I saw my grandmother standing at the foot of my bed, and this pair of hands just handing my baby to her.
>
> Q: Were you close to that grandmother?
>
> That's the grandmother that died when I was so small. I don't know. My parents tell me I was very close to her, so maybe. The only thing, I don't even remember her at all. I was like three when she died. But the picture we have is of me with her. And that is what is strange and that is why I took it as a dream. She looked exactly as she did in the picture that I have. In one picture, she's standing right here and I'm standing right in front of her. My parents tell me that I look a lot like her and that I do a lot of things that were like what she used to do.

When Louise died, the guilt and sense of failure made it difficult to feel the same solace of Louise in heaven with the grandmother. But as the pictures went up on her wall and Louise's things went into Ann's hope chest, Tasha has become more peaceful with the thought of Louise in heaven with her grandmother. She has grown away from the simple beliefs of her youth, however, and the image of the baby with the grandmother is at variance with other images of heaven she has. Heaven is now, like earth, a place of self-sufficient and responsible human beings.

> I believe my daughter is in heaven, and there's a feeling that I can always be sure where she is. But it is not judgmental. They've got to live out their lives and be judged on them now. I've come to the realization that I've done and tried as much as I can. I'm not going to blame myself anymore for what mistakes they make. I will try to help them through the mistakes. But they are going to make them and they have got to grow out of them.

CLIFF

Cliff's youngest daughter, Cynthia, died at age 17 of an infection that did not respond to antibiotics. She was a healthy adolescent one week and dead the next. Cliff still does not have a clear understanding of the cause of death but has reconciled himself to the belief that he never will. Cliff's wife attended Compassionate Friends frequently, but Cliff rarely attended. We interviewed him 5 years after the death. Cliff is a successful businessman who began his career in a large company and moved up. Three years before we interviewed him, he left the company and with another man began a consulting partnership. He said the change in career was in the works before Cynthia's death, and that her dying really only delayed the change. Cliff's wife, Alice, went back to school after the children were in high school and she now has a job as a legal assistant. They have two surviving children, both of whom are now out of the home.

As the children were growing up, Cliff was devoting long hours to his career:

> My job always kept me traveling quite a lot, so I wasn't at home as often as I'd like to have been. I was jealous of those fathers who were; I was jealous of the fathers who had a closer relationship to their kids than I was able to get. I like to go out with them now; I love to go out just with the kids. I get a big kick out of going out with them one-on-one, which I didn't get to do nearly as often as I wanted to.

He remembers Cynthia and says:

> She was a neat gal. I felt very close to her, maybe even a little closer to her than to my other two kids. I think I liked her just a little bit more than my other two. I got more hugs, kisses, and attention than I got from the others. As I said, she was really a beautiful gal.

Cliff is ambivalent about how his grief interacted with his work. At one level, he feels that it impaired his performance and that he was using the grief as a way of not dealing with what he was supposed to handle.

> I was going through some problems at work; it just seemed to make everything worse. I was using that as a crutch, I'm sure. "How can they bother me when I have this sorrow?" Later, I realized that wasn't fair. They would have bothered me anyway. It was my job to be bothered.

Things were changing in the company as new senior management was taking over. Individual people were supportive and kind, but the system did not allow Cliff to be protected in his grief. He lost a position in the management reshuffle.

> I think I was extremely upset, not only because of what happened, but that it happened while all these other things were going on and I didn't understand how anybody could do that to me. It was like adding insult to injury. They weren't caring at all, and that hurts. I worked at this company for 27 years, my daughter dies, and look how I'm being treated.
>
> I think it had to do with my age, and the salary I was making. There were also some personality conflicts, some real bad people situations. The people were very caring, so it didn't have anything to do with that. It was the "powers that be" that were very insensitive. But like I said, in retrospect, I think what happened would have happened, and it is probably working out for the best with the new consulting work.

Since Cynthia's death, Cliff finds that he is not as confident as he used to be, though he is not sure whether to attribute the change completely to the trauma of the loss.

> I don't handle a lot of stress and conflict as well as I used to. I used to be able to go pretty far without getting upset. Now it seems that I can't go as far anymore. I'm not as patient as I used to be. Maybe it's age, maybe it's because of Cynthia. I know that I no longer have the financial security that I had when I worked for the big company.

There is a part of Cliff that does not accept the reality of Cynthia's death.

> If she walked in our front door and I was sitting in the living room, I just don't think I'd be shocked. It seemes like it could happen. I wouldn't jump out of my skin, wondering if I'd seen a ghost or not. I guess that tells me that I haven't really resolved the conflict. It tells me that somehow it still isn't a reality and that there's another possible reality that happened. That would be all right with me. I'm not yet comfortable with the world in which she's dead.

Cliff and his wife, Alice, have very different coping styles. Alice has found a group of friends who can share Cynthia's death. She often finds herself crying and feels that the tears help her. Cliff wishes he could cry as freely as Alice, for he wants to feel the relief he sees the tears bring her. But he cannot. He cried at the funeral of his mother and his sister, and he cried at Cynthia's funeral. But those are the only public occasions at which he remembers crying.

> I'm not a crier and I hate that; it bothers me a lot. When I think about Cynthia and I feel sad, then I cry. I found myself, with Cynthia, crying more than I cried for my mother or sister. But I very rarely cry in front of anybody, Alice or anybody. I find myself crying, but it wasn't anything I could do in public. In private I feel that desire to share, but it's not coming out. It is not being shared. I can't pull that off.

He compares himself to Alice and feels that he does not come off well in the comparison. He worries that he has the same inadequacies he disliked in his own father.

> We have all kinds of home movies. To this day I have not been able to bring myself to watch them. That would be too painful for me. I want to, but I know that I just can't. Alice will say, "Why don't we watch some movies?" I think she's ready to try, but I have not been able to. Alice is a crier. Besides crying about awful things, she could cry about just about anything. It's always troubled me that when we do talk about Cynthia, which is not often or when we go out to the gravesite, which I don't do very often because it hurts a lot. The fact that she is able to cry about it and I'm not makes me feel a little guilty. It makes me feel like she's moving along, grieving and feeling bad. It seems to me that because I'm not crying, I'm not grieving. That troubles me a little bit. My dad never cried. I never saw him cry when my mother passed away.

But, he says, as much as he would like to, he does not derive comfort from talking and crying.

> Talking about Cynthia doesn't bring comfort, and I wish it did. I wish we could talk about old memories, and that would be comforting and warm; but now the memory just hurts.

For Cliff, Cynthia's death represents a real spiritual and existential/intellectual question. Cliff has maintained an active religious life although his connection with religious institutions has been perfunctory. His God is the one who establishes order in the universe, and when things seem disorderly, he could say a prayer and it seemed to him that order was reestablished. He described his response to the other deaths of people close to him and to a serious illness he had several years ago.

Whenever I lose someone or if anyone got sick in the family, it always seemed to spur up a little prayer from me. I remember when I was sick. It gave me some reason to say a few prayers, and everything worked out. It seemed like when you really needed it, you could say, "Okay, God, work this out; take it out of my hands." It seemed like the system worked.

But the old system did not work out when Cynthia died.

There's no explanation for why this happened to a kid who didn't seem to deserve it. I tried to rationalize it in every way, and no matter what way I went, there was no rationalization for her to be taken away. There are kids who go out and get drunk and get in a car and kill themselves, and it's horribly tragic; but there is a reason for it: It's something that they weren't supposed to be doing, or somebody else did something. But in Cynthia's case, nobody did anything.

Cliff now finds some solace in believing that there is order in the world; that our deaths are preordained; but that we cannot know the nature of the ordering principle or the particulars of the preordained events.

It just seemed important for me to rationalize it. I guess I've taken it out on God, but He is the only one to me who could ever do it. God is supposed to be the order keeper in the universe. The only rationalization that I've ever been able to deal with in my own mind is that I convinced myself that I now believe in the Book of Life; that, whatever living being comes into this world, there will always be a way this being will leave it. He inscribes your time from the day He creates you and that's the way He did it. But the "why" of it I have never been able to sort out. Why is there a bus crash and 100 people die? I wonder if He wrote that one in the Book of Life. I don't know if He does or doesn't.

But Cliff is not really sure how much the predestinarian beliefs help him. The beliefs seem to him to be an explanation that allows him not to live in an irrational universe, and in that sense, the explanation is solace. But the beliefs are not an enduring comfort in the face of the reality of his missing Cynthia.

It is all preordained. I have not been able to figure out any other reason. I just know that she didn't deserve it. I'm still angry. But He's still God and I'm still me. I know I harbor those feelings still and when I can't find anybody else to blame, I still blame Him, but I figure it's not doing me a lot of good.

Cliff is not without solace. He now has a personal relationship with Cynthia. She is a living presence to him when he is alone.

I drive a lot in my business. I use the car to think through what's going on in my business and what I'm doing. When things are not so hectic, I'm always just sitting there having a conversation with Cynthia. I always picture her wearing the same clothes as I last saw her wearing—a little sweat outfit that she always had on. There was always a position that I remember her in. She would get onto a little hassock at home and watch TV and prop her head up on her hands. It was a very uncomfortable position, but that was the one she was in a lot. I picture her in that position wearing those clothes, and that's the way I see her when I talk to her. We just talk about whatever is going on at the time. I tell her what's going on with all of us here. If somebody has passed away recently, we talk about that. Her friends, my friends or relatives, whatever. I just lost an aunt, so I talk to her about that.

He also has a linking object that he shares with his wife. They both feel that when they see a mourning dove Cynthia is with them. His wife was quoted in Chapter 3. Cliff recalls the day of the funeral, when they saw the mourning dove on the deck:

I said, "That's Cynthia, as sure as I'm sitting here. She's come back to us." I believe it to this day; it's one of the irrational things that I think about, though normally I'm a very rational person. I always pooh-poohed ghosts and stuff like that, but I really believe that this mourning dove was Cynthia. About a week or so ago there were two mourning doves; I backed out of my driveway and there were two little mourning doves standing on the sidewalk about eight feet from where I was. I stopped and spent about ten minutes talking to Cynthia. I figured the other dove was her boyfriend. I bet if the neighbors looked out and saw me sitting there talking to these birds they would really have a party talking about what happened to me. They know me as the guy next door who is positive and objective. I opened the car door, which I thought would scare them away, but it didn't. I must have gotten within four feet of them and these little birds wouldn't fly away. I felt it was really getting ridiculous and I took another step and they finally did fly away. I feel that is Cynthia's way of letting us know that everything is all right. Alice thinks I'm a little crazy. When I said the other dove was Cynthia's boyfriend, she thought that was pretty silly. But being a little crazy is okay.

He also takes comfort in his remaining family. His remaining children are successful in school and in their new careers and the

bond with those children is strong and real to him. But he especially
finds solace in a grandson.

> This baby was born about a month or so after Cynthia died. I had lots of
> talks with God about that one. He takes one away and delivers another one
> for you to care about. That's been kind of a help. There's a certain amount
> of replacement there. I guess the average guy sees it as a plus. For me, it
> replaced a little bit of what I lost with her. I'm not sure that I can explain
> that. I can't really put my finger on it, but there is something there that,
> when I'm with that child, I feel as if some of the hurt has been made up.

II

Parental Grief
in Four Contexts

Introduction to Part II

The second part of the book portrays bereaved parents in four different contexts. As we see parental bereavement in each of those contexts, we gain a deeper understanding of the dynamics of the process. If we see a student only in our class, we understand less than if we also have seen the student at home, on the athletic field, in the dorm, and at work. In the same way, we can understand parental grief best if we can observe it in different contexts, for each context brings different aspects more clearly into focus.

Chapter 5 is an ethnographic study of The Compassionate Friends (TCF), a self-help group. TCF is an organization that grew from within the dynamics of parental bereavement. The study of TCF is the longest chapter, for it was within TCF that I first began to understand parental bereavement. Chapter 6 is a study of another self-help group, Parents of Murdered Children (POMC). Within that context we can see rage and a political resolution of that rage. In Chapter 7, a study of the role of bereaved parents in a support program for pediatric cancer patients and their families allows us to see the dynamics of finding authentic existence within the experience of having a child die. Within that context, we can see a religious resolution more clearly. Chapter 8 examines parental bereavement within psychotherapy. Because psychotherapy is a relationship that focuses on the individual life history, it is a context that depicts the complexity of the parental bond and the complexity of the individual resolution.

These contextual studies are the basis for the abstract and theoretical understandings of parental bereavement in Part I. The larger structure of parental grief began to emerge as I was trying to understand what was happening in TCF. Several years later, the dynamics within POMC and the hospital program deepened this understanding of parental grief. As I began seeing bereaved parents

in private practice, I began to see more clearly the connections between the parent's history and the issues in grief. Clearly, I did not
enter these four contexts *tabula rasa*. What I knew from TCF could be
applied to POMC. What I learned from the hospital program could be
used in psychotherapy. The understandings from each context in-
fluenced the understandings from the other contexts.

5

The Anatomy of
Social Support:
The Compassionate Friends

Most of the understandings of parental bereavement in this book were first formulated within the ethnographic study of a local Compassionate Friends (TCF) chapter. TCF is a fruitful setting for understanding parental bereavement. First, it is a forum in which a great many parents share their frustrations and their resolutions. Parents go to meetings expecting to open themselves to each other. As the months pass, the changes within the individual members and the changes within the members' social networks are clearly visible. Second, TCF is a good setting for understanding parental bereavement because it is a social organization molded to the realities of parental bereavement, one that sustains itself on the energy that comes from the resolution of parental bereavement. We can understand parental bereavement in TCF not only from the individual lives of the members, but also from the organizational patterns that TCF has developed, the ritual interactions we find in the meetings, and the bonds that develop between members. This chapter is an attempt to describe the TCF process as parents move toward resolution within the process.

As we noted in Chapter 2, the most common finding of research on bereavement is that social support is the most significant factor in the resolution of grief. The study of TCF is a closer examination of the way social support functions. The process is complex because it involves the reestablishment of the self in a changed world, and it involves the transformation of the inner representation of the dead child. The parent brings his or her whole self to TCF and the complexity of the self is mirrored in the complexity of the process.

TCF is a self-help group. As such, it should be understood as distinct from support groups that have predetermined outcomes and a strong separation between helpers and helpees (Powell, 1975; Schwartz, 1975). It also should be understood as distinct from professional counseling or therapy that is based in specialized scientific knowledge about human functioning (Klass, 1982, 1985; Klass & Shinners, 1983). Lieberman and Borman (1979) give the most adequate definition of self-help groups:

> Their membership consists of those who share a common condition, situation, heritage, symptom, or experience. They are largely self-governing and self-regulating, emphasizing peer solidarity rather than hierarchical governance. As such, they prefer controls built upon consensus rather than coercion. They tend to disregard in their own organization the usual institutional distinctions between consumers, professionals, and Boards of Directors, combining and exchanging such functions among each other. They advocate self-reliance and require equally intense commitment and responsibility to other members, actual or potential. They often provide an identifiable code of precepts, beliefs, and practices that include rules for conducting group meetings, entrance requirements for new members and techniques for dealing with "backsliders." They minimize referrals to professionals or agencies since, in most cases, no appropriate help exists. Where it does, they tend to cooperate with professionals. They generally offer a face-to-face, or phone-to-phone fellowship network usually available and accessible without charge. Groups tend to be self-supporting, occur mostly outside the aegis of institutions or agencies, and thrive largely on donations from members and friends rather than government or foundation grants or fees from the public. (pp. 14–15)

THE COMPASSIONATE FRIENDS PROCESS

We can understand TCF process by looking at four phases of membership: First, we examine the decision to attend the group. Second, we examine the interactions among those who decide to affiliate. Two dimensions of interaction seem to be operative in the decision to affiliate: (1) an interpsychic dimension—that is, identification with others or a particular person in the group; and (2) an experiential dimension—that is, sharing solutions to specific problems. Third, we examine the decision to help others. The TCF process hinges on a discovery most people make: that helping others is a way of retaining a relationship with the dead child and a way of healing the self. Some of those who make that decision take on organizational leadership. Fourth, we examine the decision to drop out of active participation in the group, or to lower the level of participation. Quotations with names are from taped interviews. Quotations without names are from informal conversations or comments made at meetings.

Attending

Parents come to the group from a variety of referral sources, but all come with timidity and more than a little ambivalence. For some, the decision to come is merely an acquiescence to an invitation or suggestion from someone else.

> Irene: Well, I enjoyed the newsletters, but I really didn't want to come to the meetings. I didn't want new friends. I wanted my girls. I didn't feel I needed anyone. I had been independent all my life. But Cathy called and invited us for dinner and said "Tell Sam to come over from work and bring his good clothes. We are going to a meeting." So, we went. Sometimes I need a little push.

> Frank: First a fellow at work whose son had died told me about it. Then a relative who had a son killed had notified someone who sent us a newsletter. I talked it over with my wife and we went to the first meeting.
> Q: Did you go willingly or reluctantly?
> Frank: I would say reluctantly. My wife wanted to, but I didn't. There was a lot of emotionalism over my son's death between my wife and myself that was impossible for us to talk about. We were extremely polite and quiet with each other, but there was a lot of unspoken anger.

Sometimes the newly bereaved parents feel an inner sense of rightness about their going to their first meeting. Messages from the unconscious seem to play a part in bringing many TCF members for the first time.

> Helen: I would say the crash came in June—maybe May—because May was when I saw the article on TCF and first attended in June.
> Q: What took you there?
> Helen: Mainly because by then I didn't like myself. I was screaming and hollering at the two kids and taking everything out on them. . . . I didn't know why I was acting this way. I asked the doctor about support groups. He told me what he knew, which wasn't really a lot. He didn't know if it could be helpful. Things got progressively worse at home. That became the only thing I could think of doing (going to TCF). When I found the listing and realized where it was I said to myself, "That's right in my back yard, so God must be giving me a sign to go."

Grace: We went fairly early. I think in December. One of the reasons, which was probably a silly one, was that the meetings were at the same address as N. once worked. The association made me feel that maybe I was meant to go.

Donna: I went for the first time the following February. I didn't know anything existed like that, but somebody had sent me a newsletter. I read it, but thought, "Oh, this stuff is not for me. There's no way I could handle this group." I left it lay there, but about an hour before the first meeting started, I suddenly decided I was going to the meeting.

Sometimes there seems to be a rather strong feeling of estrangement from the natural support system that moves people to find places where they will fit in.

Alice: My friends didn't understand and I felt lonely. I felt I needed somebody or something but I didn't know what. I wanted to talk to someone who had gone through what I had gone through. I felt it would be best to get out and get involved in some activities, since I had so much time on my hands. O.'s care had taken up a great deal of my day, so I suddenly didn't know what to do with myself. I had read about TCF in the *North County Journal*. My son took me to the first meeting and attended two or three meetings with me after that.

For some, attending the first meeting is part of an inner conflict which is about accepting the fact that the child is really dead. One person was sent a notice of the TCF meeting with a sympathy card a few days after the child's death. She tore up the card. Then she received a newletter that featured articles on getting through the holidays. She tore that up too.

Cathy: There were not going to be any holidays for me! Finally, though, out of sheer desperation I had to do something. I couldn't survive the way I was going. I had lost 15 to 20 pounds, and the doctor was angry that I wouldn't take any medication. I simply couldn't function when I attempted to take the tranquilizers, so I told him, "I've dealt with things my own way for too long to begin dealing with them your way. I'll survive." He said, "I don't think you will."

She went to her first TCF meeting 2 months after the child died. She sat resentfully and quietly through the first meeting. She vowed not to return, but did, and at her third meeting she began to talk about her loss.

For a significant number, this is not the first experience of a self-help group. For one person, the recommendation to TCF came from another TCFer in Al-Anon.

> Bob: I'm glad you mentioned Al-Anon. Someone there who had lost a child told me about TCF. Al-Anon provided tremendous support right after E.'s death. Thus going to TCF was a very easy step.

Another had been active in Parents Without Partners:

> Joan: In PWP, people bare their souls and talk about everything that bothers them. Having been in PWP and having met people who had gone through and were getting out of crisis helped me in my decision to attend TCF.

There is a connection between TCF and the self-help experiences that some parents have had during their child's illness. Other TCF members had previously been active in the cystic fibrosis group and in the Cerebral Palsy Association. One of the local groups was formed as the bereavement group in a parent support program at the children's hospital. The group elected to stay together, rather than to integrate with existing TCF groups, because the bonds between them were already strong. The group voted to join TCF as a subchapter and to participate with the larger group in the newsletter, steering committees, social events, and holiday services.

Some TCF members have been in professional counseling or therapy at some point in their lives, whereas others have not. Some try professional counseling as well as TCF after the death of the child. Sometimes professional intervention seems to help and other times it does not.

> Bob: Chuck's anger showed up in May. Six months after E. died, he began acting out his anger, which was taken out primarily on his brother. We agreed to go to a counselor, a psychotherapist. She insisted on working with us as a group.

> Joan: The kids have been greatly touched by T.'s death, but I don't think at their young age they can ever know for sure how much so. I went with my youngest daughter to a counselor for some months.
> Q: Was the counselor helpful?
> Joan: No, not at all, not to me. He couldn't relate at all to what my problem was. He didn't know how to relate to a teenager, either.

Other TCF members have sought counseling prior to the death, usually for marriage counseling.

Losing a child seems to be a random happening. It can come to rich, poor, urban, and rural families. It is difficult to know the percentage of people in the general population who have had experience with self-help groups or with counseling. Thus, at this point, it is difficult to know whether those who affiliate with TCF have had more self-help or counseling experience than has the general population. Studies on a wider population might be helpful here, but, as we have seen, the new members come ambivalently and in response to messages from the unconscious. Clearly, neither counseling nor previous self-help experience make attendance a simple matter.

Affiliation

We define those who have *affiliation* with TCF simply as persons who return to the group four or more times within an 8-month period and who say that they find the processes within the group helpful in their grief. Yet obviously this simple definition points to some very complex matters in a person's life. At any given meeting, one third may be attending for the first time. Rarely is there a meeting in which there is not at least one new attender. They come rather hesitantly and often are accompanied by a very supportive friend.

Affiliation A: Interpsychic Dimension

The newcomer asks, "Are these people like I want to be?" while those who have been there longer say, "I was like that, but I am different now." It is this sense of identification with fellow travelers on the road through the valley of the shadow of death that we have called the *interpsychic dimension*. One's identification with others in the same condition moves one toward transformation of the inner representation of the dead child in the ongoing life of the self.

In a study of professional therapies, the study of the interpsychic dimension would largely center on *transference* and *countertransference*. Transference is the emotional attachment to significant figures in one's past that is projected onto a person in the present and therefore is available for use in the therapeutic interactions. In TCF, that interpsychic dimension remains in the present, for there is very little sense of continuity that the bereaved parents feel with their personal pasts as they try to come to terms with their loss. The time factor, which may be several decades in the type of transference characteristic of therapy, is in TCF a matter of months. The self that is brought to the TCF meeting is not the old familiar self, for whom social skills and social position are well established. It is a new self, one that is not pleasant to behold and whose future is frightening to project. That new self is isolated from the interaction patterns of the familiar self. But the discovery that the new self can be socially validated within a group of others who share the same condition provides a beginning place to rebuild.

The parent-child bond is part of the interpsychic dimension. Not only have other members experienced the same life crisis, but the group is a place in the present that includes the attachment the parents still feel with the dead child. It is not that parents reach into the past for the significant figure they will bring to the new attachment. The child is real to the parents, and the child can be real within the group. Because the inner representation of the child is available within the TCF process, the inner representation can be transformed within the process.

In group psychotherapy, the interpsychic dimension would be understood in terms of group cohesiveness (Yalom, 1975), but in self-help groups of bereaved parents, the group will stand far less internal stress than do therapy groups. In the self-help group, positive identification of others in a similar life situation is part of the decision to affiliate, whereas it is discovered in the psychotherapeutic group as the process matures. The investment of the energy formerly invested in the child seems unique to these self-help groups. Dutch psychologists van der Avort and van Harberden (1985) found *identification resonance* as the central theoretical construct in understanding self-help. The concept seems similar to what is here called the interpsychic.

> Bob: The one thing that is probably the most helpful is that when you are with other parents who have lost a child you have a common base. It has nothing to do with the reason the child died. It has nothing to do with your socioeconomic status. And it has nothing to do with anything in life except that you are all level at one point. It is similar to Al-Anon. You are all there for one reason, which is a very leveling thing. It affects you in different ways. You recover from it in different ways, but you all have a common base. I think that is what is TCF's single most important factor. We all have different levels of devastation because of our character and our relationship to the child. But that isn't nearly as critical as the fact that you are all leveled and all are rebuilding lives that are shattered—attempting to get them back to some normalcy.

Because everyone else there has lost a child, the child who is dead is the bond between the bereaved parents. Thus the identification can have some of the emotional energy which was part of the bond with the child.

> Helen: One thing that appealed to me is that I knew I could go there and not say anything if I didn't want to. . . . The leaders had lost a baby son named V., so there was an immediate rapport. I thought, "Here's someone that understands!" It was a great feeling. I was very frightened of the introduction, but I thought, "Well, this is one place I get to introduce *him*, I don't even have to mention the other two. This is for V. . . ."
>
> It was like a magnet I was drawn to each month. It wasn't always something I wanted to do. I wasn't always up to it because I knew there would be new pain each time, but it was the one time of the month I could talk about my child.

> Irene: I didn't think I would say anything, but it felt good to be able to talk about the girls. It was good to be able to say, "I'm their mother." You don't have anything else left, but you are still their mother.

One of the activities which bonds members of TCF to each other is sharing pictures of the dead children. At the national conferences, there are boards on which parents can pin a picture of their child. Those boards become a gathering place for many parents. At a regular meeting about twice a year, our chapter has a picture-sharing session. Photographs are brought and passed around while stories are told about the occasion of the picture—the summer camp, the family baptism gown, or even the body after the tubes had been removed. It is hard to know what to say when people share pictures of living children, but these pictures of dead children seem to evoke appropriate admiration in the TCF meeting. The emotional attachment to the child, which has become part of the bond with the other TCF members, becomes part of the reason to remain with TCF in the helper role.

> Eva: It's the one place I can talk about Y. freely. One mother couldn't understand how I could cry so openly in a group setting and she couldn't. What she didn't know was that I couldn't cry about Y. openly at home, so the group was a release for me. Also, by doing something to help other grieving parents, it gives Y.'s death a reason.

> Alice: You feel if you can do something for someone else, it helps put some meaning in the heartache you have gone through. If you go through all sorts of hell and don't learn anything. . . .
>
> I tell myself that O. would have been pleased that I do this. He was a very caring person. He would have felt that helping others in this way was a good thing to do.

The emotional energy of the interpsychic dimension has elements in addition to the emotional energy of the parent-child bond, and not all of the bond to the child is given to TCF. However, it is clear that at least some of the affiliation with the group is in the form of energy attached to the child. Such a transference, therefore, has a radically different temporal aspect from the transferences that are the usual focus of therapeutic literature. As TCF members often remind each other, "When your parent dies, you lose your past; when your child dies, you lose the future." When TCF members affiliate, they are not drawn back to the past. Their affiliation with parents who share the same condition is a decision about the present and about the future. The focus of TCF is on dealing effectively in the present and in opening up the future.

The interpsychic aspect is concerned with grief as a disequilibrium in the relationship of the bereaved to the inner representations of the deceased. This reworking of the inner representation seems similar to Lopata's (1979) *sanctification* and Marris' (1975) *integration of hermeneutic structures* in the resolution of grief. The connection members make between the bond to the child and the bond to the group seems to be a continuation of the link between the quality of the bond of the mother to the neonate and the strength of her social support system (Ainsworth & Bell, 1970; Rutter, 1981; Stayton & Ainsworth, 1973).

In discussing their relationship to the group, parents move in their description among a sense of unity with those whose lives had also been shattered by the death of a child, the feeling of being in a familylike community, and the sense that the group is an appropriate place to which energy formerly attached to the child might now be attached. The TCF credo makes that mixture explicit.

> . . . . We reach out to each other with love, with understanding and with hope. Our children have died at all ages and from many different causes, but our love for our children unites us. . . . Whatever pain we bring to this gathering of The Compassionate Friends, it is pain we will share just as we share with each other our love for our children.

"Pass It On," written by Fay Harden, and often put to music for TCF gatherings, also contains the mixture:

> With open hearts we took the love our children gave us.
> When another stands alone we reach in understanding.
> The love our children gave us is what we'll share now.

So pass it on, Compassionate Friend, the love goes on and on.
Pass it on when you are strong, the love our children gave us.
Because you've been there too, afraid and broken hearted.
Because we've traveled on that road, we now can show the way.
So, pass it on, Compassionate Friend, the love our children gave.
Take the love our children gave and share it with another.
Pass love and kindness on in tribute to our children.
The love our children gave us is what we'll share now.
So pass it on, Compassionate Friend, the love goes on and on.

The words read at a Christmas candlelight memorial service were:

We are here tonight as Compassionate Friends because our beloved children lived and because they died before us—their parents. As we light a candle in the memory of each of our children, we do so in eternal gratitude that they lived. They are no longer physically here on this earth, but they are still with us in spirit and will always be. They are here in spirit to give us the courage to go on with our lives in a positive stance. It has been said—"Compassion is not pity that looks down: it is love that shares and divides the poignancy of pain." As we light the candles tonight in rememberance of our cherished children, we do so as Compassionate Friends who care, who share, and who remember.

Although the elements within that bond between bereaved parents seem disparate on first hearing, the relationship of parenting to social support shows that the parent-child bond is not an individual matter, but rather that it is embedded in the bonding within the larger social network. In bringing together those elements, the significant number of parents who find TCF useful demonstrates that the relationship of social support and the bond with the child is operating in the resolution of parental grief. Just as having other people share the joy of parenting is important to the quality of the bond established between parent and child, the sharing of parental grief is important to the quality of the resolution of parental bereavement.

The interpsychic dimension also has the universal human element of community sharing in a time of crisis. Many bereaved parents report a sense of isolation from their usual intimate networks. For many, TCF fills that void.

Donna: After the third time, I knew I wanted to stay. It was kind of like having a family. No matter where I'm at, it hits me that I'm different. I feel apart. There was this horrible thing that happened to me that makes me different. With TCF, though, we are just all alike. We are all a family. You can act so together, but if I break down with my friends, they don't understand and think I should be more together. If I break down at TCF, they don't think anything about it.

The new self that the bereaved parent brings to TCF feels strange, so the fear of insanity is present even when it is warded off with humor.

Helen: The most helpful thing was finding out that there are all these other people dealing with the same things. I got a lot of hope by seeing people who had made it. They hadn't ended up on a funny farm.

It is not a group in which the child is forgotten, but TCF is rather a group in which the parent can develop a full life that includes the child. The sense of being accepted within a community that includes the dead child is seen in the social programs the group holds. At a spring picnic, a man reported that his grandchild, the son of his murdered daughter, did not cling to him but ran and played with the others. "He fits in here," the man reported. Later in the day after volleyball, softball, and other games, a clown passed out balloons to all the children at the picnic. As the day neared its end, the clown gave each parent a balloon with the dead child's name written on it. The parents gathered and released the balloons together. The group silently watched until all the balloons had floated out of sight. Then they went back to the tables for a snack before breaking up to go home. The dead children were not excluded from the picnic. In the parent's minds, they were very much present in the life of the group. But as they are supported by their bonds to the group, the parents can also let the child go. That presence and letting go was ritualized in releasing the balloons.

For some members, the identification with the group is heightened by finding very close models for behavior in the group. At the TCF national conventions, special sessions are held for parents of specific kinds of children's deaths. Informal networks form continually in any TCF chapter as parents whose experiences are very similar seek each other out. The group attempts to foster subgrouping by occasionally offering meetings aimed at one specific group, for example, the parents of suicide deaths. On occasion the group facilitates such hookups by having a meeting in which a panel of parents representing different kinds of deaths presents short speeches, following which the group breaks into smaller groups with a panelist leading each.

As the local chapter developed, there was a split in the group along geographic lines. Chapters were formed in various parts of the urban area. But the group also split according to experience. A few years after the local chapter's formation, a group of parents whose children had died as infants began meeting separately. A group of survivors after suicide was formed. Another set of parents whose children had been murdered formed the Parents of Murdered Children, but still kept their affiliation with TCF. Parents whose children died of cancer already had a support group at the hospital, but they voted to join their group to the local TCF chapter. Thus, the interpsychic dimension seems to be fostered by having a bond between parents whose experience is similar. Although in TCF meetings there is a constant recognition of a shared bond between all bereaved parents, in the dynamics of the self-help process the bonds between those who have shared the same kind of loss seem to be important. Often we find that a person in the group who has experienced a similar death but is a little further along in the process is the focus of a more specific identification for a newer member.

> Eva: It was during the second meeting I attended that Darla and I talked. It had been about a year since Darla lost her baby. We started calling each other and that helped a lot.

> Cathy: For the first three or four meetings I just stored their words of hope and advice for later because I wasn't ready to accept them at the time. Then I noticed that June, another mother whose child was killed a month before mine, was beginning to heal. I wanted desperately to be like her. I didn't know what to do to make it any better, but decided I was going to try.

The sense of unity with those whose lives have been shattered, the sense of hope at seeing that others have made it, the sense of finding an appropriate object on which to attach the energy of the parent-child bond, the sense of family in a supportive community, the sense of the shared loss of the individual's child, and the special relationship with someone very much like the self but further along are all part of the interpsychic dimension. That dimension allows for great intimacy by which the healing process can work.

It seems, however, that for some individuals, the intimacy of the TCF process does not open up the self in identification. Rather, intimacy threatens the defenses by which the pain is kept at bay. Knapp (1986) finds some bereaved families he calls *isolate families*. They are internally atomized and nonsupportive. An isolate family is a closed system that does not interact within the larger social environment. When we called those who did not return after attending one or two TCF meetings, we found that some said they already had the intimate relationships that they saw in TCF. But a significant minority of those we called were isolate families. They said that they found attending the meeting stressful. They found no relief of the pain in the meeting and reported that hearing of the experiences of others only made them feel worse. Characteristic of these people was that they did not communicate about the child's death even within the family. Several of these parents indicated that the conversation with us was stressful, one saying, "Why don't you call The Compassionate Friends. They like to talk about it there" (Hoeppner & Klass, 1982). Without the interpsychic dimension, pain could not be shared, and others' pain could not be an occasion for expressing one's own pain. Instead of reaching out, the parents attempted to hold the self from pain even if that entailed cutting the self off from potential healing relationships and from the inner representations of the dead child.

Affiliation B: Experiential Dimension

The temporal perspective of the interpsychic dimension in TCF is oriented to the present and future. As in all the interactions in TCF, the basis for that temporal orientation is complex. We have already noted the transference of the attachment from the child to the group. The sense of shattered self also contributes to the temporal perspective. In effect, life starts over for the bereaved parent. As one of the members said, "Your life has changed. It's like moving from one town to another. You can't go back. Even if you did go back, it's not going to be the same." How does one learn to live in this new town—in this new self? One must learn by experience, and from the experience of others, how to find one's way around. It is this learning that we have called the experiential dimension of affiliation with TCF.

The *experiential dimension* is a sharing of solutions to concrete problems that confront bereaved parents (Borkman, 1976). When the child died, the parent was cast into a world for which there are few role models. In the experiential dimension, bereaved parents help each other explore the pitfalls and possibilities of that world. The importance of the experiential seems to be one of the characteristics that differentiate this self-help process from professionally led group therapy in which "tools for action" are considered by group members to be far less important than are other factors (Dickoff & Lakin, 1963).

The experiential is concerned with grief as a disequilibrium in the social world of the bereaved. This can be understood as the loss of environmental psychobiologic regulators, as does Hofer (1984), or as the loss of habitual roles and the resultant dysfunction of the re- pertoire of responses, as does the Bowlby group (Bowlby, 1961, 1969–

1980; Parkes, 1972; Parkes & Weiss, 1983). The task in the experiential dimension is to adapt to the environment by forming new attachments or finding new psychobiologic regulators within the existing field of attachments and social roles.

To an observer with a psychotherapeutic background, many of the interactions in a TCF meeting would appear rather directive. A person newly bereaved may cry and tell the story of the death. The group listens with little interruption. But after the emotions are drained out, a rather direct question is likely to be asked by one of the newcomers. "Does anyone else have problems going into the child's room?" or "What have other people done with the child's things?" After the emotional catharsis of the earlier part of the sharing, these practical and rather objective questions seem, to the psychotherapeutically inclined listener, to be too simple. It seems that valuable group time should be spent on issues more central to the core of the self. Yet many TCF members see the practical advice they received as one of the most helpful parts of the process.

> Joan: I came into TCF with all these blank problems that had no solutions. Such things like, do we hang the stockings? Do we have the Thanksgiving dinner? I was so relieved to hear people at the November meeting talking about the stockings and how they handled it. It was a big thing to me, yet you certainly don't go to a friend with this problem. They would think you were stupid, or nuts, or both. . . . I remember reading in Ann Landers about someone, after the death of a child, asking how many children the parents should tell people they had. To me it seemed foolish. I could not even see how this posed a problem for them, yet that turned out to be the biggest problem I had. I was always so proud of my five kids, and it absolutely broke my heart to ever speak the words, "Four kids."

The experiential functions first to define the problems as normal. Because the problem may not be seen as important by the larger society, many bereaved parents have difficulty because seemingly small matters are causing them major stress. A newsletter article says:

> It is true we cannot take away the pain entirely, but we can help in healing the emotional wound we have all suffered. We learn that we are not alone, that others have experienced the emotional upheaval we are going through, and that these are normal reactions. Parents share answers to such commonly asked questions as: What shall I do about my child's room and possessions? How do I answer the question: "How many children do you have?" What can I do to help my other children?

The two issues that seem to recur most often in the group are what to say when asked "How many children do you have?" and how to celebrate the holidays. Often when the TCF members speak of there being no right way to grieve, they are not talking about emotional expression, rather they are talking about how to deal with the practical issues that the death of the child raises in this culture.

Frank: I don't see where it would be possible to deal with it constantly in the same setting [therapy], but can see that you could go to TCF for years and continue to get something new out of it. It's also less pressure oriented. You are also taking a risk in going to a counselor in only hearing one viewpoint. With TCF, the actors keep changing, so you hear a variety of viewpoints.

Cathy: It is the only place you can go and talk about your grief and your child as openly as you want. No one is going to make any judgments on you about how you are handling the situation. They reassure you that there is no right way or wrong way. Whatever helps you the most is the right way. You take all the information and sift through it for what you need. Also, where else can you go to discuss major issues such as when someone asks how many children you have what do you say.

The holiday issue is probably clearer to the nonbereaved parent, for most people have faced Christmas with someone being away from home, and it is generally recognized that significant occasions such as birthdays or holidays are reminders of one who has recently died. Each year, TCF has a meeting just before Thanksgiving in which the topic is "Getting through the Holidays." Parents tell what they have done in the past that was helpful, and other parents try to make plans that will suit them. For example, one parent did not know whether to hang up the stockings, so she went to her son's drawer and found 19 socks. She put a present in each and sent them to the VA hospital. Another parent wanted to remember the child, but did not want to make the rest of the family more uncomfortable, so she attached a black bow among many colored bows to the wreath outside the door. Some parents find it helpful to put a Christmas tree on the grave. Parents often measure themselves by how well they are able to deal with the holidays, and the experiential advice given at TCF is central to that measuring.

Alice: After a year, I was beginning to be able to get on with my life. I was able to have the Christmas celebration back at my house.

Irene: I also learned how to cope at Christmas. A lot of people had different suggestions on what worked for them. Putting a tree on their graves was helpful to me. We put on all the girls' homemade ornaments, then I could go home and have Christmas with the rest of the family.

Some experiential solutions are simply advice and permission. A newsletter account of a meeting reported different responses to the question "How to vent anger."

When one of our members asked this question, she started a discussion everyone wanted to enter. Here are some of the comments and suggestions we came up with.
—Newly bereaved parents are afraid to let it out for fear they'll lose control. You won't, and letting it out really helps.
—One member recalled how another had told her that when she was home alone she would beat the floor with a towel and scream.
—Another kicked a pan around the basement because the noise was so satisfying.

Some of the experiential sharing is very specific but of great existential importance. A large article in one newsletter is devoted to tips from a professional photographer on care for "our special photographs."

Your most treasured photos should be copied; the negative should be a *black & white negative*, because it will *never* fade. It should be "sleeved" (or put in a zip-lock baggie), and then put in a safe deposit box.
To remove crayola, lipstick, smoke damage, etc, use KRYLON WORKABLE FIXATIVE—it can be purchased at an art supply store. Apply with a cloth to damaged area and follow directions. It works like magic, really.

The curative qualities of the experiential dimension are linked to the existential stance the bereaved parents take within their world. The question about what to say when asked, "How many children do you have?" is an example. At first, it seems a rather practical question. But in fact the question reaches deep into the nature of the parental bond. What does it mean when people say they "have" a child? After all, only under specific conditions do children understand that they "have" parents. Yet even if we were to "work through" the nature of that bond in therapy, the parent is still left with the problem of what to say in the social situation in which the question is asked. It is a casual question to the one who asks, while to the bereaved parent it is an issue of the degree of intimacy there must be in a relationship before the loss is shared. The issue of the degree of intimacy is related to factors in the culture that bring on discomfort in people when they hear about the death of the child, that is, it raises the marginal social role of a bereaved parent in a death-denying society.

In the group are others who have faced the question and found answers. Not all the answers are the same. Each answer positions the parent differently toward the underlying nature of "having" a child and toward the problematic social role of bereaved parent. When TCF members say they listen to the information or opinions of others and then decide what might work best for them, they are saying that they are finding ways to position the new self in the world. The parent with the problem can thus choose a position from several available models in the group. At the point of choice, the underlying issues are understood clearly in a way that is both concrete to the social situation and congruent with other existential positions the person takes in life. It is interesting to watch the faces of the individuals who ask the question at a meeting, for very often when the option they will choose is mentioned, they nod and grin in a way that shows instant recognition of the issues involved and the solution that is now lined up. The problem is not that the parents need to understand what it means to "have" a child. They understand that all too well. They also understand deeply the marginal nature of their social role. What the experiential dimension has given them are options for existential action.

We might understand the experiential in another metaphor. Objective knowledge can analyze bodily movement and the effects of air-pressure differential on moving objects. But the batter in a baseball game must integrate both those into one experience when watching a pitch. Like bereaved parents at a meeting, the ball players work on their "stance" during practice. During the game they do the best they can, knowing that they can go over the problems later at another practice session. If they go into a slump, they may want to try a different stance for a while.

The experiential dimension does not provide answers set in stone, for different answers may work at different times in the grief. A newsletter on preparing for the holidays had the following report on hanging stockings:

> What a torment! Funny how you worry what your friends will think. For days I worried and finally I hung three on the fireplace wall, and laid one gently on the mantle.

But that was last year! This year I shall hang all four above the fireplace. For this year the confusion of the mind has found new answers—with conviction! For it does not really matter whether my oldest daughter lives in Tucson, or my youngest son is dead—these are my children—our family—and as long as we hang the Christmas stockings, we shall hang them *all* . . . with love.

The experiential dimension of affiliation with TCF is thus not a decision to act in a particular way. Rather, it is an understanding that TCF members have gathered some experience about the problems of being a bereaved parent, as well as a decision to use the experience of other TCF members as a starting point for learning to manage the new self in the world. The experiential dimension is also, as the affiliation develops, a decision to share experience from one's own life with those who follow by a few months.

Antze (1979) used the concept of *ideology* in his analysis of TCF. The idea is more simple and didactic than what we have called experiential knowledge, for it seems to be based on the reinterpretation of self and world that is found in Alcoholics Anonymous (AA) groups. The principles for TCF published by the national organization are specific in maintaining freedom of belief and action: "We understand that each parent must find his or her own way through grief," and "We never suggest that there is a correct way to grieve or that there is a preferred solution to the emotional and spiritual dilemmas raised by the death of our children." In TCF, the experiential dimension is sharing discoveries, not promoting conformity to an ideology.

Transition to Helping

Does one get over being a bereaved parent? The answer seems to be no. What, then, is the continuing relationship with TCF? While parents do not get over it, neither do they remain in the condition that brought them into the group. A newsletter article comparing parental bereavement to the grief of an amputee concluded with:

> In time, the pain in our hearts will gradually ease, and we can learn to live again without our beloved child. Our lives will never be whole, but they can become full once more.

Transition A: Experiential Dimension

The transition toward fullness, if not to wholeness is, in part, also a transition in the relationship of the member to the self-help group.

The transition within the group is a turn of energy toward others. Videka-Sherman (1982) identified "altruistic behavior" as the coping mechanism that characterized TCF participation. She found a positive relationship between altruism and lowered symptoms. The death of her subjects' children, however, had occured no more than 30 months earlier, so the full resolution is not seen in her study. The experiential dimension is a part of the transition to the helper role, for just as members were given options for existential stances in relation to difficult problems, they now present the options to others. Sharing a solution can be as simple as a sentence in a meeting or over the phone or in a short newsletter article, so it is an easy step to take. By listening to others and offering the solution to the other's situation, the TCF member puts her or his own life experience in perspective, for the individual can see the self more clearly when it is reflected in the lives of others. The sense of competence is gained by showing others that one's own life experience is worthwhile.

> Cathy: Between 6 months and a year, my motive for going to TCF changed from taking to giving back—not that I ever quit getting something from the group. . . . I find that giving to others in the group is a healing in itself. It helps to give some purpose to I.'s death. At one point I decided that he couldn't be completely happy in heaven while he knew I was so unhappy.

Writing for the newsletters and talking to newly bereaved parents on the phone are important ways which many people find to give back.

> Irene: Writing the letter that they printed in the newsletter was helpful to me. I really like writing, but it wasn't until I was in the hospital that I took the time to write that letter to the girls. It also helps me to know I have helped others. Some people have told me that just seeing that I have survived has helped them.

> Donna: My writings have really helped to get it out of my system, and the fact that TCF thought enough of what I wrote to publish it. People would let me know that I wrote just what they were feeling and it helped them to read it. That helped me a lot. With others it's different, though. My kids don't read what I write. I think it's too painful for them. With my family (mother and sisters) there has been a lot of fussing about my writing. They ask, "What do you write that stuff for? It just keeps reminding you." I don't need to write to be reminded.

The experiential resolution of grief is the general recognition of the changes in the social world and the decision to live in that changed world in as creative and positive a way as possible. Thus, in the resolution, the specific existential issues, such as hanging stockings or telling the number of children, are integrated into a whole view of the new world that is known and in which the problems can be managed. A newsletter report by a father reads:

> I came to realize that I could accept the things that I could not change or I could become a bitter old man. I refused to become that and made a conscious decision to go on living, to survive. I read books, I cried, I talked with bereaved parents who had lost chidren, I cried, and a day at a time, I began to heal. The day came when all the mirrors that surrounded me, that reflected at times and events back onto me and my tragedy, began to become windows and I could see again out of myself and into the lives of others; first into the lives of other bereaved parents, but then gradually into all those whose lives touched mine. . . I came to realize too that in trying to help others I was helping myself, that a very important part of the healing was putting love back into my life.

A mother reported in a newsletter:

> The situation that I faced after J.'s death was unalterable and frightening. The days kept coming and I had to continue my life without the very person that gave it meaning and joy. After much sorrow and contemplation, and with the support and love of family and friends, including The Compassionate Friends I came to the decision that I was going to try to use my gift of life to the utmost as J. had used his.

Transition B: Interpsychic Dimension

In the *interpsychic dimension*, the parent transforms the inner representation of the deceased from the role it played in the bereaved's life before the death to the role it will play in the new intrapsychic equilibrium. The inner representation is not simply memory, but is, as Fairbairn indicates, a part of the ego, the characterization or thematic memories of the object, and the emotional states connected with the characterization (Fairbairn, 1952; Kernberg, 1976). Because there seems to be an exchange between aspects of the inner representation, we often see that activity in one affects the others. Thus, a transformation in the parental role to helping and nurturing others in the group is usually accompanied by the emergence of a more positive and less stressful memory of the lost child. We find that at the same time the parent is bonding to the group, they are also reworking the bond with the deceased child.

> Fran: I found that as I was learning to help others that the memories of H. began to hurt less and less. Rather than being afraid to remember because

it hurt so much, I began to look forward to chances to tell others about him. It seemed like being in TCF made his death have a meaning, and that made the memories better.

Bart: When I first started going to TCF, I was hardly able to say K.'s name when they went around the room introducing everybody. It just made me cry the first time, and I had to pass. The next time I could say it, and by the third time it just seemed natural the way it came out. Being able to say his name made him seem closer to me. Now he is close all the time, but then it was just when we said his name at the meetings.

As the grief progresses, active interaction with the inner representation of the deceased child is encouraged, even as the bond between the group members is strengthened. In the reworking of the relationship of the inner representation of the dead child, we can see most clearly the way in which grieving the loss of a child mirrors the process by which the bond was formed. Studies of mothers bonding to newborn infants indicate that the stronger the social support system the mother has, the stronger and less ambivalent the bond with the child will be (Anisfeld & Lipper, 1983; Chess & Thomas, 1982; Rutter, 1981). If we examine the social support in that neonatal period, it is clear that it is not so much that the mother is being supported, but that the relationship with the baby is shared. There is limited empirical data at this point, but some studies show that social support is related to the positive resolution of neonatal loss (Bourne, 1968; Forrest, Standish & Baum, 1982; Kirkley-Best & Kellner, 1982; Schreimer, Gresham & Green, 1979). Thus what we see in the interpsychic dimension is the support of others facilitating an increasing integration of the inner representation of the dead child into the parent's psychic system.

One newsletter had an account by Larry Siedl, a chaplain in a children's hospital, who on Christmas day visited a cemetery where children he had known and worked with were buried. He found a phenomenon that is common in parental bereavement.

On that day I almost thought I was at another Compassionate Friends meeting as parents freely mingled and shared among other parents who were visiting their child's gravesite. I sensed an unusual camaraderie in that other parents had a real sense of what the other was going though. It was as though each was telling the other that "you are not alone."

After a while many couples (and a large number of children of all ages) departed and I took the liberty of visiting the graves. The ensuing 20 minutes I will never forget. . . . There was the big red drum with the words, "We miss you Robbie," on the top. . . . A teddy bear, a tin soldier and manger scenes helped to fill cemetery toyland. Another child's family had Christmas cards, complete with personal messages in each, paper clipped into the ground. And, of course, numerous decorated Christmas trees with handmade ornaments made by the surviving siblings.

At the cemetery, the parents are making a bond with each other, celebrating the bond among the surviving family members, and renewing the bond with the dead child. It is done on the holiday that focuses on parent's bonds with their children.

The Nature of Resolution

The resolution such bonding to the dead child and bonding to the group is pointed toward is a permanent change in the individual. The resolution of grief is for these groups not a return to life as it was before, for there is no going back. The resolution of bereavement is a sense of a new self.

A long birthday letter written by a father to his daughter 6 years after her death allows us to see the thoroughgoing nature of the change that is the resolution of parental bereavement in these groups. The themes of The Compassionate Friends as a new group of friends, his changed religious beliefs, his changed social self, his continued use of linking objects, and the continuing role the child plays in his life are intertwined in the description.

> I think I've finally learned what real religious faith is. All the sorrow, pain, and emotional hurts of losing you has worked together to help me have some real concern for others—especially those who are hurting. . . . I'm impatient with superficiality and . . . I'm now able to tolerate and even enjoy learning from those who have different faiths. . . .
>
> I hope this doesn't hurt you but Mommy and I have had some serious problems with our marriage since you died. Little irritants that we could have overlooked in the past became mountains that couldn't be pushed aside and ignored. . . . Our new friends and our new pastor (oh, we've changed churches too) have patiently and lovingly worked with us, educating us to griefwork and all its ramifications and taught us to be tolerant of each other and our differences. It's been rough, but I think we're going to make it.

The sense of a changed self and the sense of a strong bond to the inner representation of the dead child form a resolution of parental bereavement to which the self-help process is pointed. The experiential help becomes needed less as the world of parental bereavement becomes known. The transformed inner representation becomes an accepted part of the self, hardly noticed except at those times when it is brought sharply into focus, as in a newsletter poem by Betty Stevens:

Today I saw a little boy with hair the color of sunshine and the smile of an angel, and I brushed away a tear.

I saw him reach for the woman's hand and heard his sweet voice saying, "Let's go, Mommy, come on let's go"
and I brushed away a tear.

I wanted to run over and hug him and ask his name
and tell him about the little boy I used to have so many years ago
who looked so much like him.
But he might have been distressed by the lady crying,
so I stayed where I was—
And brushed away my tears.

Formal Leadership

A great deal of the activity within TCF is premised on the transition to helper which comes as a part of the resolution of the grief, not at the end of the resolution. A newsletter is written and mailed by members. There is a list of phone numbers to call for the newly bereaved and for those who are having a bad day. Each of the chapters has a leader and some have co-leaders. Those who have been with the group for a while are likely to be asked to give presentations in the community or to appear in the media. The chapter has business meetings three or four times a year at which everyone is welcome. Generally, any person who comes to one of those meetings will go home with an assigned task.

For those who become central members in the leadership, the structure of the organizational details seems to provide a good way for them to consolidate their gains. In some cases the rebuilding of the self after the death of a child is a radical change from the self they were before the death and the leadership in TCF is a stepping stone to what Erikson (1964) calls the generative stage.

Helen: Either you feel like you've been helped and think, "I don't need that any more," or you feel like you've been helped and feel a need to give back. In my mind, TCF is a way to keep V. close to me and I like that feeling. If I wasn't involved in TCF, I think I would have a lot of sadder memories of V. But I realize that because of what has happened to me I can do this for him, with him. I can help other people. You see, I'm not typically a leader; I'm a follower.

Q: I think you are a leader, but just didn't realize it.

Helen: Perhaps, but typically in the past I would belong to an organization but not even think of being involved in the leadership. What I'm doing leading it is beyond me, but now I'm even becoming more comfortable speaking in groups. I guess the need to do this because it might help someone else has outweighed my self-consciousness and embarrassment of knowing I'll break out in a flush from the nervousness. I'm a totally different person than I was in my twenties, and I know this experience has a lot to do with it. I have rejoined the Children's Challenge group and put down V.'s name and introduced him. Another mother then introduced her deceased daughter. I thought, "Well, good, maybe I gave her the courage to do that."

GRADUATIONS

As they find resolution of their grief, some parents who do not move into the formal organizational leadership of the chapter become more irregular in their attendance. But those people who have stopped attending regularly do not seem to feel as though they have stopped being members, and most of them keep in regular contact with other members. The difficulty seems to be that although they are over the grieving in the medical model sense of that word, they are not over the loss. The loss of the child is not something to be gotten over, any more than one could get over the amputation of an arm. So when parents leave the group, they do not leave as they were before the death. On special occasions, birthdays or holidays or when they see a child about the same age or hear of a similar accident, the grief returns and it seems as if it were "only yesterday."

Donna: It wasn't something I wanted to do. To this day I still miss the group. I had to go to work a year ago when my husband left me, and I have to work nights tending bar. At first I arranged to be off on the meeting nights, but as of this last summer, I wasn't able to work it out anymore and had to stop. I miss it something terribly. I feel so left out.

Q: Over the period of time you went, did TCF's role change for you?

Donna: I still need the group and get a lot out of it. I still need to be able to talk about it and be able to say the things I still feel. But I also need to be able to do something for someone else. Then I don't feel like I'm a total failure in life. If anything good came out of this whole thing, it's being able to help others. It bothers me very much not to be able to do that now. I still want to write, but haven't because I am exhausted from working, yet I still need to do that. It will be three years soon, but at the same time it was only yesterday.

Other people see TCF as a continuing source of strength in their lives, but do not move into formal leadership. A woman whose daughter was murdered was active before Parents of Murdered Children was formed. She had stopped attending, but when the trial drew near she began attending again.

> Grace: Part of why we went to TCF was to get in shape for the trial. It was a year and a half before it went to trial and it was important to us to be there and be prepared to handle anything that came our way. . . .
>
> Q: How long did you attend TCF, and why did you quit going to the meeting?
>
> Grace: We went pretty regularly when it was close, but after it moved up north we didn't go. The last time or two was after the trial. It helped us keep our equilibrium during that time. I felt we had to be reasonably strong before the trial so we wouldn't fall apart. I'd still like to attend at times, but one of the results of all this is I'm very uncomfortable going out alone at nights and my husband doesn't want to attend any more.

Those who have moved to formal leadership positions also find that there is a time when they want to move on:

> Ellen: It was hard for me to decide to give up my role in TCF, because I felt that was a place I could give back. But I found that I was starting to do it from obligation and I didn't like that feeling. Besides that, it seemed to me that I had other things I needed to do with my life. If G. had lived, he would have moved out of the house and it would be time for me to do other things. This feels like what other people do with the empty nest.

But they do not sever their ties with TCF. The holiday candlelight memorial service has the feel of a reunion as old members return with their families as a way of keeping their child as a part of their holiday celebrations. The phone networks that were developed when they were active in TCF seem to remain intact, for those who attend often have updated reports on those who could not attend. Parental bereavement is a permanent condition. The parents have reached resolution by learning to live in the world that includes the fact that children die, and especially that their child died. They have found a place for the dead child in their ongoing life by introjections and identification. They have found new equilibria in the world and in themselves. But they are forever changed and, for them, TCF is a part of that change.

CONCLUSION

Many bereaved parents seem to find self-help to be an effective intervention. We have attempted to understand the TCF process in terms of the decision to attend, the nature of affiliation, the transformations within the group, and graduations from the group. The decision to attend seems to be rooted in a variety of expectations. An invitation by parents who are already members or the support of friends and family members is often involved, as often are messages from the unconscious. New members attend who have a variety of experiences with professional interventions and other self-help groups. Affiliation has, first, an interpsychic dimension that entails a sense of unity with those whose lives have also been shattered, a sense of hope at seeing that others have made it, a sense of finding an appropriate object on which to attach the energy of the parent-child bond, and a sense of family in a supportive community. Second, affiliation has an experiential dimension that is an attempt to develop an existential stance in a problematic world, based on shared solutions to concrete problems. The decision to become a helper is the key to the TCF process. Helping others helps the self, for it allows the interpsychic dimension to become complete in internalizing the dead child and allows the experiential dimension to change from using the experience of others to sharing one's own experience. As time progresses, some members move to formal organizational leadership while others tend to become less regular in attendance, though they do so with some ambivalence. The leaders also at some point find that they have resolved the grief and they get on with their changed lives. The TCF process is self-renewing, for taking the place of those leaders who move on are people who a year or two ago thought they might not survive the death of their child.

6

Rage and Political Resolution: Parents of Murdered Children

The Parents of Murdered Children (POMC) was begun in 1981 at a national meeting of the Compassionate Friends (TCF). Although it is self-help, the dynamics of POMC are somewhat different from TCF because the aftermath of murder not only includes the grief at the death of the child, but it also puts the parents into the police and court system for several years as they try to win justice for their child's death. The grief itself has a special quality in that the narcissistic wound that is a part of all parental grief was caused by someone. Someone killed their child. Many murders are committed by family, friends, or acquaintances of the victim, so the parents have often known or heard of the murderer. The drive to revenge as a way to compensate for the narcissistic wound is strong in many parents whose children have died, but it is a central issue for many parents whose children are murdered. The justice system is designed to protect the rights of the accused and has over the years become a maze of legal rules and procedures. Parents need help in understanding the system, and then they need help in demanding their place within the justice system.

Homicide plays a central role in the American psyche (Kahn, 1984; *President's Task Force on Victims of Crime*, 1982). In stories reported in the news or in the plots of prime-time television, murder is familiar to us. Yet little attention has been paid to the survivors of those who have been murdered. When the death has been by murder, parental grief is complicated by special factors. In this chapter we will first outline the unique issues in the lives of parents of murdered children. Then we will show the unique ways in which POMC functions as a means to resolve the grief.

The dynamics of grief after a murder are not different from those we see in all parental grief, but in murder the sense of powerlessness and rage is stronger. The grief is prolonged by the criminal justice system. The fears in an unsafe world are stronger. Thus the study of POMC helps us not only understand the particular dynamics of bereavement after a murder, but also in POMC we can see more intensely some issues that are present in other parental bereavements.

THE AFTERMATH OF MURDER

Anger and Revenge

Murder does not seem part of the natural order in modern society. It is violence that cannot be put into a larger set of meanings, as can killing in war. It is death that cannot be ascribed to the vagaries of bodily malfunction, as can cancer. It is death for which medical science is not likely to find a cure. It is a death that did not have to happen. It is a death that was directly caused by someone. The narcissistic wound that is a part of all parental grief is exaggerated and focused when the death is by murder. Parents of murdered children experience an overwhelming anger and drive for revenge. The majority of murders are committed by relatives, friends, or acquaintances (Danto, 1982). Thus the survivors often know or know of the killer, who may even have been trusted as a family member. The anger has an immediate focus and transforms itself into revenge. The parents' power to protect their child has been challenged and they wish to reassert that power by diminishing the power of the killer in an act of vengeance.

> Sam and Gloria's married son was stabbed brutally by his wife, Anne, who had been accepted and loved by the family. Anne had a chaotic childhood, but Gloria felt that she had provided the mothering Anne never had. During the trial, a local women's group befriended Anne and counseled her to claim that she had been an abused wife. She was found guilty and given a light sentence of 3 years in jail. Gloria says she never thought she was capable of such hate as she now feels toward Anne. Occasionally, she fantasizes about methods to torture and execute Anne. She also has great hostility toward the women's group, asking, "Am I not also a woman; have I not suffered as a mother? Why

do they not care about me and my son?" Over and over she describes the gruesome details of the murder and her continuing need for retaliation. Her husband, Sam, experiences his anger in the opposite direction—he supresses it and refuses to deal with any of his conflicting feelings. He says the past is past and life must go on, but within the home, they remain at loggerheads.

Joyce attends the group without her husband. Her daughter Tina was murdered after being raped when she left her job as a cocktail waitress late at night. The body was found after several days. Tina had a stormy adolescence, but Joyce believes strongly that in the few months before the murder, Tina had "started to get her act together," and was maturing and beginning to resolve some of her problems. There had been a reconciliation between mother and daughter. The suspect was apprehended quickly, found guilty, and given a 50-year sentence. This decision was reversed and in a new trial a lighter sentence was given. "They have destroyed my life and family. We will never be the same," Joyce says. "It never gets any better, it just keeps getting worse." She feels her daughter's reputation was smeared in the newspaper reports of the trial. Joyce directs her anger at the suspect, the criminal justice system, and the news media. The combination of hurt and loss make it difficult to make any movement in her grief. If she gives up the hurt and the protest that the hurt motivates, she must give up the sense of herself as battling for her daughter's reputation and for justice at her killing. A great deal of her selfhood is now invested in the anger.

The Criminal Justice System

The police and court systems are properly charged with providing the justice the parent's seek. Historically, the victim's family had the responsibility for punishing the murderer or the murderer's family. Such a system still exists in some cultures. However, in the Western world, the Biblical injunction "Vengeance is mine says the Lord" has come to mean that the state takes to itself the power and responsibility for revenge and retaliation (Bowers, 1940; Jacoby, 1983). But the biblical injunction is both a prohibition and a promise. If the individual is to leave to God and the state the power for setting the world aright, then the individual expects that justice will indeed be done. This promise does not seem fulfilled in the experience of members of POMC. Within the criminal justice system, the victim's family finds they have no legal standing, for the case is the state versus the accused. The system is designed to protect the rights of the accused, whereas the survivors have no rights. The burden of proof rests with the prosecution. The legal system is a procedural labyrinth for which family members often have insufficient guides and un-realistic expectations.

Parents feel very strongly that a conviction and a harsh sentence are psychologically necessary for them. Thus, until the trial has been completed (often 1 to 2 years after the death), the parents seem unable to begin to resolve the grief. Yet the process often ends in either acquittal or short sentences. In murder trials, there is usually an appeal, resulting in a second trial, which can prolong the process for 2 or 3 more years. The person accused of a crime has the right to a speedy trial, but there seems to be no place in the American legal system for the victim's right to a speedy resolution of the legal process. In the second trial, parents' wounds are reopened through another step-by-step account of their child's gruesome death. Parents are aware of the parole system and know that even a 25-year sentence can mean only a few years served. They resent the court's weighing the value of their child's life as worth only 7 to 15 years of the killer's life. Even those parents who get a conviction and a long sentence are not satisfied, for, as one father said, "So he gets three life terms; that still does not pay for my son's life. Even if he was executed, it would not bring my son back." Thus the legal system seems to pro-mise a satisfaction of revenge, but cannot usually make good on the promise. After conviction, the killer is in jail, but often still has rights to communicate with other family members, including children. The murderer is seldom out of the life of the family of the victim.

Jane is from a very small town where "everybody knows each other." She attends POMC, sometimes with other family members, including parents, but she has been designated by the family as the person who will manage the family affairs concerning the murder. After her broth-er's murder, despite repeated requests, her family were not given any information by the police. It was as if the investigation was halted. After members of POMC marshaled political pressure on the police and prosecutor, Jane was able to obtain information. That moved the in-vestigation forward, but then at the hearing, she and other family members were barred from the courtroom even though they had a right as members of the public to be there. After political pressure was applied, the trial was scheduled, but the State's Attorney built his case around the testimony of a friend of the accused who would turn state's witness. Three years after the murder, it is still not clear whether the person will be willing to testify, for it is not clear that the person can be protected in prison from friends of the accused.

Nina's son was shot in the head by her daughter-in-law while he was asleep. The evidence was firm and the trial speedy. During the trial, Nina was put on the stand by the defense because of her strong moral/religious beliefs, which the defense said interfered with the marriage by controlling the son. The defense claimed wife abuse, though there were no witnesses. In addition to having to defend herself, Nina was forced to stare at a piece of trial evidence—her son's blood-soaked pillow—while she testified on the witness stand. The sentence was 3 years. Nina now has custody of her three-year-old grandson and is fearful that the mother will regain custody when she is released. Psychologically the grandchild has taken the place of her deceased son. The court has demanded that the mother be allowed to visit with the child while she is in prison, and Nina must take the child there periodically even though the drive is nearly 300 miles. The child regards Nina as a mother. It is difficult to know the nature of the child's attachment to the mother. Nina reports that the child is upset for several days after the visits. The court has upheld the mother's right to see her child, but has refused requests for psychological evaluation of the child to assess the effects of the visits on the child.

Fears in an Unsafe World

The act of murder reduces life to predator and prey (Kahn, 1984). This brings survivors back to the basic fears from which civilization is supposed to protect us. The fears are both for the self and for other members of the family. Because the killer is out on bail or because the court process results in the killer's being on the streets in a short time the fear does not seem unrealistic. In a larger sense, murder takes away the basic sense of power over our lives that democratic society is supposed to provide. In the developed world, we are supposed to be able to make assumptions about the safety of our children. But murder takes away that pretense.

> George and Sharon's daughter and son-in-law were murdered mysteriously in another city, but the granddaughter, who was a witness, was left unharmed. They now have custody of the child, and the murder has remained unsolved. The police have quietly told them that it was mob connected, and to leave it alone. They fear enough for the child that they have changed their names and moved to a new community.

> Lila and Steve's daughter was attempting to separate from her husband. She was found dead in the bathroom by her twelve-year-old daughter. The son-in-law remains the prime suspect, but he remains free because all the evidence was immediately removed by incompetent

police and prosecution was impossible. The granddaughter now lives with Lila and Steve. The son-in-law is now attempting to reestablish a relationship with his daughter. He has called and threatened Lila. The daughter has a need for a relationship with her one remaining parent, so Lila and Steve fear that they will alienate her in their hatred for her father.

Alan had been active in ward politics in the city for several years and had been a leader in a trade group that often lobbied for legislative measures. His son was shot in a parking garage. There was an arrest, and during the trial Alan attended the group. Alan dominated the first few meetings he attended. Over and over he told of the inept police work in his son's case and recited the list of politicians and important people he knew. It seemed as if he were trying to convince himself of his own power over the court system. He stopped attending when the trial ended in acquittal.

The Social Role of the Parent of a Murdered Child

The parents of a murdered child are in a new and unknown social role. They search for a way to cope and survive without the benefit of role models. The taboo character of the death cuts off usual support systems. While the search for role models and the loss of support systems is part of all parental grief, it seems to be exaggerated in the case of murder.

> Gene and Barbara's daughter was murdered in another state. Gene has an influential position and is highly respected in the community. Barbara has just finished a graduate degree and has begun a new profession. They report that they had to take the responsibility for reestablishing relationships with friends and colleagues. After the murder, they found themselves isolated and alienated, with few support systems. They sensed the fear and apprehension that their presence created in their social circles. Gene said in a meeting, "I would be walking down a hallway and see people avoiding me. People don't like to know what has happened to us, because they don't want to admit it could happen to them. It brings it too close to home."

> Mark and Linda were the object of daily newspaper and television coverage when their two daughters were abducted, raped, and murdered. Since that time, they have lost any privacy. Wherever they go, even on vacations, people recognize them and their grandchildren from newspaper pictures. It should be mentioned that there was so much notoriety about their case that when they attended POMC early in the life of the group, several members recognized them and responded to the newspaper stories and not to what they were really saying.

THE POMC PROCESS

A great many of the interactions observed in a POMC meeting seem familiar to one acquainted with other self-help with bereaved parents. In the study of TCF in Chapter 5, we examined two dimensions of the self-help process. First there is the experiential, in which solutions to problems of living in the new world of parental bereavement are shared (Antze, 1979; Borkman, 1976; Lieberman & Borman, 1979; Powell, 1975), for example, the question of what to say when asked how many children you have. Second, in an interpsychic dimension the emotional attachment formerly invested in the child is transferred to the group in a way that allows the inner representation of the child to be transformed (Fairbairn, 1952; Kernberg, 1976; van der Avort & van Harberden, 1985). Both these elements appear present in POMC, but there is an additional dimension in this group. The powerlessness, the drive for revenge, and the mazelike justice system produce anger and rage that is far greater and more specific than the anger associated with bereaved parents in TCF. Further, the survivor after homicide is still involved in the process. That is, the ongoing police and court activity is a continuation of the process of the death. Thus, only a minority of the members can feel that the death is behind them and the grief phase is at hand. The drive for revenge that grows from the radical sense of powerlessness and from the sense of being caught in the legal system that is supposed to bring vengeance forms the basis for a third dimension of the self-help process in POMC. We call that the *political dimension*.

The Political Dimension

Anger and rage are channeled into action within POMC. Two kinds of action are an important part of the group's activity. First, members help each other with their ongoing problems within the criminal justice system. Second, the group works toward reform in the criminal justice system.

Problems with the criminal justice system form the common thread that unites POMC members. The ritual opening of the meeting is, like that of TCF, to have members introduce themselves, give the child's name, age, and death date, and say something about their present psychological state. In POMC the present status of the case in the criminal justice system is also given. If there have been significant developments since the last meeting, they are announced. Reports of arrests, indictments, trial dates, and convictions are greeted with expressions of congratulations.

About half the meeting topics involve education about the legal system. Speakers have included judges, prosecuting attorneys, and police officials. Each stage of the judicial process is examined, so the parents learn the system in a way they can respond most effectively. For example, many parents are incensed when low bail is set for the accused killer. "They set the bail at $10,000," complained one man to the judge who was the guest speaker. "Here my daughter is dead and they only value her life at $10,000." The man had raised the issue of the low bail several times earlier in the group. The judge explained that bail was set based on the likelihood of the person fleeing prosecution and on the possibility the person was a danger to the society. Because the accused is not yet judged guilty, the size of the bail has nothing to do with the value of the victim's life. In theory, that value is weighed in the sentence. The bereaved father now had to decide on the appropriate way to direct his anger. If he kept being angry at the bail that was set, he was tilting with windmills. The judge's explanation seemed to satisfy him, for he did not raise the issue again and explained it several months later to a newcomer to the group.

The group maintains a close relationship with the the prosecuting attorney's office and with some police officials, so that on occasion political pressures can be exerted to gain members their rights. On a few occasions when the murder has occurred in another jurisdiction, phone calls from the group's political friends to their colleagues have been made. It is difficult to trace exactly the causal relationships of such actions, but it has appeared to the member having problems that the police or prosecuting attorney has been more forthcoming after POMC intervention. Sometimes the political pressure is in the form of a letter from the chapter to the police or prosecuting attorney, and sometimes pressure is in the form of letters to newspapers. The group also lobbies in cooperation with other victims' rights organizations for changes in the law that will give them more standing within the criminal justice system.

Although these activities can be understood in terms of social support systems, the deeper understanding of the dynamics of POMC is found in the way the group deals with the issue of vengeance. The dynamics of vengeance lead us deep into the human psyche. For most of human history, revenge was recognized as the legitimate basis for the actions of the murder victim's family against the murderer or the murderer's family. A life must be paid for by another life. Although the modern world has rejected vengeance by the family on the murderer, we seem not to have worked out a public philosophy of the place of vengeance in the treatment of the criminal in the court and prison systems. The POMC members, then, have no well-established guidelines by which to channel their need for vengeance when the state does not seem able to make good on its promise to bring justice.

The philosopher Friedrich Nietzsche gives a useful analysis of the interaction of vengeance and powerlessness. In *On the Genealogy of Morals* (1967), Nietzsche argues that love and forgiveness is a slave morality invented to disguise to the self the powerlessness of those too weak to defend themselves. Knightly aristocrats had no need to turn their vengeance into hatred, for they had the power to do the deed that would set their world aright. They could respect their enemies because the enemy could have power like their own. Their vengeance was good because it was an extension of their power in their world. But those who were under the power of the State had to trust in God to bring their justice. That powerlessness resulted in hatred.

Forgiveness that grows within the resentment of powerlessness is directed toward those who have demonstrated power over us. To turn the other cheek implies that someone had the power to slap the first cheek. In the politics of oppression, love among the powerless is always a problem, for rage that cannot be directed toward the rightful object is displaced onto those who also have no power. For Gandhi and other nonviolent leaders, the greatest challenge is to maintain peace and unity among the followers, not to show courage in the face of the power. To ask, therefore, that forgiveness be the norm among the parents of murdered children is to ask for a level of sainthood that has been achieved only rarely in human history and that has never been sustained within ongoing political relationships such as those found in the criminal justice system. It asks them to embrace their powerlessness, to accept the narcissistic wound. No external voice can say that. The authority of the voice would depend on a power greater than the parents of murdered children. The authority would be a power beyond the parents, but it is the lack of power that creates the rage; the external authority would only increase their sense of powerlessness. Some parents do forgive, though their love often has rage within it as they love the killer in order to "heap burning coals upon his head." But such forgiveness cannot be a norm in POMC.

The process within POMC takes the dynamics of rage and vengeance and applies them in a more pragmatic way. The in- terpsychic dimension is based on the identification of the powerless with each other. That is, the statement that everyone is equal in the face of the murder of their child and in the frustration with the criminal justice system means that love and mutual respect can be shared among the members. The acceptance of others in the group transcends some rather obvious social barriers. Some of the children murdered were innocent victims in the wrong place at the wrong time. Other children had been involved in illegal activity. Other children had become involved in problematic interpersonal relationships. There are also large social class and racial differences within the group. But the group self-consciously overcomes those differences in their identification with each other. Thus, within the group, anger and rage are directed outward toward their rightful object rather than displaced.

Whereas the individuals within the group may have little power, as an organized group they can demonstrate a great deal of power. The system does not seem to work for justice, and POMC is becoming an action group working for reform. Several state legislators have been invited to meetings. The focus of those meetings has been to inform the officials of the members' experiences. POMC members have gone as a group to the state capitol to lobby for bills aimed at securing victims' rights and to effect more speedy justice. Representatives of the group have testified before the Presidential commission on crime victims. The group is also represented in state victims' rights organizations. Victims' groups as well as prosecuting attorneys have been influential in passing state laws that give the family of the murder victim a place in the judicial system. The law gives the family a right to make a statement to the court prior to sentencing, about the suffering the crime has brought and about the character of the person who was murdered. Each time the murderer is brought before the parole board, the family has the right to make a statement about the continuing effects of the crime. If the state has taken over from the family the duty to seek vengeance for murder, POMC is working to restore a place for the family in the process.

The political dimension is about the restoration of power in the face of the powerlessness the parent of a murdered child experiences. When the parent experiences a sense of power, the vengeance can be freed from the hatred that made it so useless before. Like Nietzsche's knightly aristocrat, the parent can incorporate the sense of vengeance into the power to set the world aright. The parent can demonstrate competence by keeping pressure on the police and prosecutors to press their child's case fully. The group aids the parent in that mission by giving information about the system, supporting actions the members have taken, and helping members mobilize the needed political power. The parents also transcend their individual need for power as they act on behalf of the group to restore rights within the system. Like the more overtly political groups of parents of children killed by drunk drivers, the parents of murdered children are finding resolution of their grief within the sense of competence and self-esteem that comes from being a citizen whose voice is heard.

Experiential Dimension

The political dimension of POMC shades into the experiential dimension, for parents of murdered children are dealing not only with their grief, but are also caught up in the legal system. Thus, the experiential sharing is often as much about legal issues as it is about grief issues. The grief issues are not different from those we have already described in the TCF process, so we will not repeat the discussion here. The experiential dimension of the group process in terms of the criminal justice system is somewhat more specific than the broad experiential advice in TCF.

The political savvy that some members have developed in their own encounter with the law is put at the disposal of all. In POMC there is a rigorous questioning of the facts in the case and of the possible areas of action.

Alice: I am so frustrated. I just know the police are not doing anything. I call them and they never return my calls.

Fred: What exactly are you saying when you call?

Alice: I ask for Sgt. Jones. He is in charge of Bob's case. He said he would call if he found out anything, but I know he talked to some people who know something and he didn't call. I'm sure he thinks I'm just a bother, but the whole family is relying on me to get the information, and things are just a wreck around home.

Jane: Well, you know, they are in the business of solving crimes. If you just seem another burden on them, of course they will not want to call you.

Alice: But I need to know. I just can't stand it, thinking nothing is happening on the case.

Fred: Then I suggest that you go down there when he is in and tell him that you want only fifteen minutes in which he will brief you. Be businesslike with him.

Alice: Well, I'll try it.

The members know a great deal more about the specifics of each others' situations than is common in TCF. As members gather for the meeting, they ask about court dates that were discussed in previous meetings.

Interpsychic Dimension

The interpsychic dimension of POMC would also be familiar to those acquainted with TCF. The members share the bonds with the dead children as a way of bonding with each other. Periodically, pictures of the dead children are brought and passed around as lovingly remembered stories are recounted. It is clear that the solace of introjections and identification in parents of murdered children are similar to the solace of all bereaved parents. But in POMC, the shared desire for revenge and the shared experience with the criminal justice system provide further opportunity for identification with each other in the present.

The parents are bonded to each other in their shared anger. In a meeting, an expression of rage and demand for revenge is supported by the members. One man told of his feelings about the killer. He said that he needed to be careful of his feelings in the courtroom because any outcry would lead to a mistrial. Another man responded:

> You have to be careful about letting it out. But I know what you are feeling. If I ever got my hands on the guys who raped and murdered my daughter I'd kill them and kill them slowly. I didn't think I was capable of such thoughts, but after I heard what they did to her, I don't care if I go to jail or they kill me for it. I would just like to get those bastards.

A woman then shared:

> Paul [her dead son's child] and I often just sit and imagine what we would do to Lucy [his second wife, who killed him] if we could ever get her. I would just torture her like she did my son.

The drive to revenge is a forbidden feeling in modern society. Yet it is a feeling that parents of murdered children share. One of the interpsychic dynamics is in sharing the validity of the feelings. It is difficult to know the degree that such bonding in anger normalizes the feeling as a part of the ongoing life of the parent or to what extent bonding in anger holds the members within the rage and prevents them from working toward a resolution. In answer to the question, one father said:

It is like the holocaust of the Jews. You can't just get over that. That stays with you forever. We must remember and feel it every day. We must be witnesses to the injustice that was committed.

On the other hand, a woman whose son was murdered 9 years earlier and whose killer was never found reported: "I had to give up my anger and hurt too. I finally said, 'They have taken too much from me already. I will not let them take the rest of my life.'" She did not give up the anger in an act of forgiveness; rather, she gave up the anger in an act of self-preservation. Whether rage channeled constructively into political action is counted to be as healthy as letting go of the rage or as healthy as forgiveness probably depends on a value system that is outside the analytic that is used to understand parental bereavement. In our observations, it appears that when parents can understand themselves as having power to effect real change in the criminal justice system, their functioning in the rest of their lives is enhanced.

Parents of murdered children are also bonded in their struggles with the criminal justice system. Trial dates are announced at the meetings and in newsletters. Often, members will go to court as an act of support for other members. Just as the interpsychic dimension changes the question in all parental grief from "Why me?" to "Why us?" it changes the pronoun to the plural form in the encounters with the police and courts.

The sharing of the battles in the criminal justice system allows the members to share victories and defeats. One victory is victory for all.

Mary's daughter was murdered by a boyfriend with whom she had broken off relations several months previously. Some of the evidence cannot be used in court. Thus, the killer was on the streets for 2 years. Mary often shared her fear of the killer. She said she had a gun under her pillow and shared the bed with with one of her teenaged daughters. She reported that she always runs from the car to the store or office, and that she always feels as if she must look over her shoulder. The killer was arrested for killing another person, and in the process, the police were able to get evidence that could be used in Mary's daughter's case. The report was in the newspaper a few days before the POMC meeting. As she arrived at the meeting, she was greeted by hugs and kisses from several members, but especially from two people for whom their child's killer was still at large. "Well, congratulations," said one. "You got your arrest. I am so happy for you. I think it is just wonderful."

On the other hand, those whose cases have gone well are tempered in their satisfaction because they know it might have gone otherwise. One father reported after the conviction:

> We were lucky. The police did a professional job. The judge was just as careful as he could be. He said he didn't want any grounds for mistrial and he bent over backwards to give the defense every opportunity. They brought in the guilty verdict and he got 50 years. Now I hope somebody kills him in there. I feel good, but I know we were just lucky. When I hear these other stories, I know it could have been different.

Sharing victories and defeats in their individual battles with the criminal justice system allows the group to remain united in their political action. Those who have not had an arrest or who have not been able to get a conviction can take satisfaction that some people do. Those who get arrest and conviction can know that others don't. Thus, the energy of the members can remain focused on the political dimension and not be dissipated by jealousy on the part of some members or self-righteousness on the part of others.

CONCLUSION

Every death of a child is a narcissistic wound to the parent. In POMC, the rage and sense of powerlessness brought on by that wound are focused because the death was caused by someone. The rage becomes a drive for revenge, but the criminal justice system is a poor vehicle for the psychological satisfaction of vengeance. Rather than empower the bereaved parent, the criminal justice system contributes to the parent's sense of powerlessness and impotence. In addition to the dynamics of experiential sharing and intrapsychic identification that we find in the social support of other self-help groups, POMC offers a political dimension. By learning to cope with the criminal justice system and by working to change the laws and rules of criminal proceedings, POMC members gain the power of citizens whose voices are heard.

7

Discovery of Authentic Self: Bereaved Helping the Dying

This chapter will examine the lives of beareaved parents who are part of an ongoing support program of children and their families in the oncology unit of a large pediatric hospital. Through this examination, we can see more clearly a resolution of grief that promotes socially valuable interactions. We will focus particularly on the dynamics of social support and the dynamics of the internalization of the dead child.

THE CONTEXT

The unit has an average population of 7 to 10 inpatient children and over 100 outpatient children receiving active treatment. The hospital also follows several hundred other children who have completed treatment. The average time spent in treatment is 24 months, though the variations are great. The focal point of the unit is the outpatient clinic, where the children come from one day a week to every day for treatment. In the clinic, there is a great deal of activity which is aimed at helping parents communicate with their child, helping the children develop peer support for each other, and helping the parents develop a social support system for each other. A large parent-run organization is active on the unit. The organization implements many of the programs for families. Parties for Halloween, July 4, Valentine's Day, and other holidays are held on clinic days. Several bereaved couples played Santa, Mrs. Claus, and the elves for Christmas last year.

In the summer, there is a camp for older children in treatment and a family camp for younger children, their siblings, and parents.

There is also a 3-day family camp. Most siblings attend family camp, so the group is over 100 people. Some of the counselors at the camp are bereaved parents, some of the counselors are older teenagers with cancer, and other counselors are older teenagers who are "graduates." The bonds between the counselors and the campers are strong, and several of the teenagers come back on clinic days to visit the younger children who were in their group. Among the parents in the clinic, the camp experience is a high point. For several months, their small talk and banter is full of references to the weekend.

The nursing staff is included in this large supportive network. There is a staff support group/inservice training group for the nurses. In that group they are allowed to ventilate the emotions they feel toward the physical and emotional damage the treatment imposes on the children, the stress they feel in the slow progress of some patients, and the pain they feel at the death of the children. They can share meaningful experiences and have their experiences socially validated.

Bereaved parents are a central part of this whole mutual support system. The bonding between parents of sick children is carried over to the bonds between parents whose children have died. The bond the parents share with each other's children is transformed into the shared loss when one of the children dies. On the other hand, when one of the children recovers, the bond between parents and children allows the joy to be shared just as the grief is shared.

If a child is to die in this setting, it is seldom unexpected. There is a follow-up after the death of the child, which is aimed at retaining the social support that was given during the illness.

First, when a child dies, a staff member attends the funeral or funeral-home visitation. Thus the bonds between the newly bereaved parents and the social support system are strengthened and affirmed immediately after the death.

Second, the bereaved parent receives information. Within a week after the death, the staff sends a sympathy card that notes that a packet of information will be arriving in a few weeks. The information packet is mailed about 3 weeks after the death. The packet was developed by The Compassionate Friends chapter. A copy of Schiff's *The Bereaved Parent* (Schiff, 1977) is also included.

Third, there is a bereavement group to which the parent is invited a month after the death. The bereavement group meets at the hospital, though in an area some distance from both the clinic and the inpatient floors. The drive to the hospital is a familiar one, a familiarity that has several meanings to the bereaved parent. It is a reminder of the loss, but it is also a well-worn path. Though the hospital is associated with the death of the child, it is also associated with the supportive community there. The bereavement group is a subchapter of the local Compassionate Friends.

Two characteristics of this bereavement group seem slightly different from other TCF chapters. First, there are more men at the meetings. This seems to be because the fathers knew each other during the care of the child, so they are used to getting support from each other. Second, there is a fuller social life. This seems to be an extension of the parents' social life together when the children were included. Thus, the observer at the meeting feels even more like an outsider. At the same time, the community seems more familylike than other TCF groups.

What makes it possible for bereaved parents to come back to the place their child died and work with parents whose children may very well die? We interviewed two couples who have been active in the program. One couple devotes a great deal of time to the hospital, volunteering in the clinic and helping in the bereavement group. The other couple has been active for several years and is now "retiring" as a new generation of parents come into the group. For both couples, the transformation into the helping role has been a central part of their lives. We found a rather consistent pattern of resolution.

For these parents, strong social support during the child's dying facilitated a thoroughgoing change in the parent's self. Within the community that developed around them and the child, the parents found new core values. These new values are associated with a sense of the divine presence, which is strong and solace giving. The inner representation of the child is merged with religious solace the parents gained in the dying process, but the inner representation is also held closely. They find meaning in helping, as an extension of the social support they found as the child died. Helping others is a way of giving meaning to the death of the child and as a way of authentically engaging in the present.

GIVING UP AND KEEPING: RELIGIOUS SOLACE

The inner representation of the child is integrated into a positive ontology of religious devotion; that is, the child is strongly experienced as being in heaven. Yet at the same time, the child is experienced as a present personality. That paradoxical introjection seems to energize the parent while at the same time it provides a great deal of solace.

We can see the complexity of the introjection in an interview we did with Hans. His daughter's wish before she died was to see the ocean. Bills for her treatment had already taken all the family savings, but with the financial help of friends, the family had driven to the coast, where for the first and last time the child played in the ocean. The next morning the father awoke early and walked out on to a dock. There he gave her up, but he did so remembering when she was given to him at her birth. At the same time, he held on to his daughter, for he felt her close to him in memory and in the merger of inner representation of the child with the representation of God.

> Hans: I still picture myself on that dock, still asking for a miracle which would give her back to me; yet I knew by the same token that, "If this is Your will, I know where she is going to be. I can be happy with that."
>
> Q: It sounds like you had a pretty intense talk with God.
>
> Hans: I became closer to God than I think I have ever been; I think that since she died and went to be with Him, it's just gotten stronger. I can truthfully say that I was never mad at Him during her illness. I don't know if that's hard to accept, or maybe there's a part of me saying, "Well, you do hate him for that." But I can't bring that out. . . .
>
> Q: As she became sicker, more and more you felt in touch with God. You were having conversations with Him. It started out with, "Give us a miracle," and ended up with, "Take care of her."
>
> Hans: It ended with, "I give her back to you." I also thanked Him because He gave her to me for 11½ years. I knew that sooner or later we are all going to die. At that time I felt at peace and I felt relief. There are times now even after 5 years that you choke up. The tears are there. You see other kids and that will remind you of her. The tears just come to your eyes.
>
> Q: It's something that you never really get over.
>
> Hans: I don't want to get over it.
>
> Q: Why not?
>
> Hans: Because she meant so much to me that I never want to put her in a closet and close her up. I always want her there fresh. . .I want those happy memories.
>
> Q: If you let go of the sadness, you have to let go of the memories?
>
> Hans: Yes, it's like that. And, it is that I had such a love for her that it was like, "If I really let go of everything, I'll forget her." I don't want to forget her.
>
> Q: So you feel, "I'll take the pain that goes with the memory because the memory is so precious?"
>
> Hans: Right, and it's something that's inscribed in my heart because she was my daughter. I can remember when she was born and they brought her out. She wasn't even cleaned up yet. They showed her to me. I

kind of related that to when I was out on that dock. I can remember the nurse standing there with her, showing her to me. It was like she was giving her to me and now, after 11½ years, I had to do the same thing with God. I had to give her back.

He now feels a continuity between God and his daughter. His child does not feel far away, rather, the merger of God and the inner representation of the child makes God feel closer. His daughter is not alone, for there are other children to whom he feels bonded.

My picture of God is that F. is up there running through a field picking flowers and bringing them. And Jesus is sitting there on a rock. She is gathering flowers for Him. I feel that she is right there in his lap. I feel that even though I still grieve and still have the pain and the tears, I have this picture of Jesus on a rock with a little girl on his lap. And all these other little kids there, and Him telling them stories.

Hans' vision of his child with Jesus supports a new view of himself. He can cry in a way he could not when he was macho.

It's comforting. I think I need the tears, though. When I say this I mean that I feel that it's so hard for men to cry and it's a way of getting your feelings out. . . . I'm not ashamed of it. I don't like the word macho. The reason I don't like this word is because everybody thinks that men are supposed to be macho. But if those men would lose a child, would they still be macho?

We asked a mother we interviewed how she had come to the point at which she could let go of her child. She cast the answer in terms of other attachments. She feels attached to God and to a strong community of other people. Within those other attachments, she experiences the continued active bond with her son.

Jane: I think a lot of it was just seeing him become sicker and sicker and the realization that it really was the end and he was going to die. If there were to somehow be a miracle (and I have great faith in the Lord), and I will certainly say that our religious faith carried us through that time—and our friends, and everything else—but I felt that it was time. It was strange. The night he died, I wasn't panicky, and it was a beautiful experience— and yet it seems crazy to say this—but it seemed like a good death. I was holding his hand and I could tell when the spirit left him. I was absolutely contented, although it seems like a strange word. I wasn't hysterical or anything, I was just calm.

But even as the child was given up, Jane feels a direct communication with her dead child. The child represents her best self.

> Jane: I'll be on the highway in a traffic jam and I'll say, "Okay, G., get me out of this. I'll go by the cemetery and talk to him, or I'll be thinking about something and I'll talk to G.
>
> Q: You say you hear him sometimes. How do you hear him?
>
> Jane: Just in my mind. I'm trying to stop smoking and I say, "My God, you've got to help me through this." When I get ready to buy a pack of cigarettes, I say to myself, "Don't buy those." I know it's in my own mind.
>
> Q: That's the place in your mind that he occupies; he's the best part of you.
>
> Jane: I think about the times when G. was so worried about me. His concern was for me. He was strong, and a wonderful example for me. He just loved us and we could feel it. G. brought us the example of showing love and now we continue that in our other children. The kids all recognize it too. It's a beautiful experience. We believe in heaven, and that G. is where he should be. We feel that his purpose has been fulfilled; and for us, we are still working on it.

The presence of the child in heaven is experienced in that part of the self that is beyond social relationships. The child is experienced as both inner and outer reality in the core of the self.

> Kirstin: There are parts of grief that I believe you can share and you can go through together. But where it was F. and me, that could not be shared. I still feel the oneness of the relationship. She's still a part of me, so I communicate with her in a way. I never sat down and said, "Now I want to communicate with her." It's like a presence. Her presence is still with me. . . . To a person who has always been blind, colors cannot be explained. That's how I feel about trying to explain my feelings about F. It's almost unexplainable. . . . It's not my imagination and I'm not pretending that she's there. She is there and I'm not trying to make a bigger deal out of it than what it is. She is just there—always. Just as your children who are alive, and may not be in your presence at all times, they are still there.

The sense of the child both as in heaven and as a present solace would be disturbed by a less-than-caring God. Even as the sense of God has been enlarged by the merger of the inner representation of the child, we also find that the faith is in a less-than-omnipotent God. Though the God of their faith early in the illness was a God of miracles, the God of these parents is not to be controlled by the wishes of humans, but nevertheless God works for human good.

Kirstin: I don't know that I've ever suffered the, "Why me," syndrome. . . . The curiosity of "Why me," not the martyr of "Why me." I wonder why this happened in our lives instead of someone else's. I wonder what the purpose of it is, or whatever. I never felt like God did this to her, but I feel that He allowed it for a reason. . . .

Q: Are you willing to talk about an answer to the question, "Why me," with what you are doing now? "Why me—so I can do this?"

Kristen: Yes, I think He has got to be part of that. I still don't feel that God would take her so that I could do this; I don't think that He's that kind of a snatching God. But I think that all things work together for the good. I don't think that God uses people as little pawns to move about here and there. He gave life to Adam in the first place so that He could share. And I don't feel that He would put a little life on earth and watch it grow, and then snatch it away so that something else could happen. I know He could do that, but I don't think he would.

The parent must wrestle with the seeming disparity between a God who can do anything and the death of the child. The theology by which the disparity is resolved is firmly rooted in the intellect.

Q: Did you think that all that praying would bring about a cure?

Curtis: Yes, ask Jane about this too, because Jane is kind of a realist and I'm kind of a dreamer. That was the one area we had some conflict. She realized that it was coming to an end. . . .

Q: How did you come to terms with this? It sounds to me like you stayed in touch with your religious faith, but there must have been a transition when the cure didn't happen.

Curtis: I guess I'm realistic enough to know that it is not something that happens all of the time. I'm also enough of a realist to know that many people don't believe that it ever happens at all. I truly believe that there is a God to be with sometimes, and I don't challenge His logic for one thing. He's helped me so many times on request, but never the way I wanted, but in the way that was best for me. I kept thinking, "Are You going to do it? But if He isn't, He isn't."

Q: Was that a hard transition to make after G. died?

Curtis: No, I don't think so: I just know that G. is there in heaven.

Q: How do you know?

Curtis: Well, for one thing, I'm an engineer and I do a lot of testing. I guess that I've tested God enough, and He's answered enough things for me. I couldn't put it on a graph, but I've been on my knees in the hallway and have said, "God, I've screwed up, and I don't know what to do. You do it for me." And He has done it. I've done that enough to know that He's there.

CONTINUITY IN SOCIAL SUPPORT

Strong social support facilitates the solace-giving inner equilibrium these parents have found. In the hospital and in their communities, they found that as the child died they were surrounded by a community that wanted to help and that cared for the parents as well as the child. Within the child's dying process, the parents reoriented their values. The encounter with death was for them the most authentic existence they had ever known. For them, the edge between life and death was not a place of abandonment—an existential abyss. For them, it was a place of true living, a place where authentic community exists, a place where they sorted out the important from the unimportant in life. The new self these parents found as their child died is sustained on the outside by the social support they still maintain. The new self is sustained on the inside by the sense that the child is in heaven and is close at hand.

Helping other parents within the hospital program enables these parents to maintain and express the new authentic self. But the transition from the social support of the child's dying to an ongoing lifestyle is not smooth. The death of the child is also the loss of community.

Social Support and the Changed Self

When the child was dying, the parents felt themselves at the center of a caring community. They found people reaching out to help them, and in accepting the help, they found a sense of authentic community which they had not felt previously. Within that community and in the face of death, the parents found an authentic existence which they had not known before.

> Curtis: These friends of ours down the block have five cars. Our car wasn't working, and I said, "Oh, the heck with it, I'm going down and ask them if I can borrow one of their cars." You would have thought that I had given them a million dollars. They had been wanting to do something for us to reach out and didn't know what to do. After that time, anytime they left town, they would say, "I'm bringing a car down to leave in your driveway." They didn't know what they could do to help us. It told me that everyone likes to give, but nobody likes to accept help. You can't give it unless someone is ready to accept it. Now, if someone offers something, I take it. I talk about what I call the big circle theory: Someone says, "I'm going to pay you back." A helps B and B helps C, and they go all around the world, but it will come back. I really believe that.

The closeness the parents felt to their dying child and the closeness they felt within the social support was for them a fuller way of
being themselves. The social support mediated to them a larger bond
with their world. Religious faith became more meaningful.

Curtis: We go to church, and during the 3-year period as the word got out
that we had a son who was ill, different people knocked on the door. A
friend of mine who is a neighbor, but I hadn't seen for about five years,
knocked on the door and came to tell me about the group that he and his
wife belonged to. He was the last guy in the world who I would expect to
belong to a prayer group. He invited us to come to the meetings. Another
friend of mine invited me to join a Bible study program, which I did. . . .
The afternoon of the prayer group was January second. We called her and
told her we were coming. There was an inch of ice on everything. The folks
didn't tell us that they had canceled it. We went out to the home of two
perfect strangers and we must have talked for 3 or 4 hours. We attended a
prayer group at their home for about 6 to 8 months. They came into our life
at that time, but I haven't seen them since.

Jane: We didn't hug or touch or even say, "I love you." Curtis and I
both came from the same kind of family. My mother died last year and I'd
tell her I loved her, and she couldn't write to me, "I love you too." I grew
up in a family who never hugged or said those words and, really, Curtis
did too. We began to see the importance of showing our feelings. Every
time we would cover G. up, he would say, "I need a hug." We would hug
each other and say, "I love you." After a couple years of this, it really
reconditioned us and our whole sense of values changed.

Initial Loss of Social Support

When a child dies after a long fight with cancer, one of the things the
parent initially loses is the supportive community they found during
the years of the illness.

Kirstin: There's a family relationship that's built around the hospital as you
go through it with your own child. Most parents lose that. They lose the
friendship; of the staff at the hospital and the other parents and the other
children that they have become attached to. After a child dies, normally
you are not back in that situation and you totally lose a part of your life—a
big part, because you have been spending most of your time there. . . .
What we experienced right in the very beginning was not only her loss, but
the loss of our lives. Whatever our lives were for the past eight months are
gone. We are not going to spend our time doing the same things. We are
not going to spend our time with the same people. We are not going to
spend our time at the same places. We are not going to spend our time

planning the same kinds of schedules. What do I do now? Where do I go? My whole life has changed. I have all this time on my hands.

Jane: For me, the hospital had become an extension of our family. I was talking to Bonnie the social worker every day. As G. became more ill, the chemotherapy was destroying his brain, so he had to have this brain surgery, and so we were in the hospital a lot for the last 6 months. We had decided to keep him at home and they were preparing us for all the eventualities and there was a tremendous communication. The people at the hospital were part of our family, and when G. died, all of a sudden that's over with.

Helping and Holding

The death of a child creates an empty space in the life of the parent. To some extent, the hole can be filled with a continuation of the new meaning of life the parent learned when the child was dying. The death of the child is, for these parents, both a loss and a gain. The child has been given up and incorporated into a larger sense of bonding to the world in religious faith. Yet the child is retained as a solaceful presence in their lives. In the caring for their child through the cancer, they gained a new sense of meaningfulness in life and a new way of relating to a supportive community. The experience of giving up and keeping the child, the experience of finding a new sense of authentic community, and the experience of finding a more meaningful sense of their own life is continued by forming support groups of other bereaved parents and by remaining in the community of the hospital where they can help other parents whose children are now fighting cancer. Life as a bereaved parent thus becomes a continuation of the new life that was learned when the child was dying.

Jane: I sat around with nothing to do because he had taken so much of my time. When he was gone, the contact with the hospital was gone, and the kids went back to school, but life has to go on. . . . There was a big hole in my life and no way to fill it up. To this day I can't fill that up.
   Q: What did you do with the loneliness that you felt; not knowing where to put yourself after G. died?
   Jane: We had a business which had pretty well gone to pot. We put energies into that. We had our other children. I became active in the church. Then they opened the Ronald McDonald House and we threw ourselves into decorating that whole house. It was wonderful, and of course we met nothing but lovely people. That carried us through the next spring, that one big project. We painted and papered and had a wonderful time and it was good therapy.

I became very involved with a mother who had a son. Her name was Fran. A woman who lived in Alabama brought her son to the hospital here for treatment. They gave her my name and she called me. Her son had lung cancer; they told her that they had probably arrested everything, but it came back. I became very close to her, and was a big help to her. I didn't go back to the hospital anymore, but I missed the people there like friends.

Kirstin: I felt a need to go back and see people, to visit. It happened to work out because our son had to go the the hospital for a minor operation. We had more excuses to come to the hospital and visit everybody while we were there. That helped fill the gap of the loss. Doing other activities like joining bowling leagues or something seemed so empty, and after experiencing the death of a child—who cares what your bowling score is? You get to the point in your life where everything else seems so trivial and stupid. I wanted to do something important.

It appears that when the social support is strong for parents during their child's dying and in the early months of their bereavement, they can pass on that social support to others. The needs of a friend whose child died in an accident led to the formation of a potluck supper group.

Curtis: Another couple's son lost his life in a motorcycle accident and the husband was having a tough time. She asked if Jane and I belonged to any organizations. We put our heads together and made a list of our friends who had lost children and we were surprised that three kids out of G.'s eighth grade class had passed to the next world in violent accidents. We invited couples over here. We sat around in a circle like a bunch of teenagers. We are all roughly the same age, in our fifties. Nobody was talking much. Jane and I went in the kitchen and said, "This is really a flop." Everyone was waiting for someone to start. At the end of the evening, the couple we had this for said, "Well, when do we meet again?" Like they had been invited to join a club. We looked at each other and said, "Maybe we will have a potluck supper at our house in a few months." This time, when we had the potluck, everybody opened up and shared.

The group met for several years.

The degree to which the inner representation of the child is a central part of the ongoing helping role seems to vary. We asked the man who had played Santa Claus at the hospital what had been his relationship to his dead child as he spent a whole day going from bed to bed.

Hans: She was right next to me. Every time I touched one of their little heads, because that was the thing between F. and me. Even mom wasn't allowed to touch that all the time. When I got to kiss or touch a little bald head, it was like having F. back. I can get right down to the level of the kids, and she's there. But I also know that the child who I am playing with is not F. Even though F. might be here, that child is not F.

Yet for his wife, who played Mrs. Claus, the basis of involvement was different. She is motivated by the sense of closeness she found in the hospital as the child was dying and by the sense of authentic life that a meaningful involvement in the world motivates. Though she has an active sense of her child's presence, the inner representation of the child is not really involved in the helping role.

Kirstin: I feel she is the reason I do this only because I wouldn't have known or understood it before. You can sense that I didn't have a real happy childhood. Then going along in our marriage and becoming happier, and probably becoming happier when I became more in tune with the Lord. As our spiritual lives grew, our communication grew, our love for each other grew, our love for our family; and joy comes with all that. I felt strong enough to reach out to areas of my life that I didn't feel strong enough to do before. I feel that I have found where I am supposed to be in life.

CONCLUSION

The resolution we see in these bereaved parents who are active in helping in the hospital where their children died is very complex. The inner representation of the dead child is introjected both as a living presence and as a merger with their sense of the presence of God. They find great solace in both aspects of the introjection. For these parents, the time their child was dying provided them more authentic living than they had known before. The social support they felt as their child was dying provided the most authentic community they had ever known. Helping is, for them, a continuation of membership in the supportive community and a continuation of authentic living in the face of death.

Although this resolution appears to be a relatively stable psychological configuration, the elements within the configuration are not unique, for the centrality of social support and solace of introjection we see in these parents is found in other forms and combinations in the resolution of most parental bereavement.

8

Uncovering Complexity: The Psychotherapeutic Process

Bereaved parents bring a variety of problems and expectations when they seek help from professional counselors or psychotherapists. This chapter is not an instruction manual for professional counseling and therapy with bereaved parents. Rather, it is an attempt to understand the dynamics of parental bereavement that are seen more clearly within the context of professional intervention. We learn the complexity of parental bereavement from the uninhibited flow of thoughts and feelings, the exploration of past and present relationships, the transferences between therapist and client, the concerns for the future, and the changes which come with the resolution of the bereavement. Together these data form a fuller portrait of the meaning of one death and of the dynamics of one resolution. We will first set out problematic elements in parental grief that bring individuals into therapy. Then we will present five cases that illustrate these elements. Finally we will examine the etiology of pathology in grief.

TWO ELEMENTS OF PSYCHOTHERAPY WITH BEREAVED PARENTS

In the early chapters of the book we found that the resolution of parental bereavement is in the establishment of a new equilibrium in, first, the parent's relationship within a social world that has been made poorer by the death of the child, and, second, in the establishment of a new equilibrium in the parent's relationship to the inner representative of the dead child. As they work toward those equilibria, bereaved parents have many tasks that are part of their griefwork: accept the reality of the loss, ventilate the emotions the grief raises, find new attachments by which to reorient their lives, find ways of reestablishing a sense of competence, integrate the loss into a philosophy of life, learn the pitfalls within the social role of a bereaved parent, rework the relationship with the child's other parent, separate out their inner representations of the child, and internalize the representation of the dead child.

The therapist may be called on to help in any or all of those tasks. But in general, it is not the simple inability to accomplish one or more of those specific tasks that brings a bereaved parent to seek professional intervention. If the grief is difficult enough to call for extended professional therapy, there are two elements that can be complicating the grief. First, there can be problems in the social support system. Social support that is weak or characterized by conflict does not allow the parent to move toward resolution. Second, the grief can be complicated by ambivalences within the inner representations of the dead child. The parent's preexisting personality dynamics were also operating in the relationship with the child. Especially if the parent has not adequately differentiated the inner representation of the child from the self-representation, we often find multiple and conflicting inner representations of the child. When we do grief therapy, the personality issues that are the center of the therapy are also issues within the bond with the child.

Problems in the Social Support System

As has already been noted in this book, the most important factor in reaching those new equilibria is social support. A major task of some work with bereaved parents will be rooted in the inadequate social support system (Alexy, 1982). For some bereaved parents with a history of psychological problems or with social relationships full of conflicts and guilt, the bond with the therapist may be the primary social support in the parent's life. In those cases, psychotherapy with bereaved parents is similar to the friendship contract Feigenberg (1980) uses with some terminally ill patients. The therapeutic bond is characterized by (1) psychological nearness in which the ordinary barriers between professional and patient are lower, (2) dialogue on a full range of emotions, thoughts, and recollections, and (3) the concept of "new friend." The new friend is a contact of great intimacy, but is one with no previous history to contaminate the relationship. The intensity of the relationship within the friendship bond transcends the usual limits of the therapeutic frame. This kind of therapy is a common, yet unresearched basis for a great deal of work with the bereaved in settings like Elisabeth Kubler-Ross' intensive workshops.

For most parents, however, social support comes within their natural support system. The therapeutic relationship serves to help the parent maintain and improve the natural support system. As Weizman notes, the individual needs of the family members may be so overwhelming that a "therapist is advisable to help the family learn to share their feelings, support one another, and take care of each other in a new way" (1985, p. 122). In some of those cases, the therapeutic focus may be limited to problems within the individual parent's response to the death. The family relationships then can be reworked outside the therapeutic frame. In other cases, the therapeutic task may be to open communication within the natural support system, or within subparts of the natural support system, for example between the married couple or between parents and surviving siblings. The death of a child changes the family system. One of the tasks of therapy may be to help the members of the family to create the system as it will be without the dead child (Fulmer, 1983).

Personality Patterns and Parent–Child Bonds

The second element in psychotherapy with bereaved parents is rooted in the parent's preexisting personality pattern and, by extension, in the problematic elements in the bond between the parent and the now dead child (Krell & Rabkin, 1979; Mawson, Marks, Ramm, & Stern, 1981; Melges & DeMaso, 1980; Volkan, 1971; Volkan & Showalter, 1968). Separating out conflicting or ambivalent inner representations of the dead child is a step in some cases of parental grief that lends itself to the sustained critical analysis of psychotherapy. The connections between how the parent was parented and how parenting was given the dead child can be examined by the recollection of the past. The parts of the self that were developed in parenting can also be issues within the therapy hour. Questions of the preventability of the death raise the issue of the parent's inability to protect the child and of their loss of a sense of competence and self-esteem. Those issues are often rooted in larger issues of competence and self-esteem. The question of preventability in the therapy session can be an occasion for separating out the particular events of the death from the long-term problems with competence and self-esteem. The religious meanings that parenting holds are called into question after the death of the child, and the exploration of meaning can be a useful activity in some therapy with bereaved parents.

We have seen that the resolution to the grief after the death of a child is not a simple restoration of the *status quo ante*, but is rather a full change within the parent's interactive patterns in their social environment and within the parent's psychic organization. The bonds between parent and child reach to the center of the parent's self. The bonds are rooted in the history of the parent's being parented, in the parent's significant bonds with others in the world, and in the intricate relationship of the parent to the child's other parent. Thus the issues of the grief are intertwined with the central issues in the parent's selfhood. When a bereaved parent enters into a therapeutic relationship with a mental health professional, the grief is examined and resolved within the whole of the life.

The death of a child offers some possibilities for major changes in the dynamics of the self. The birth of a child is the occasion for investment of a part of the self that transcends the self. We have noted, however, the degree of separation of the child from the self is a difficult matter in some parenting. The child is both the parent's best self and the possibility of the parent's worst self. The child represents both the parent's past and the parent's future. The bond with the child reaches deep into the parent's self, so when the bond is reworked after the child dies, the parent has an opportunity to come to terms with issues central to the self. The internalization of the dead child either as solace objects in introjection or as enriching the ego in identification offers an opportunity to establish a different interpsychic equilibrium than existed before the death. An inner representation of the child that has not been fully differentiated from the parent's self-representation can be used in a changed self-representation when the inner representation is internalized by introjection or by identification.

One of the satisfactions in working with bereaved parents is to watch the growth which often emerges from the grief. There is in this growth, however, a strange equation which never seems to balance. I asked one man, for whom the death of his son had occasioned a real sense of depth and wisdom, whether the pain had been worth it. He replied:

> No, I can't say that. I do not want to say that S. died so I could have this new way of living. I don't want his life to be only for mine. I feel like I have grown a lot since he died, but I would give all that up in a minute if I could have him back.

Like the solace that comes with the internalized child, the growth that comes from parental bereavement is always a consolation prize.

THE THERAPEUTIC PROCESS

There is a wide variety of techniques that can be used in psychotherapy with bereaved parents. Clinicians will find that most of the techniques can be adapted to work toward the resolution of parental bereavement. Clearly some techniques lend themselves more to problems of inadequate social support, and other techniques lend themselves more to the problems of preexisting personality issues. But because the two elements are intermixed in any individual therapy, different techniques can be used at appropriate times. At different times I have used techniques from family therapy, marital therapy, gestalt exercises, dream analysis, reality therapy, play therapy, and art therapy. Sometimes the sessions are nondirective, and other times the sessions are directive. Often the psychotherapy includes didactic moments about the nature of grief. It is not unusual for me to hold parents tightly in my arms as they cry for their child. Other times I maintain more therapeutic distance.

One technique we have adapted from Volkan's re-griefing therapy (Volkan, 1971; Volkan & Showalter, 1968) and from activities in self-help groups might be mentioned, for it has proven effective in a wide variety of cases. In the second or third session (though much later in a few cases where other material is pressing) we ask the parent to bring pictures of the child. The parents usually also bring artwork the children have done. We go slowly through the pictures. As the parent tells about the picture, the therapist tries very hard to reconstruct the child in his or her mind. In effect, the therapist bonds to the child in a way that the bond the parent feels can be shared. Comments and questions about facial expressions or response to events and individuals in the pictures focus the conversation onto the child and make the bond between parent and child real within the therapeutic situation. The parent is in control of which pictures are brought, and the parent controls the order of presentation. Sometimes the parent chooses not to show recent pictures until later in the sessions. We have found in long-term therapy that the parents often spontaneously begin bringing pictures as they reach turning points in their resolution. The parallels between this technique and the interpsychic dimension of the self-help process are obvious.

There are no established norms for the extent of grief counseling/

therapy because the therapeutic issues are so diverse. In my own practice, in cases where the natural support system is to be the primary one, contacts have ranged from a 1-hour informational session for the family a few weeks after the death, to a relationship that lasted 3 years with once- and sometimes twice-weekly sessions.

CASE STUDIES

Because the data within individual and family counseling is so complexly interwoven, it seems best to present some cases in all their complexity. We will begin with a fully developed case of psychotherapy. Many of the dynamics of parental bereavement can be seen in Ann. After discussing Ann, we will move to a shorter examination of other cases that have somewhat different foci in therapy.

Ann

Ann's 10-year-old daughter Beth died after a 1-day illness while on a vacation in Ann's hometown. She was buried there. A full autopsy, which Ann got 6 weeks after the death, could find no explanation for the death. Six months before Beth died, Ann's husband Alvin had died after a 2-year battle with cancer. She has one surviving child, Judy, who is eight. She had received supportive counseling during her husband's illness and for a time after he died. She made her first appointment two weeks after Beth's death. She said she knew she was in shock now, but that she would not "make it through this without a lot of help."

Factors that came out during the early sessions were: (1) Ann's mother had consistently criticized Ann for being "too needy." That meant that the mother did not accept her less-than-happy moods. When Ann felt sad, afraid, or insecure, she was denied intimate access to her mother. At the same time, Ann's mother had hoped to have her own frustrated ambitions of education and a high-status marriage fulfilled through Ann. Ann had, in fact, gone to school and married Alvin, who climbed the corporate ladder to a vice presidency before he was taken by cancer at age 42. But her mother criticized the way Ann handled the role of affluent wife, feeling that she could do better than Ann did. (2) In her early twenties, Ann had three long-term relationships with men in which she learned to express the emotions her mother had forbidden. She met and married Alvin, whose quiet solidity was the anchor for her emotional life. (3) Beth (the child that died) was "Ann's daughter" in that Beth was much like Ann—emotional, exuberant, intuitive. Judy (the surviving child) was "Alvin's," for she is a quiet, rational problem solver. Ann was proud that she had raised Beth differently than her mother had raised her, for the beautiful emotionality she saw in Beth was not stifled, as Ann felt her own had been. Beth, thus, had been Ann's hope for fulfilling her best self. Ann felt that Beth, until she died, had been what Ann had not been allowed to be. One of Ann's dominant memories was a confrontation with her mother in which Ann had defended her child-rearing practices. In her mothering, she felt a sense of competence, in that Beth would not be raised as Ann had been, and in that competence, Ann kept the inner representation of her mother at bay. (4) Ann's internalized mother/critic was not conscious early in the therapy. Rather, the critic came out in what Ann called "mindbenders." Mindbenders were obsessive thoughts about her unacceptability because she might be boring, mean, stuck-up, and so forth. In the mindbenders, she felt hazy and out of touch with reality. In her marriage and motherhood, the mindbenders were held in check by the security she felt in her relationship with Alvin and by the positive sense of herself she saw in Beth. In the early sessions, Ann described the mindbenders and reviewed her history of trying to understand them in counseling.

The insecurity with her emotional life that grew in Ann's early bond with her mother, but which was overcome in her marriage and motherhood, returned with the death of her husband and daughter. A great deal of the continuing therapeutic process involved assuring Ann of the normality and acceptability of her feelings, both the feelings she had in her grief and the general insecurity she felt in her new social role of widow/bereaved parent/single mother. Without her husband and daughter, the mindbenders were difficult to handle because there was no sure reality against which to check them.

Even though Ann was still in a state of shock when she initiated the therapy sessions, she was already anticipating the pain she would feel later. She was experiencing a general feeling of disorientation that included memory loss and an inability to concentrate, especially to read. She dropped a college course in which she had enrolled before Beth's death. Later she started and soon quit a part-time job. During this early period, we established a relationship between Ann and me and Beth, her dead daughter. We spent several sessions with pictures and tapes of Ann's family when it had been intact. Beth was shared through her artwork and writing. The aim of this activity was to make Beth and Alvin part of the therapeutic relationship. This was a way to make the social support of the therapy relationship as strong as possible and to bring the inner representations of Beth and Alvin into the therapeutic relationship in anticipation of internalization.

An early problem for Ann continued for much of the next year and a half. She had received nurturance and an emotional anchor from her relationship with her husband and a sense of competence from the roles of wife and mother. Without Alvin there, her emotions were frightening to her. She attached to one man who was not available for full romantic involvement, so with difficulty she withdrew from that relationship and entered another with a single man, Floyd. In part, establishing a secure relationship with a man was learning to live in the changed world, for she regarded her ability to relate to a man as an area of competence as well as a source of nurturance and support. Yet she had not "played the single game" for several years, so a great deal of time was spent on that aspect of establishing a new equilibrium in the social environment. For a time, she joined the images of Floyd and her deceased husband in her mind. Then gradually the husband's image was withdrawn from the male friend and she mourned her husband. She did not use the therapist for that substitute husband, because the fee was her way of making sure the therapist would not reject her feelings as her mother had, and as men could potentially do.

The relationship with Floyd provided Ann with someone who cared, but the relationship was the focus of many therapy sessions because Floyd did not share Beth's death. He tried to empathize with Ann by recalling the death of his mother 4 years earlier, but the reality that Ann felt was not a shared social reality in a way that could help transform the inner representation. Yet she needed the solidity and nurturance Floyd offered, and learning to trust his caring was a long-term issue in the therapy.

Ann's relationship to her mother was also a therapeutic issue, much the way it would have been in therapy with no grief aspects. Ann was no longer protected from her internalized critic/mother by her marriage to Alvin and by the daughter who could be the reincarnation of that part of Ann's self that the mother had rejected. Periodically, Ann spent time during the therapy session using the empty chair technique to talk to her mother. Slowly Ann was able to connect the mindbenders to her mother's early demand that Ann not feel insecure or afraid. The feelings in the grief were linked to the feelings from her childhood. She was again the frightened little girl. The mindbenders could be signals to her of her present insecurity.

Several sessions were spent reviewing the relationships by which she was able to develop from mother's rejected child into adulthood. In losing her husband, and now the daughter who was the best part of her, she had lost a great deal of her sense of self and her sense of competence. Because she was building again, we went back to examine how she had built her senses of self and of competence earlier in her life.

For the first 5 months after Beth's death, Ann had a difficult time feeling in touch with Beth or with the reality of her death. As the holidays drew near, she began to think more of Beth. The first feeling was a dread of the emptiness she sensed in her self, and she spent a few weeks building up to letting that sense of emptiness in. She used the image of falling into a pit. She feared she would never be able to get back out of the pit. For three sessions, she asked to be held and she sobbed deeply. In the third session, she curled up and whispered softly, "I'm at the bottom and I am not afraid." For several weeks she returned periodically to that sense of despair, admitting it as a permanent residue of her losses.

Shortly after that, Ann slowly began to integrate Beth's inner representation in preparation for internalizing it. She started to sort out Beth's belongings, but she had trouble "getting in touch" with her. I suggested she find a linking object, briefly explaining the concept. The next week she brought in two stuffed toys with which she had begun sleeping. As we talked, she held one like a baby for the whole session. She was at the same time reviewing the feelings she had had when she was Beth's age and feeling the nurturance she had received from intimate friendship. Thus, the bond with her daughter and the sense of her self in her own childhood were being brought together.

At Christmas Ann had returned to her hometown, where her daughter was buried, but she felt only emptiness at the grave. Almost a year after the death, she was working on the inscription for the headstone and planned a visit for its dedication. She went to the cemetery with her grandmother who had been a nurturing figure in Ann's childhood. On the way to Beth's grave, the grandmother pointed out the graves of other significant family members and friends. At the grave, Ann felt the presence of her daughter melded into the sense of continunity her grandmother and the graves of family represented. "It was like there was my grandmother and me and my daughter. We are all part of the same continuing reality. It's hard to explain." The same weekend, she attended a high school reunion and gained a real sense of her continuing self. Comparing her life to the reports of classmate's lives, she could affirm herself as a competent and worthy person. Ann continued to feel Beth's presence consciously for several weeks as she slowly sorted out Beth's things and began to change the house to better serve the two remaining members of the family. She put up pictures of Beth and Alvin as part of the redecoration. Often she felt as if she had put Beth somewhere that she could not find, but at other times she was deeply conscious of Beth as she expressed anger at Beth's leaving and a sense of rejection that Beth had chosen to join her father and thus to reject Ann.

After the anniversary of Beth's death, Ann came in saying she felt that Beth was somehow at the center of Ann's self. She said she did not know the words to explain what she meant, but she put her hands to her stomach to indicate it. She said she simply felt Beth in her, and that the feeling would never leave. She used the therapy sessions to reinforce this new sense. Such an inner resolution, however, brought the relationship with Floyd into question, for he could not share that. She felt isolated from many of her friends for a few weeks while she learned to manage the feeling of having her daughter inside her. The change was shown a few weeks later when three times in the session she said "When my daughter died" as a way of referring to the anniversary of the death. Thus, the recognition of the reality of the loss was accompanied by a new relationship of the inner representation of her daughter.

Subsequent sessions focused on general therapy issues. She moved forward in small ways, went back to her earlier insecurity, worked through the old feelings, and then moved forward again. Each cycle lasted a few months. Ann found that her new independence and sense of selfhood demanded that she find a new way to emancipate herself from the judgmental mother, and to find a bond with her more mature mother in the present, as well as to find meaning in the mothering she herself had given to Beth. The inner representation of Beth added strength to the desire to live now as her daughter would have lived. The introjection of the linking object now moved to identification.

Near the second anniversary of Beth's death, the now well established identification with the inner representation of Beth brought a new phase in the bond with Floyd. She was seeking with Floyd the kind of maternal nurturance she had known with her husband, Alvin, but had not known with her mother. But Floyd did not give fully accepting love, as Alvin had. Floyd insisted on maintaining regular nights away from Ann with his own male friends. He did not freely share his inner life with her. Ann now acted toward Floyd as, she later reflected, Beth would have. She courted rejection by demanding closeness. "I will thaw him out," she said, and she did to a great extent. The conflict invigorated her. She reported that the relationship with Floyd was the most exciting she had ever had with a man.

A crisis in the relationship came when Floyd rejected her because he thought she was too uninhibited at a party. Ann, in retrospect, said her actions were very much in Beth's character, though not typical of Ann's previous way of acting at parties. She fought Floyd's rejection, insisting that they talk and that he examine his hang-ups that made him reject her behavior. Thus she fought in Floyd the rejection that she had experienced in the relationship with her mother.

The fight lasted a month. When it was over, Ann found that the mindbenders were less troublesome, for though the obsessive thoughts were still there, she felt less hazy and out of touch when she was having the thoughts. With the mindbenders less problematic, Ann began to renew ties with friends "from my old life." She joined a group of single parents for social life apart from Floyd and for activities with Judy, her surviving child. She found her bond with Judy was clearer than before. Thus, the fight with Floyd focused her new self, a new self which now included the identification with the inner representation of her dead child. The dead child was the self Ann thought she would have been had Ann been parented differently. That best self was no longer an extension of the self in the child. It was reincorporated in a new way into Ann's self. With this new self, Ann was able to meet the demands of her new world more adequately.

Ann has the psychiatric history and social relationships characterized by conflict and guilt that could have led her to a less satisfactory resolution of her grief. But within the therapy, the longstanding psychological issues were isolated at times from the new experiences in the grief. At other times, the longstanding psychological issues were used to illuminate for Ann how she was responding to the changed social situation and to the new relationship with Beth's inner representation. The loss of Alvin and Beth was the occasion for renewed psychopathology, for her social environment had changed in a way that took away the stability she had built. That increased psychopathology provided the occasion for Ann to reresolve the basic psychological tensions in her life. Being on her own caused her to find again a social equilibrium that was less dependent on Alvin and Beth. The psychotherapeutic work she did on her childhood relationship with her mother was part of achieving a new interpsychic equilibrium. The inner representation of Beth ceased being just a memory and became part of the ego. The internalized inner representation could thus become a source of strength to free herself from the mother she had early in life internalized as a critic. It is impossible to know whether, if Alvin had not died, Beth's inner representation would have been internalized in such a health-giving way. Later she discovered that some interactions with Floyd were like her mother's critic messages. On discovering that, she found a real sense of being centered when she continued to state her needs and desires in the relationship in the face of his seeing them as illegitmate.

Ann was an experienced therapy patient. She had used therapists and counselors at other stressful points in her life. Because she paid a fee, she could be sure her feelings of insecurity would not be rejected. In doing so, she could regulate the degree she felt she was imposing on her remaining natural support system. Transference was limited to "the expert on her side." I accepted that role, though I signaled acceptance and a closer relationship by offering a second session per week at no cost during her difficult times. When the insurance ran out and she was put on reduced fee, Ann brought up the limitations of the relationship several times by offering to pay for extra sessions and by asking for a more consistent adherence to the 50-minute time limit on the session. As the sessions progressed into the second year, Ann relaxed in the relationship and began to seek a parent-like acceptance by sharing good grades on the papers she wrote for a college class she was taking. As she could free herself from the inner representation of her critic/mother, aided by the ego strength derived from the identification with her dead daughter, Ann could accept a less controlled relationship with the therapist even as she was able to develop a more mutual relationship with Floyd.

Samantha

Samantha is a forty-year-old woman whose only child, Tammy, aged nine, died 13 years before Samantha began therapy. Tammy was born with a congenital heart defect that was diagnosed at 18 months. At that time the physicians "gave her a 90% chance of dying." As she grew up there were several operations. When she was nine, the physicians were telling Samantha that the child "had a 90% chance of making it"; however, that year Tammy died after another operation.

Samantha's mother became psychotic shortly after Samantha

was born. The mother is still institutionalized and Samantha is her guardian. During Samantha's childhood, her father would bring her mother home for a few weeks and demand that the family act normally. When the mother would begin to lose contact with reality, he would reinstitutionalize her.

Samantha's father was remote from the children most of the time. He was brutally frank a few times. When Samantha was eight, he told Samantha that he would provide for her physical needs, but she could expect nothing else from him. She worked hard to be invisible, for her father only noticed her when she did something that "bothered him." "I raised myself," Samantha reported. As early as she can remember, she was getting meals and taking care of her own clothes. She was tired most of the time. In retrospect, she thinks that she was malnourished during her childhood.

Samantha was depressed when we started therapy. It was for her a familiar feeling. A memory that emerged was at age 11, coming home from camp, standing by a window, and deciding that nothing would ever be better. She had looked forward to camp and had a wonderful time. But when she returned home, nothing had changed. Samantha also remembered at about age seven deciding that if she wanted to she could kill herself and that it was her choice to live. She still keeps that option.

At 17, Samantha married and became pregnant. Her husband was immature and irresponsible. Shortly after Tammy was born, Samantha made a vow that no matter what it took, Samantha would make sure that her child would not grow up as she herself had. Tammy would be loved and cared for. Samantha spent the next 9 years fulfilling that pledge. She got divorced and worked to support herself and the child. Tammy was sick, but the helplessness of the baby fueled Samantha's sense of obligation and determination. She reported that, especially after the diagnosis, "It was the two of us against the world, and we were going to make it." Pictures from Tammy's childhood show Tammy as a happy child, smiling directly at the camera or directly relating to someone. Samantha looks tight and frightened in the pictures.

Although it is clear that Tammy was invested with a large part of Samantha's ego, Samantha experiences the child as very separate from herself. After the death she found Eastern philosophy helpful. She described Tammy as "an old soul. She was spiritually far above me. She loved everyone and everyone she met loved her. I hope someday I can be reborn at her level." She also said several times that she had a deep feeling that "Tammy was sent to teach me something.

I feel frustrated because I don't know what it is." I understood the belief to mean that the inner representation was of Samantha's best self, which was cut off from her present self. The interpretation seemed confirmed later when I asked if Tammy would be proud of what Samantha had accomplished in her career. She said the opposite was true, for she often had a sense of falling short of Tammy's standard. She could never live up to the level of Tammy. It seems then that within Samantha's depression, the introjected dead child functions as a judgmental ideal.

Samantha has only a few memories of when Tammy died. The moments after the death are remembered as if a nightmare. She began running through hospital corridors until she came to a dead end, and there she collapsed. She remembers no comforting embraces, no sharing, no human contact. She went into shock and for several days was unaware of her body or her surroundings.

When Tammy was alive, Samantha had thought about going back to school as a way to provide for Tammy's future. A few months after Tammy died, Samantha started school in computer programming. She felt compelled to complete school, even though she worked two jobs to support herself and to pay tuition. She graduated near the top of her class. She now feels that she had such drive because she needed to escape the pain of the grief. There was nothing behind her but pain, and nothing but pain when she relaxed. She filled her days with hard work and activity so she would not feel the pain. After school was completed, life again felt empty and meaningless. Relaxation meant pain. She met a man visiting from the West Coast and, after a month's dating and corresponding, agreed to marry and join him. She says that she knew she didn't love him, but thought he loved her and that would be enough. She now feels she was escaping the pain by running as far as she could go. The marriage was very unhappy, though she found fulfillment in a good job. Samantha divorced her husband and continued her career. When her father died, she returned to the home of her childhood and assumed guardianship of her institutionalized mother. She began a master's degree as another escape into hard work. Shortly after the master's degree was completed, she initiated therapy.

The fear of losing control of her emotions was the theme of the first two months of therapy. The first release of emotions and attempts to repress them again brought severe headaches. We explored her childhood and marriages. Any references to Tammy were met with, "That was a long time ago. It feels like a lifetime away." After several months, I asked her to bring in pictures. The next session she brought them and threw them in my lap, saying, "Here, you wanted these." I did not deal with that feeling, but asked her to take me through the pictures. The next session she allowed herself to feel the pain of the death. It was so intense that it clearly could not be integrated in its present form.

The therapy had two goals. The first was to help Samantha stop using in the present emotional responses that had been useful in her neglected childhood. The second goal was to lessen the gap between Samantha's self-representation and the inner representation of Tammy. The child was an ideal by which the mother judged herself. It was a standard that seemed to be at the base of a great deal of the depression. If the inner representation could be brought closer, it could be transformed by being introjected as solace, or by being made part of the self-representation in identification.

Cognitive psychotherapy was used for responses in the present. Samantha did not assimilate positive feedback from her environment, but she was hypersensitive to negative feedback. Together we read an outstanding evaluation she was given at work. We reviewed her professional interactions to learn to sort out meaningful feedback from nonmeaningful feedback. She found old report cards, and we read comments teachers had made about her as a child. I took an active role in reinterpreting her experience, and slowly she began to share the reinterpretation. I genuinely felt that, given her background, Samantha had triumphed. The present was reframed in terms of her accomplishments. Childhood memories were allowed to surface, and with those memories old pains were shared. The father's message to be invisible was reviewed and critiqued. Interspersed with those sessions were sessions in which we shared the inner representation of Tammy. Samantha's competence as a parent was stressed, as was the emotional closeness between mother and child.

Slowly the depression eased. During one period of several weeks when she was feeling good, Samantha began redecorating her house. In the process, she found many of Tammy's belongings in a closet, as well as many of her father's possessions. She discarded the things that belonged to her father. Her spontaneous smile as she recounted the act showed the inner meaning. She had a somewhat harder task with Tammy's things. She discovered that now she had both good and bad memories. A ball, for example, reminded her that although Samantha had felt very badly that Tammy could not fully play with the other children, Tammy had been thrilled that she could kick the ball. "I could never feel what she felt," Samantha said. "But I can get a sense of it now; before, it was just the negative. But I feel both the positive and negative now." She found a picture of Tammy, but had difficulty choosing the right frame. It took a few weeks of shopping, but she found a beautiful frame. She took a few more weeks to select the place to hang the picture. "I don't want a shrine," she said. "I want that to be in the past." When she had almost finished redecorating the whole house, she found a place to hang the picture.

Late in the second year of therapy, Samantha began to enlarge her interest in Eastern religion. She began to meditate with a well-known Buddhist master. In the meditation she found a technique for feeling and letting go of emotional pain. The therapy process speeded up as she augmented our sessions with daily meditation. Several very emotional sessions were devoted to her recalling many painful memories of Tammy's hospitalization and her anger at several insensitive medical staff. The inner representation of Tammy was transformed within the meditation. She reported, "When I can let go and accept the impermanence, Tammy seems part of the impermanence." She could let go of the immediate and painful attachment and begin to find solace in a more amorphous, but very real bond to a larger, ever-changing world that included the life and death of her daughter. The words of the Buddha's first noble truth, "All life is suffering," and the second noble truth, "The cause of suffering is desire," became very real to her. "Yes," she said, "I did desire Tammy. And in some ways I desire the pain because she is at least in the pain."

There was more therapy to do, for depression occasionally returned. But it seemed that when Samantha could come to terms with the pain of her own childhood and with the pain of Tammy's death, she could identify with positive elements in the inner representation of her dead child. The newly integrated inner representation of the child could now be in the service of living more fully than Samantha had done before.

Lillian

Occasionally we learn something of the dynamics of parental bereavement in the psychotherapeutic encounter, even if the therapy is not successful in any conventional sense and when the agent of change is not the therapist. In Lillian we can see some of the dynamics of the child's being a continuation of bonds from early in the parent's life. The introjection of her dead child allowed her to maintain the bond with the child in a way that did not disturb the complicated set of psychological relationships she had with the child.

Lillian was a 43-year-old woman who sought treatment 5 months after her 18-year-old son, Ron, was killed in a motorcycle accident. A faulty steering mechanism caused the cycle to veer into oncoming traffic. Lillian felt responsible for the death in that she had encouraged him to buy the motorcycle and had given him money to go out that night. The reason she knew she needed help was that she was unable to say the word *dead* in relationship to Ron. She explained her problem by spelling out the word with great difficulty. She had forbidden members of the family from referring to Ron as dead, and she made it a condition of therapy that I not use the word.

Lillian's brother's daughter had committed suicide 6 years earlier. The sister-in-law was still on heavy dosages of prescribed drugs. Lillian did not want to be like her sister-in-law. Before coming to me, she had been to a psychiatrist who prescribed drugs and did nothing more for her. Lillian felt that she was out of control and did not want the drugs—just as she said she would not now use marijuana or alcohol because she was afraid of getting on a "trip" and being unable to come off it.

Lillian had been married four times. When I asked her to tell me about the marriages, she said they just happened and that there wasn't anything to tell. Two of the divorces were because the husband "just turned out to be too crazy," and one was because "I just didn't love him." She was currently married to Simon, an alcoholic. Since the death, they have not communicated well and he is spending most of his time away from home.

Ron, her oldest son, was three years old when his father left. Since that time, Ron had been Lillian's main emotional relationship. In talking about him, she recalled his talking to her and caring for her when she was depressed. She also described him in some erotic images, for example, his beautiful body as he stood in the hall in only his briefs. She described Ron as her "partner, best friend, and husband." That formula was repeated several times during the four sessions we had. There were very few images of Ron in a childlike relationship to her. The erotic images of Ron, along with Lillian's inability to get distance on her marriages and divorces, indicate that Lillian habitually acts impulsively on dynamics rooted in her early childhood.

Lillian had found religious faith several years earlier in an evangelical charismatic protestantism. She prayed several times a day, she said, and in doing so had a strong sense of being both in touch with God and in touch with Ron. She did not seem to distinguish the sense of God's presence and Ron's presence.

Lillian began a twice-a-week intensive therapy routine. The aim was twofold: First, I wanted to find the multiple inner representations of Ron so the multiple resolutions could begin to occur. I especially wanted to find the connection between her marriage to Ron's father and her holding Ron as a "partner, best friend, and husband." The erotic inner representations of Ron were contrary to her charismatic protestant faith and would have to be carefully handled. Second, I wanted to provide a safe, accepting atmosphere for Lillian to regress to a more dependent relationship than she was able to find in the natural support system. The bond with Ron seemed to be rooted in a need for someone to depend on. I told her that I would strongly support her desire to grieve without prescription drugs.

After the intake session, we had two therapy sessions the following week. In those we looked at photographs of Ron and read cards and letters he had sent to Lillian over the years. Toward the end of the second hour she softly said, "You know, I really know he is dead, but it hurts so."

The fourth session was her last. She reported that a man making repairs at her house had said to her that he thought she needed prayer, and that he had been sent to her. He was a minister, though she said she had not known that when she engaged him to do the repairs. She told him of Ron's accident and her difficulties. They kneeled down and he put his hands on her head and prayed that she be able to "let Ron go, to give him up to God." At that moment, she said, she felt she let go. She said she knew at that moment that Ron is in heaven waiting for her and that she will be with him someday. She was clearly calmer than she had been the week before and could say "dead" with ease. The new religious interpretation did not seem quite secure, for when I suggested she might find Compassionate Friends useful, she said she did not want to go because she felt that was a lack of faith. She said that though God had given her this new peace, the sessions with me had been helpful and she wanted to continue. She missed her next appointment, and when we rescheduled she missed that too. A phone call confirmed that she felt she should rely on faith alone to manage her loss.

Lillian's inability to say the word *dead* and her refusal to allow the word to be said in her presence might be interpreted as denial, as an inability to recognize the reality of her life. But she was aware of her inability; indeed, it was that awareness that brought her to therapy. To accept the reality of the loss, Lillian found a new reality in the solace of an eternal relationship with Ron. In the prayer with the repairman/minister, Lillian had given Ron up to God. That is, she was able to introject Ron into her psyche in such a way that the multiple and complex bonds she had with Ron could be maintained indefinitely. He could continue to be her partner, best friend, and husband. Just as she could not feel the difference between the presence of God and the presence of Ron in her prayers, so in the introjection, she will not be able to tell the difference between her former solace objects and Ron's presence. Whatever bonds from Lillian's own history that were projected onto Ron in a way that made him an adult in her life from the time he was three can now be transferred to the introjected Ron. She can have drug-free grief because she has an ongoing source of solace. She had been afraid to take drugs or to drink or smoke marijuana because she was afraid she would get on a trip and not get off. In the introjection, she seems to have found an acceptable "trip." But she must be careful of not getting off. She must guard this interpretation of reality against other interpretations. Gordon and I found such guarding to be characteristic of a common form of transcending experience in the encounter with death (Klass & Gordon, 1978). Lillian does this by not going to Compassionate Friends or continuing therapy, where she might find others who interpret their world differently.

It is difficult to know the degree to which the interactions between Lillian and me in our three sessions before her meeting with the minister were preparation for the prayer session. She had rejected the psychiatrist who offered only drugs. She apparently found our interactions less threatening, for she returned. But the minister offered her a mythos and a mechanism by which she could find the instant relief from pain she sought. The erotic elements in the bond to Ron could remain safely hidden in the religious reinterpretation of her situation. Those elements, if brought to light in therapy, would probably have been too threatening for easy integration into her self.

Melody and Leo

The role the therapist plays in the life of the bereaved parent may make up for the deficiencies in the parent's natural support system. Leo and Melody had a marriage that was satisfactory to both of them. But it could not function well when their child died because Leo was phobic about death. On the surface, I was doing simple grief counseling with Melody for most of our relationship, but actually I had entered rather fully into their marital relationship and was the instrument by which Melody made Leo act in a more supportive way toward her grief.

Melody was referred by the social worker at the hospital after her son died at four days from a rare infection. The social worker said in referring, "If ever there was the death of a hoped-for child, this is it." For as long as she could remember, Melody had loved children and dreamed of the day she could have her own. When she married Leo, they immediately began to make plans for a family. She conceived twice, but miscarried both times. Leo and Melody decided they would never have children of their own, so they began adoption proceedings. They were 2 months from getting an adopted baby when Melody became pregnant. They stopped the adoption and fixed up a room in their apartment. The baby was named Leo, Jr. Little Leo died after 4 days.

Melody's grief was normal and expectable. The first question for her was "Why?" For her that was a religious question, and she doubted the God who had been so important to her in her life. As if to prove her defiance of the Almighty, she reported that she had become drunk and smoked a joint one weekend. We spent time talking about the fairness of God. Melody's religious problems were heightened by remarks made by people in her church. They questioned whether she had done something wrong that this would happen or whether she had not taken adequate care of herself while she carried the baby. We went over the pregnancy in some detail to reassure her that she had not caused any harm to the baby. The autopsy report was read closely, twice. We also examined her moral life and thoughts, especially in comparison to a friend whose life was less exemplary, but who had delivered a thriving child.

Most of the therapy time was spent remembering in detail the short life of little Leo. Melody told over and over how she had given him permission to die and how she missed him. For her, those 4 days were a lifetime and no matter how many other children she would have, little Leo would always be remembered. She remembered other lost children—her miscarriages and when a baby she had cared for as a teenager moved away. The therapist's role was that of a supportive friend.

Melody found peace with the religious question as she found the community in her church became supportive after she was able to give a medical explanation of the death. But she became more and more angry at Leo, Sr. He had not gone to the hospital to see the baby after the death had been predicted. He had not wanted a funeral for the baby, though he had given in to Melody's demand that there be a full funeral. He could not talk to her when she was crying. Finally, one day she demanded that he come in to talk to me. He was a big, gentle man who had recently been laid off and rehired. He had started a small home-repair business when he was out of work and was continuing the business on the side. He said that he did not "want to get into that crying and boo-hooing because, if you do, you could not come back." He said he hated anything to do with death. He remembered his grandfather's funeral when he was 12 years old. His grandfather was an important model to him. He said he cried at that funeral and thought he could never stop crying, until he remembered his grandfather saying, "Let it go by the side," meaning not to let anything bother him. From that time on, he had removed himself from any stressful situation involving death. He had attended no funerals since his grandfather's. We talked of his life and of his work. I rather directively told him that his wife needed him, for although he could avoid death and grief, his wife couldn't. I assured him that crying was good for her, even if he did not cry. I assured him that when Melody cried, she would stop after a time, and that his holding her did not make the crying last longer.

Two sessions after I talked to Leo, Melody decided to terminate the regular meetings. I had been holding that as a possibility for her for two months. She said that Leo was being more considerate at home, and that they had decided together to reopen the adoption application. A few weeks after that, Melody dropped by the office to announce that she was pregnant. She called periodically during her pregnancy and then called to inform me that she had delivered a healthy baby girl. I knew that the baby's room was still set up, so I said, "You know this baby is not little Leo. This baby is her own person." She replied, "Oh, I know. For little Leo I had Winnie-the-Pooh stuff. I put that away. For this baby I have Mickey Mouse."

There is no history of psychopathology in Melody. The marriage proved problematic because of Leo's phobic response to death. The therapy sessions provided Melody a safe outlet for thoughts and emotions that were not acceptable in her church community. But she probably could have done as well with a sympathetic neighbor as she did with me. In some ways I was a substitute husband in the one area where her husband could not be supportive. Leo was a good mate for Melody, but his need to avoid the grief and her need to deal with the grief were in conflict. She used me to work through the grief, and then she brought Leo in as a message to him to be more supportive. When he became so, she could terminate our sessions and call me with reports on her progress.

Cases of delayed grief have been noted in the literature for some time (Worden, 1982), though little attention has been paid to the factors in the delay. My colleague, Samuel J. Marwit, has reported a case of delayed grieving. I have left the report in the first person, but all the case material is Marwit's. In the case of Mr. and Mrs. H. it appears that questions about the preventability of the loss (Bugan, 1979) were important in bringing on the delay. Just as important, however, seems to be the inability of the mental health professionals to be an adequate social-support system in allowing the parents to focus on their grief. This was compounded by the prescription of drugs over several years.

Mr. and Mrs. H.*

Mr. and Mrs. H. had been referred to me 10 years ago for conjoint marital therapy. At that time, I was not so knowledgeable in the area of grief therapy as I am now, and so, while focusing on recent infidelities and misguided marital communications, I failed to pay significant attention to the drowning deaths of both of their children 1 week prior to Christmas approximately 2 years prior to our meetings. This same "oversight" was true of the referring psychiatrist, who could not understand the current actings out after almost 2 years of intensive psychotherapy. My attempts at marital treatment were met with severe resistance, and what I saw as premature termination took place after only a few months.

Twelve years after the drownings, Mr. H. contacted me again, saying he was extremely depressed for reasons he could not identify. He was thinking of selling his business, which he had spent years nurturing into a success, was again experiencing marital dissatisfactions, and was snapping at his nine year old son whom he clearly adored.

At this time, as we explored his history, the loss of his sons reemerged as primary material. The children had drowned in a river behind the house he and his wife had recently purchased. The accident took place on a day that Mr. H. had uncharacteristically allowed his boys to stay home from school because he sought their company. They had drowned while he left them unattended to make their lunch.

Their dog had also disappeared under the ice and, as Mr. H. reconstructed the incident, he believed that the boys must have thrown a stick that the dog chased, causing the dog to fall through the ice and the boys to follow in an attempt to aid their pet. Mr. H.

*Used by permission of Samuel J. Marwit.

described dealing with these deaths by never crying or allowing himself to mourn the losses, by drinking for a full year and a half, by blaming his wife for making him buy the river property, and by other similar denials and projections of his grief. Prior to contacting me again, he and his wife had never visited the cemetery. She, by the way, had been existing for 12 years on large doses of tranquilizers and antidepressants administered by a local psychiatrist.

As we explored the past few months, it became clear that Mr. H. was dealing with a delayed grief reaction, the precipitant of which was a visit 1 week prior to Christmas by his sons' former friends who were the same ages as the two deceased boys. Once Mr. H. saw the parallels in dates (pre-Christmas) and ages, he could begin to acknowledge the possibility of a delayed anniversary reaction and could start to focus on his "hidden feelings." Through a series of imagery exercises and sharing photographs of the boys, he was able to "relive" the events of twelve years ago and to attach his current sadness to these circumstances. The circumstances of allowing his boys to be home from school were recast by me in terms of his being a kind, loving father who wanted to play hooky with his sons and to enjoy their company on a lovely, snowy day. He was encouraged to consider all of the times that he had permitted the boys to go to the river unattended with no adverse consequences, so that he could see that this was not an isolated incident for which he had to continue to punish himself. With time, his guilt decreased and his affection, longing, and sadness for his sons were expressed. He began to cry openly. His wife, seeing this progress, requested to come in and asked for help in reducing her intake of medication. Together they planned visits to the cemetery and found this relieving. Mr. H. and I effected an agreed-upon termination many months after we began, an ending that was far different from that of our sessions 10 years prior.

Marwit's report points at resolution of the grief, beyond that which took place within the therapy session. In the visit to the cemetery both parents recognized the reality of the loss and began to locate the children in their world. Mrs. H.'s lowered medication level will allow a kind of social support within which the newly discussable deaths can be mourned, and within which the memories of the dead children can become a new bond within the family. But none of that had to be part of the therapy, for the task of therapy was to open the grieving, not to be a part of its full resolution. Within the therapy, the technique of sharing photographs of the dead children was a means for the therapist to share in the bond with the dead children. Thus, the therapist becomes bonded to the children and, within that shared bond, Mr. H. could rethink and thus rework his role in the deaths. Having transformed the inner representation he carried of the children from bad parent to good parent, the way was open to internalize the children in a way that he and his wife had not been able to do before.

THE ISSUE OF PATHOLOGY

In part, the reason bereaved parents seek professional help is the psychotomimetic quality of severe grief. It mimics psychosis in its deep catatoniclike depression, hallucinations, morbid thoughts, bizarre behavior, and suicide thoughts or threats. Professional intervention in helping bereaved parents raises the problem of the definition of pathology in grief, for often psychotherapy is recommended for behavior, feelings, or thoughts that seem to fall outside the normal. We need, therefore, to examine the nature of psychopathology in parental grief.

In grief, it seems, pathology is in the eye of the beholder, not in any objective norm. Alice Demi and Margaret Miles (1987) did a complex research project with 30 subjects who were scholars actively involved in teaching, research, or counseling about bereavement. First they asked the subjects to propose terms for manifestations of grief that "fall outside the normal parameters of grief." They then asked the subjects to choose the five best terms from the generated list. The results show no agreement on the nature of pathology in grief. Half the subjects chose the term *pathological grief*, but the term is meaningless because it has no content of its own. In the other terms chosen, the bases of judgment are very different from each other. Some judged on internal issues in the bond to the deceased (*unresolved* = 50%). Some judged on behavior that might be either within the grief or within preexisting personality patterns (*self-destructive* = 45%). Some judged on how well the person was adjusting to the changed social environment (*dysfunctional* = 41%). Some judged on the basis of one of the stage theories of grief (*fixated* = 27%). Demi and Miles' research shows that there is no agreement among scholars on the definition of symptoms, behaviors, feelings, or ideas that indicate grief outside normal parameters.

The terms *normal grief* and *pathological grief* have been part of the scholarly study of bereavement for a long time. Erich Lindemann introduced the idea of *acute grief* as a psychiatric syndrome in 1944

(Lindemann, 1979). But a close reading of Lindemann's work shows that he is not able to establish a causal connection between issues within the loss and pathological response. Rather, Lindemann and Cobb find that the causal factors are outside of the loss itself and are not attributed directly to processes the bereaved person undertakes to resolve the grief. Simply put, the findings were (1) that people with a prior history of pathology are more likely to exhibit pathology in their grief, and (2) that when the social-support system is loaded with conflict or guilt, the bereaved person is more likely to show pathology (Lindemann & Cobb, 1979). Thus, while Lindemann identifies "acute grief as a definite syndrome," and introduces the idea that some grief is pathological and some grief is normal, in fact, in his pathological grief, he is describing preexisting personality factors and support systems. He is not describing pathology in the grief itself.

Although perhaps less widely read, Otto Fenichel (1945) arrives at similar conclusions in the psychoanalytic tradition. Pathologic mourning, he writes, is more probable if the lost object was not loved for itself, but rather was used narcissistically or if the relationship to the dead person had been ambivalent. Fenichel adds that if the griever is "orally fixated," that is, not adequately separated from the parent, pathological grief is more likely.

After Lindemann, most scholarly work on grief accepted the idea that grief can be pathological, but they ignored the causes of pathology Lindemann had identified. Rather, they found pathology in any grief that fell outside their model for health. Their models of health were not based on research with grieving people, but was one of the givens when they began constructing their theories.

John Bowlby writes that when identification with the dead person is prominent in the grief, it is an indication of pathology (Bowlby, 1969–1980, Vol. 3, p. 30). Bowlby does not offer any behavioral or psychological norm to show the grief as pathological. His theory claims that the task of grief is to withdraw the attachment bond from one object and to make new attachments within the changed environment. Bowlby is fighting the Freudian idea of making identification the end of grief. Bowlby's disciples all follow him on this point, though none offer data that would establish identification as pathological (Parkes, 1972; Parkes & Weiss, 1983; Raphael, 1983; Worden, 1982). The history of the Bowlby group's problem with identification is explored more fully in Appendix II of this book.

In the psychoanalytic school, as in the Bowlby group, pathology is defined by the internal demands of the theory, not by data that defines pathology. Vamik Volkan (1981) assumes that if there is healthy grief, there must also be unhealthy grief. But like the Bowlby group, his definition is based on the internal demands of his theory. For Freud, identification is making the lost object part of the ego. Identification is, therefore, a healthy development and where identification predominates, Volkan finds health. But there is another kind of internalization: introjection. Introjection is for Volkan pathology, not because the person functions poorly, but because the theory says introjection is less reality based than is identification. In psychoanalysis, health is based in the reality principle. In Chapter 3 the dynamics of introjection and identification are applied to data from bereaved parents. Our study indicates that a great many parents use introjection for solace. Unless the simple mental act of seeking consolation, while at the same time recognizing the harsh reality, is pathological, there is no reason to find pathology when parents gain solace in the introjected inner representations of their dead children.

Bereaved parents present a special challenge to any concept of grief pathology the clinician or researcher holds. Existing models of grief were developed in studies of widows and widowers. The time tables and expectable problems which are current in the field are based on conjugal bereavement. Parental bereavement has more intense symptoms and different expectable problems. "Bereaved parents often will be construed as having failed to appropriately complete their grief work according to the general model of mourning currently utilized" (Rando, 1986, p. 56).

We can see the misapplied label of pathology in a case discussed by Volkan and Showalter (1968), who diagnosed a woman as having a "very severe pathological grief reaction" when, 3 months after her daughter's murder, she:

> had withdrawn her emotional investments to a large extent from her two younger children, had become almost alienated from her husband and indeed seemed to be living almost entirely in a fantasy world consisting of only her deceased daughter and herself. (p. 365)

The woman had padlocked her daughter's room so no one else in the family could go in. The family dynamics that such an action indicates are not reported. At 3 months after a murder, many of the parents in our study were still in shock and hardly able to function. If the woman and her family are like many in our study, the alienation of the other children and the husband stemmed from their demand that she forget the dead daughter and return to normal. The mother seems to be communicating a rather adamant message to the family by the act of locking the room. To describe the communication as pathology seems unfair.

CONCLUSION

The bond we have with our child reaches the center of our self and is grounded in the social system within which we maintain our selfhood. In psychotherapy with bereaved parents, we see the complexity of the bond between parent and child. We see the complexity of the changes in the self that are the resolution of parental bereavement. In psychotherapy with bereaved parents, we are dealing with the interface of the loss with psychological issues in the parent's history and, by extension, with problems in the bond between parent and child, or we are dealing with the impact of the loss within a less-than-optimal social support system. Pathology may be a part of some parental grief, but the source of the pathology is outside the loss itself. Pathology may be based, first, in preexisting personality patterns of the parent that were expressed in the parent's bond with the child. Second, pathology may be based in inadequate or conflicted social support. The dynamics we observe in grief that needs professional intervention are the same as those we observed in parental bereavement in other contexts. In psychotherapy, however, we can observe the individual bond, grief, and resolution in all its complexity.

Conclusion

Parental bonds to a child are strong and deeply rooted in the parent's own history and psychological structures. The child represents to the parent both the parent's best self and the parent's worst self. Difficulties and ambivalences in the parent's life are manifest in the bond with the child. The child is born into a world of hopes and expectations, into a world of intricate psychological bonds, into a world that has a history. The parent–child bond can also be a recapitulation of the bond between the parent and the parent's parents, so the child can be experienced as praising or judging the parent's self. From the day the child is born, those hopes and expectations, bonds, and history are played out in the parent's relationship to the child.

The bond between parent and child is complex because the child is identified with so much of the parent's self. The task of mature parenting is to differentiate the child from the self. When the child is differentiated, the child is not experienced as self, but rather the child is experienced as an individual with needs and desires distinct from the self. When the child cannot be experienced as separate from the self, the parent can only respond to the child in terms of the parent's needs. When the child is experienced as separate from the self, the parent can respond to the child with empathy. Differentiation, however, is seldom complete, for the parent continues to experience the child's successes and failures as successes or failures of the self.

Parenting is a permanent change in the individual. A person never gets over being a parent. Parental bereavement is also a permanent condition, for the death of a child is the death of a part of the self. The bereaved parent, after a time, will cease showing the medical symptoms of grief, but the parent does not "get over" the death of the child. A part of the future has died. The hope for fulfilling the self through the life of the child is no longer possible.

We can best understand parental grief as two disequilibria: a social disequilibrium and a psychic disequilibrium. Social support is the most important factor in helping parents find new social and psychic equilibria. Social support has two elements: the experiential and the interpsychic. In the experiential element, the possibilities and pitfalls of the new condition of parental bereavement are mastered. The interpsychic element is more complex. Social support for parental bereavement is not simply support for the parent, it is also a sharing of the bond with the dead child. As the attachment to the child is shared, the parent can transfer some of the energy of the bond with the child onto the supportive community and, in doing so, transform the bond with the child in a way that allows the child to be internalized.

A new social equilibrium is achieved when the parent establishes new patterns of interaction and new sources of gratification that can provide stability for the social self to function in the social environment, which has radically changed with the death of the child. The parent must recognize the reality of the death and vent the rage and despair that the recognition of that reality evokes. Then the parent must reorganize the model of the self and the model of the world to match the changed reality. Bonds with the child's other parent are renegotiated after the death of the child, for although the shared loss is a new bond between the parents, the grief for the child reaches depths in the self that are beyond the bond with the spouse.

The new social self the bereaved parents achieve is not a return to their old self, for the parent has been changed by the death of the child. We find that in the death of the child, parents reorder priorities and values in their lives. As they could not protect their child, they now learn to live in a world that seems less in their control. As they find new emotional and philosophical depth, so now they are more sensitive to others. As their sense of competence was challenged by the death of the child, the parents find new ways of demonstrating competence to themselves and to others.

New psychic equilibrium is achieved as the inner representations of the child are reformed and incorporated into the ongoing psychic life of the bereaved parent. There are multiple inner representations of the child. Conflicting or ambivalent inner representations are resolved or purged. Then the representation is internalized in a way that provides solace in the world made poorer by the death of the child.

The majority of bereaved parents internalize the dead child by introjection, that is, by keeping a sense of the child and of their emotional bond with the child intact. The introjection feels other than self. For many bereaved parents, a sense of the presence of the child is an ongoing part of their psychic life. For some parents, the child's presence can be invoked by linking objects. Many parents merge the inner representation of the child to religious devotion, in a sense of divine presence that was solaceful before the child died. There is a wide variety of religious solace. We find many examples of traditional religious devotion, but nature, abstract ideas, and nationalism also have the quality of religious devotion that can be merged with the inner representation of the child. Memory is also used for solace, and we find many parents ritually evoking the memory of the child in their daily life.

Some bereaved parents internalize the child by identification, that is, integrating the inner representation of the child with the self-representation in such a way that the two cannot be distinguished.

The changed social self and the internalized inner representation of the child are provisions for a new self that is different from the self the parent knew before the child died. The resolution of parental bereavement is not a return to the *status quo ante*. The resolution of parental grief is found in the development of a new self. The new self, with its new social interactions and its new sources of solace, learns to live in a world made forever poorer by the death of the child.

Appendixes

Appendix I

The Author's Perspective

This book is an attempt to describe the journey bereaved parents make toward resolution. I began to try to understand parental grief as I attempted to help bereaved parents who were forming a chapter of The Compassionate Friends (TCF). As I fumbled for ways of helping the group, I also searched for concepts by which I could understand the human experience I was encountering. The scaffolding of the concepts in this book was set in the work with TCF. The intimacy and trust that parents granted me was within the shared work of TCF. It was ongoing interactions that forced me to examine what I thought I knew about grief. Program planning led to discussions among the group leaders about the needs they experienced. Later discussions about why one program had succeeded and another had not led to conclusions about the kind of help that worked and the kind that did not. Watching meetings and program planning for several years allowed me to see patterns that endured amidst the shifting movements within the group. As the founders moved on and new people took their places, I could see the changes in life that made leading the group a meaningful part of the self, and I could understand the possibilities and limits of the resolution to parental grief. In my conversations and occasional presentations, I was responding to their lives, even when I could not articulate it in words. As I protected myself from the pain around me, my own defenses could teach me something about the nature of the pain.

The understanding of parental bereavement in this book grew out of a particular context. The reader deserves to understand what I was doing to earn my place in the group, because knowing is a contextualized activity. There is no ontology without an accompanying epistemology. We really only understand the picture when we can also understand the camera, the film, and the developing process. The first research that Beth Shinners, then a graduate student, and I conducted within TCF was to study our places in the group. Before I could know anything about the parents, I needed to know what I was doing as the knower. The following material is a revision of that first study in light of the changes in the group and changes in the relationship between myself as professional and the group over 8 years. I hope it helps the reader to understand the epistemological context of this book.

PROFESSIONALS AND SELF-HELP

Self-help groups are "composed of members who share a common condition, situation, heritage, symptom or experience" (Lieberman & Borman, 1979, p. 2). The groups are "usually composed of strangers, having a structure and requiring those wishing to utilize their resources to spend effort and energy much as they would had they sought professional systems" (p. 4). The emphasis in self-help groups is on helpfulness to the other or to the group. Help is given in the context of mutuality and cooperation (Katz, 1970). We can think of the self-help group as providing an active role to the participant who gives service to himself or herself and to peers. This relegates the professional to a secondary role or to no role at all.

> Implicit in the self-help thrust is a profound critique of professionalism. . . . Traditionally, the professions have been characterized by (1) control of entry into the occupation; (2) colleague rather than client orientation in terms of standards; (3) an occupational code of ethics; and (4) a "scientific-theoretical" basis for occupational activity. . . . The entire ethos of the professional orientation is very different from the self-help orientation which is much more activistic, consumer centered, informal, open, and inexpensive. (Gartner & Reissman, 1977, pp. 12–14)

There was an assumption in early scholarly literature that self-help would naturally evolve into professional services. For example, Katz (1970) felt that there was a five-step evolution from self-help to a more professional organization: (1) origin, (2) informal organization, (3) emergence of leadership, (4) beginnings of formal organization, and (5) developing professionalism. Lieberman and Borman attribute the fact that these groups did not professionalize to the professionals themselves, whom they call a "new breed" (1979, p. 41). They say that those professionals who have formed or supported self-help groups have gone beyond the conventional boundary lines of their disciplines and recognized the limits of their discipline's conventional domain.

The national organization of TCF has given some thought to the question of the role of the professional and has formulated a policy statement:

> Chapters of TCF are and should be organized with bereaved parents responsible for programs and activities and with members of the helping professions serving in consulting roles. . . . Someone who has not lost a child should not attempt to play a central role in the process.
>
> TCF can benefit from maintaining a cooperative and friendly relationship with members of the helping professions.
>
> The selection of the individuals themselves is of paramount importance. They should have demonstrated commitment to the self-help principle, and be comfortable in a consultative capacity. If a professional attends meetings, he could serve as an invited speaker, facilitator, or may simply be present as a resource to be called upon if the group feels the need. The professional should be there to react, not to initiate.

Self-help groups are a challenge to the traditional concept of human services because they emphasize the power of the members to assist one another using their own cognitive and emotional resources rather than depending on professionals. The self-help process transfers the locus of control to the members. In most human service, the control stays with the professional. Commenting on the mutual exclusion of professionals and self-help groups, Katz (1970) says that the role of the professional, if it exists at all, is unclear and is minimized when complared to the usual social agencies. Schwartz (1975) finds the "role of professional leadership is deliberately minimized or even systematically excluded" (p.746). Powell (1975) sees the rejection from the other side. He notes that self-help groups "have not been widely accepted by or integrated into the professional human service system" (p. 756). Vatano (1972) finds:

> When professionals participate, their role is modified to adapt to the self-help group's distinctive culture. Thus, they are expected to act as peers and shorten the social distance between themselves and the members by diffusing the leadership function and sharing their own personal concerns with the group. (p. 14)

Vatano thus sees the professional equipped to perform three functions: (1) act as a catalyst or facilitator, particularly in the early stages; (2) do research on problems the group is dealing with and the effectiveness of the methods employed; and (3) conceptualize the group's experiences and provide the theory building and feedback necessary for further development. We found these functions to be extremely useful bases on which to begin.

The most useful theoretic distinction between professional and self-help process is that Borkman (1976) makes between experiential knowledge and professional knowledge. A self-help group is based on the premise that experiential knowledge is a primary source of truth, and, as such, experiential knowledge competes with professional knowledge, which is the foundation of expertise in most other human service organizations.

> Experiential knowledge is truth learned from personal experience with a phenomenon rather than truth acquired by discursive reasoning, observation, or reflection on information provided by others. . . . It is a conviction that the insights learned from direct participation in a situation are truth. (pp. 446–447)

Experiential knowledge leads to an experiential expertise, that is, competence or skill in handling or resolving a problem through the use of one's own experience. Not everyone in a self-help group can be said to have such experiential expertise. There are those who are defined by the group as "just starting." Others are defined as "mid-course." And some are defined as having arrived at a high level of experience with their loss so that they can be a model for others. The selection of leadership tends to be an informal process based on an interaction between the person's self-perceived growth and the group's recognition and validation of growth and change.

Professional knowledge, on the other hand, is truth developed, applied, and transmitted by an established group of specialists. Most movements for personal transformation, healing, or change in contemporary American culture are based on professional knowledge. Credentials certifying professional knowledge are only given to those who have met specialized educational and training requirements. The professional community assumes that others will accept on faith their ability to diagnose and prescribe treatment that will alleviate pain and suffering, for only other professionals are truly able to judge the work of their peers.

ROLES WE PLAYED

The controlling principle of our work within the self-help process is that the members own, control, manage, and lead the group. All the professional's activities are subordinate to the group's own process. The best indication that the professional is working effectively is that little attention is directed toward the tasks done and that attention remains focused on the processes within the group. Thus the professional not only gives up any power inherent in professional knowledge, but also forgoes, as much as possible, any recognition of her or his activities. Several other groups have reported that the intrusion of professionalism is, in the long run, detrimental to the self-help process, however necessary it may appear in the short-run situation (Schwartz, 1975).

Most of our interactions within the group have been informal. The group has never set the limits of our activities, nor has the group asked us to undertake a project or task that depended solely upon professional expertise. Yet within this informal interaction, it is possible to see some patterns in our roles within the process.

Intermediary between the Group and the Professional Community

In the early stages of the group's development, we acted as an intermediary between the professional community and the group. The intermediary role moves in both directions. We represented the group to the professional community and linked the professional resources to the group.

The self-help process is different from professional processes, but the fact is that the first contact the newly bereaved parent is likely to have is with physicians, morticians, clergy, social workers, or nurses. Given our cultural denial of death as well as the personal "It won't happen to me," it is unlikely that before bereavement the parents have heard of the group. As the local group formed, we spent some time advocating and interpreting the group's methods and goals to the helping professions. We contacted the social service and/or pastoral care departments of the major hospitals in the metropolitan area and made a presentation to as many of the staff as possible. We explained the group, showed its effectiveness in anecdotes, and spoke to concerns the professionals voiced. Because we ourselves claimed no experiential knowledge, but rather presented ourselves as socially certified witnesses to the group's effectiveness, our presentation was not a direct threat to the professionals' status.

Within 3 years after the foundation of the local chapter, members took over these presentations, for now the question had become the effectiveness of the group, not its purpose or concept. The lives of the members as they speak are the best evidence of its effectiveness.

The other aspect of the intermediary role is linking group members to appropriate community resources. TCF sets no limitations on age or cause of the child's death for membership, and parents bring a wide assortment of problems related to the death. Some of these problems could be helped by professionals. For example, an insurance executive can advise on claim settlements. We tried to have a wide understanding of the resources available in the community that members might need. We pointed people to legal services when they felt they were having problems with the prosecution of their child's murderer, supplied names of single parents' groups, and tried to interpret the role of a school counselor for a parent whose surviving child's response to the death showed up as academic problems.

As the group matured, the expertise within the group grew both because members had more experience to share and because the larger size of the group brought more broadly based expertise. Thus, there was less and less need for us to play the role of intermediary between the group and the professional community. In some cases the expertise of the group has become amazing. For example, when Parents of Murdered Children was started, the practical knowledge of the legal system within the group covered almost any new situation confronted by members.

Articulating the Group Process

Parents come into TCF not knowing what to expect. Often people assume there is "something the group can do for me," as if the member were a passive recipient of services. Parents who attend the meeting often have difficulty integrating the events or the organizational details into their own feelings about the death.

All human activity is perceived within a framework of meaning, a controlling map of reality (Berger & Luckman, 1966). Any process of human transformation must define the sufferer's problem within the process's framework and present the process in a way that opens itself to the sufferer's problem. Obviously there needs to be a link between problem and process (Frank, 1961). Because there are usually new parents at the meetings, the group needs a constant reiteration of the process. For the first few years, the leader asked the professional for a 5-minute summary at the end of the meeting. At first we thought the time should be spent in professional commentary and clarification of the issues raised within the meeting. It soon became clear, however, that such self-perceived penultimates were superfluous. We learned to simply recount the happenings of the meeting and, in doing so, to define the events and problems presented within the self-help process.

There is an interesting paradox in this role. In articulating the group's ideology, the power of the professional's knowledge is implicitly negated. The professional becomes an expert in the self-help language and, to some extent, gains new power by becoming the theoretician of the group. The professional retains a kind of "disciplined subjectivity" (Erikson, 1964; Geertz, 1973; Powdermaker, 1966) by being both involved in and detached from the process. But instead of expanding upon professional theoretical models, the professional interprets the events of the meeting within the self-help process.

As the group matured, we were less and less cast in the role of expert. It has been several years since the professional summarized at the end of the meeting. Now each meeting is opened and closed with a reading based on the TCF statement of principles. The reading defines the process and sets the ground rules by which new members interact. There is also a fund of experience among those who have attended longer; problems are more often defined within the process as they arise, rather than at the end of the meeting. The task of defining the group process has reverted to the members.

Resource in Program Planning

In the early years of the group, we were active in program planning. Self-help does not exclude professional knowledge. In planning meetings, we often suggested themes or speakers that we thought were relevant to the group. But more importantly, we attempted to identify resources within the group. Because the members often are attending to the problems of others during and after the meetings, professionals can listen for hints of talent or insights that can be shared. For example, when a member began sharing a scheme of understandings she had developed from reading several books, we suggested that she put together a short presentation for the next meeting. She did, and the meeting was a great success.

As the group matured, program planning reverted gradually to the members, for they had developed a fund of experience in what programs worked and how to find good speakers. The chapter began sending large delegations to the TCF national conventions. They came back brimming with program ideas. We still attend steering committee meetings, but as the yearly program has become more and more regularized, we tend now to just comment on effectiveness and to mirror comments we have heard from members.

Acute Grief and Psychotomimetic Behavior

Perhaps the single most common reason other professionals believed we should be with TCF was to intervene if someone's grief expressed itself in a way that the group could not handle. There is a myth, partly encouraged by some professionals, that grief is a mental illness that, if acute, puts the sufferer beyond the range of common human interaction. There is no doubt that all grief is at times psychotomimetic—it mimics psychosis—in that it includes deep catatoniclike depression, hallucinations, morbid thoughts, bizarre behavior, and suicidal thoughts. Because we are a culture out of touch with death, and because we tend to use the medical model as the prime interpretative framework for aberrant human behavior, we fear such displays of grieving and try to relegate them to the province of the professional. We discussed the etiology of pathology in Chapter 8. In sum, our finding is that pathology stems from factors outside the loss itself, and that a great deal of what is normal in parental bereavement is mislabeled as pathology within the current professionally used models of grief.

Our experience showed us that the group was quite capable of handling any acute grief presented. Indeed, the phrase, "Yes, I was like that," is a most therapeutic intervention for both the speaker and the listener. The group tends to have a far wider view of normality than professionals might hold, because the experiential base of the group rests on a more longitudinal understanding than does professional knowledge (Powell, 1975). We found that the group's tolerance for psychotomimetic behavior tends to ease the secondary stress from the fear that "I am going crazy," and allows the person to confront the primary reality that their child is dead.

We found our task was to help maintain the integrity of the group process while interpreting the psychotomimetic behavior in a way that made it accessible to the group process. We tried to avoid two dangers. First, we did not want to enter into special counseling relationships with group members, for we did not want to have the power relationship that counseling implies carried into the peer-oriented relationship with the group. Only as our role in TCF declined did we expand the private psychotherapy described in Chapter 8. Second, we avoided acting as an arbiter of normality and abnormality, for this would be claiming a power that was superior to the power of the group.

The professional power we posessed seemed to be needed by the group to assure themselves that their process was adequate. Although I introduced myself by my first name, for the first several years I remained "Doctor Klass," though the social work practicum students could be addressed by their first names. It seemed as if by lending my authority to the group I gave some legitimacy.

As the group matured, the members increasingly began to exercise their own authority and to feel more and more competent in dealing with the problems brought to the group. Slowly, members began addressing me by my first name. Further, the experiences members had with various professional interventions became a part of the experiential knowledge base of the group. Several parents who became leaders also used marriage counseling or psychotherapy to help them come to terms with their child's death. In the supportive community of TCF, they could share the possibilities and problems of professional interventions.

INSIDER AND OUTSIDER

In the early years of the group, I was a much more central figure than I am now, 8 years later. When I attend a meeting, I do not know well many of the people there. There are even leaders of the group whom I have met for the first time at a steering committee meeting, for now there are several subgroups meeting at different times and places. When I attend a holiday candlelight service or the spring picnic, I find myself gravitating to the old-timers cluster, where we speak in awe of the growth of the organization we created.

The increased distance is also reflected in my conceptual process. During the first 2 or 3 years, my knowledge was more like experiential knowledge, for I entered as fully as I could into the lives I was encountering. I simply tried to understand what was being said as clearly as I could. After the meetings, the practicum students and I would spend another few hours going over what had happened, as we tried to hold the substance of what we had been a part. We closed the bar more than a few times in those early "supervision sessions." I was too wound up to sleep much on meeting nights. As we began to see the patterns that were emerging in the lives of the parents, we tried to articulate those patterns in the "Reflections" column of the newsletter. The feedback from those brief pieces were valuable corrections to my understanding. The interviews we conducted allowed me to reflect in a more detached way as I read the typescript in my study. As I understood more, I could distance myself more; and as the theoretical model emerged, I could be less involved in the immediate interactions of the group. After about 5 years, I was surprised to discover that I could sleep when I came straight home after a meeting. I worried about myself, for I could listen to the deepest of human pain and not be overwhelmed.

The process of questioning, finding answers, and revising the question in light of the answers continued for a few more years. And in the process of conceptualizing I found an increased distance between my knowledge of parents' experience and their knowledge of their own experience.

I hope I am still in touch with the reality of parental grief. The greatest compliment I ever receive is when, after I have spoken at a TCF meeting, someone tells me that I sound like someone who has lost a child. Hearing this, I feel that I have entered their world sufficiently to try to understand. But I will make no claims. Those bereaved parents who read this book will have to judge for themselves whether I have understood the depths of their grief, the nature of their resolutions, or the difficulties of their long journey after the death of their child.

Appendix II

John Bowlby's Model of Grief and the Problem of Identification

The model of grief I have used in this book has two dimensions. On the one hand, the task of grief is to reestablish an equilibrium between the self and the social environment. On the other hand, the task of grief is to reestablish an equilibrium in the inner life by internalizing and transforming the inner representation of the deceased in such a way that it brings solace. For the first task, I have relied heavily on recent theory and research that has grown out of the work of John Bowlby (Bowlby, 1961, 1969-1973, 1980; Parkes, 1972; Parkes & Weiss, 1983; Raphael, 1983; Worden, 1982). For the second task, I have used a revised version of Vamik Volkan's (Horton, 1981; Volkan, 1981) theory of grief.

The Bowlby group's work, which is almost exclusively based on the study of widows, represents the mainstream of research on grief today. The dynamics of bereaved parents are different enough that the Bowlby model does not fit the data. Our data on bereaved parents indicate that a central issue in the resolution of parental grief is establishing the place of the child in the ongoing life of the bereaved parent. In Chapter 3 we saw that internalization of the child, both as identification and introjection, was used as a source of solace. The Bowlby model needs to be revised in a way that accounts for the retention of the inner representation in the ongoing life of the bereaved in a healthy way.

When we talk about the role of the deceased in the ongoing life of the bereaved, we find ourselves in the middle of some longstanding difficulties in the competing contemporary models of grief. The problem is that beginning with Freud (1961c/1917), the concept used to talk about the internal aspect of a relationship has been identification. For Freud, the model of identification is the Oedipus complex, in which the child gives up the narcissistic relationship with the parent and compensates for the loss by internalizing the parent in the form of the ego ideal. This is the first split in the ego and is the basis, for Freud, of all future psychological development. Freud adopted this theory when he abandoned his earlier theory that neurosis is caused by childhood trauma. John Bowlby's life project has been to restore the trauma theory by showing that attachment behavior is an innate instinct and that development, both normal and pathological, can be explained in terms of the history of the attachment between parent and child.

The Bowlby model, which used data from the study of widows, was developed specifically as a refutation of internalization of the lost object. Bowlby wrote identification out of any understanding of normal grief. The study of bereaved parents does not seem to allow us to keep this refutation. As we noted in Chapter 8, phenomena that are common in parental bereavement are labeled as pathology in the Bowlby model. In order to understand the implications of parental bereavement on the theoretical model of grief, therefore, we need to understand the history and possibilities of this controversy in grief theory.

In this appendix I will: (1) describe Bowlby's model of grief as it relates to Freud's concept of identification; (2) briefly examine the concept of identification in Freud and in Freud's followers, especially Vamik Volkan; (3) trace the problems in accounting for phenomena associated with identification by those using Bowlby's model: Bowlby, Colin Murray Parkes, Beverly Raphael, and William Worden; and (4) examine the possibility for modifications of the Bowlby model in the work of nonpsychoanalytic scholars Thomas Attig (1982), Helena Lopata (1973, 1979), and Peter Marris (1975).

BOWLBY'S MODEL OF GRIEF AND THE PROBLEM OF IDENTIFICATION

After the completion of his three volume *Attachment and Loss* (1969–1980) Bowlby discussed the events and influences of his career in several reflective articles (1979, 1981a, 1981b, 1982). He began as one of the second generation psychoanalytic psychiatrists. For that group, Freud had opened horizons with his idea that primary relationships during childhood determine the structure of the adult. Led by Freud's daughter Anna, it was a generation that was more interested in the ability of the ego to build, cope, and grow than in the darker examination of id impulses and cultural pathology. It was a generation for whom the psychoanalytic insights could be a vehicle for curing individual and social ills. Childhood determinism was an occasion for reforming childrearing practices.

"My choice of career had been determined," Bowlby says (1981a, p. 2), "by what I had seen and heard during the six months that I had spent in a school for disturbed children between my pre-clinical training at Cambridge." During that time he also read widely and "had been exposed to hypotheses, derived from the 'new psychology' emanating from Vienna, regarding the role of childhood experience in their origin." Hoping to understand those children that had so affected him, he entered training in psychoanalysis. But he found that he was mistaken about Freud's theory.

> Although my training as a psychoanalyst had been undertaken in the belief that Freud attributed the emotional problems of his patients to the traumatic experiences they had had within the families of origin during their early years, I gradually realized that he had abandoned that opinion long since and had concluded instead that the events he had believed important had not occurred in reality but had been the products of his patients' imagination. This was then, and until recently has remained the dominant view in the psychoanalytic world. . . . I thought otherwise. (1981a, p. 2)

Bowlby's theoretical project became to reintroduce the reality of the child's individual history back into psychoanalysis.

> If we were to understand our patients' present difficulties, I felt sure, it was just as necessary for our discipline to include the study of the way children are really treated by their parents and its effects on them as it is to study the internal representations of parents that the children or grown-ups we treat now have. . . . Believing that progress would be possible only if we have far more systematic knowledge about the effects on a child of the experience he has within his family, I concentrated my attention on that area. (1981b, p. 244)

An assignment as a postwar consultant to the World Health Organization on the needs of homeless children provided the opening for Bowlby's own work. He discovered the ill effects of maternal deprivation, which became for him the most central of the real experiences a young child could have. Children who were deprived of

mother's care for long periods and children who were institutionalized showed the effects of that trauma all their lives. The response
of the child to separation from the mother would henceforth be the
paradigmatic human experience for Bowlby.

Two scholars from very different branches of the study of animal
behavior were useful to Bowlby in understanding the meaning of that
childhood trauma. First Harry Harlow's experiments with infant
monkeys separated from their mothers or raised by artificial mothers
allowed laboratory confirmation of the response to maternal deprivation (Harlow & Harlow, 1963). Second, and more important to the
theory, Konrad Lorenz's (1966) ethology allowed Bowlby to jettison
Freud's metapsychology. Rather than the dynamics of impulse and
repression, Bowlby could now have instinctual behavior. The instinct
is attachment behavior which, as Bowlby says in the first volume of
Attachment and Loss (1969–1980), "is regarded as a class of social
behaviour of an importance equivalent to that of mating behaviour
and parental behaviour. It is held to have a biological function specific
to itself" (Vol. 1, p. 179).

Bowlby does not consider, as we have had to in this book, that
parental behavior (or mating behavior) is also involved in grief. He
does not, for example, record the parent's behavior when separated
from the child, which is different from the child's behavior when
separated from the parent. Thus, his model of grief only considers
attachment behavior.

Attachment behavior is simply "what occurs when certain be-
havioural systems are activated" (Bowlby, 1969–1980, Vol. 1, p. 179)
and can therefore replace the whole issue of drive and instinct in the
psychoanalytic system. The behavior is to keep the mother in close
proximity for protection from predators (p. 226).

Attachment behavior follows a distinct sequence when the child
is separated from the mother. First, the child protests and tries to get
back to the mother. Second, the child despairs returning to mother,
but remains preoccupied with her. Third, the child loses interest in
the mother, and, should she return, the child initially will be emo-
tionally detached. Those three phases of the response to separation
for Bowlby replace Freud's metapsychology, for, as he says in the
second volume, each of the phases is related "to one or another of the
central issues of psychoanalytic theory. Thus the phase of protest is
found to raise the problem of separation anxiety; despair that of grief
and mourning; detachment that of defense" (1969–1980, Vol. 2, p.
27).

It was an understanding of mourning that allowed Freud to open the full development of his metapsychology in his paper "Mourning and Melancholia" (1961c/1917). In that work Freud relies heavily on the process of identification—that is, making the relationship with the lost person a part of the ego. Identifications form the mature ego.

Bowlby uses the concept of attachment to account for some of the same phenomena that Freud accounted for through the concept of identification. There is a critical period in early childhood, Bowlby says, in which lasting personality changes are made depending on the adequacy of the environmental response to the behavior (Bowlby, 1969–1980, Vol. 2, p. 210). The attachment behavior is, however, not outgrown.

> During adolescence and adult life a measure of attachment behaviour is commonly directed not only towards persons outside the family but also towards groups and institutions other than the family. A school or college, a work group, a religious group or a political group can come to constitute for many people a subordinate attachment-"figure", and for some people a principal attachment-"figure." In such cases, it seems probable, the development of attachment to a group is mediated, at least initially, by attachment to a person holding a prominent position within that group. Thus, for many a citizen attachment to his state is a derivative of and initially dependent on his attachment to its sovereign or president. (Bowlby, 1969–1980, Vol. 1, p. 207)

In *Group Psychology and the Analysis of the Ego* (1922), written shortly after the paper "Mourning and Melancholia," Freud uses identification to account for the relationship of the individual to institutions. Like Bowlby, he saw the sense of oneness with the group mediated through a sense of personal oneness with the leader. Freud also uses identification to explain "falling in love," which would presumably be a special case of attachment for Bowlby.

Thus Bowlby uses attachment to account for the same phenomena as did Freud with identification in situations not connected with bereavement. The basic patterns of personality that Bowlby sees formed by the quality of the environmental response to the child's attachment behavior, Freud saw growing out of the resolution to the primary relationships, that is, identification with parental figures. It should not surprise us, therefore, that Bowlby goes to some lengths to avoid any admission of the concept of identification or any of the phenomena associated with it into his model of grief.

In adopting Freud's trauma theory but rejecting his other work, Bowlby was indeed, as he claimed (1982, pp. 668), setting out to provide a new conceptual framework in Kuhn's sense (1970). More recently, Jeffrey Masson has also called for a restoration of the trauma theory (1985). The question with Bowlby, as with Masson, is simply: If we rule out all psychodynamics except trauma theory, have we adequately accounted for the entire phenomenon of the human experience we observe? To ask this question is not to claim that Freud or the Freudians are right in the way they understand the relationship of the bereaved to the lost object. Indeed, I will later note other options in non-Freudian theories. The case I am making is simply that identification—or something like what Freud was trying to describe with the term *identification*—is an aspect of normal grief, is in the Bowlby group's data, but is not adequately accounted for in their theory.

Bowlby's basic understanding of the problem death brings to the organism is a "state of biological disequilibrium brought about by a sudden change in the environment" (1961, p. 322).

> Mourning is best regarded as the whole complex sequences of psychological processes and their overt manifestations, beginning with craving, angry efforts at recovery, and appeals for help, proceeding through apathy and disorganization of behaviour, and ending when some form of more or less stable reorganization is beginning to develop. (Bowlby, 1961, p. 332)

The new state of equilibrium and reorganization is understood to be of the individual in relationship to the environment rather than in the relationship of the individual to the lost object. It is when the individual ceases searching and trying to restore the lost object that the work of mourning is complete. At that time, the individual rebuilds life by attaching to other objects.

> Just as a child playing with Meccano must destroy his construction before he can use the pieces again (and a sad occasion it sometimes is), so must the individual each time he is bereaved or relinquished a major goal accept the destruction of a part of his personality before he can organize it afresh towards a new object or goal. (Bowlby, 1961, p. 335)

The inadequacy of this formulation of the nature of grief is that if the problem grief raises is in relationship to the environment, how do we account within the theory for settling the relationship between the bereaved and the lost object? That is, though to be sure a death does cause a disequilibrium within the social world of the bereaved, there is also a disequilibrium in the inner life of the bereaved. That inner disequilibrium is settled by some sort of renegotiation of the relationship with the dead person. Bowlby's model only accounts for the rearrangements in the social world.

FREUD AND THE FREUDIANS ON IDENTIFICATION AND GRIEF

Freud spoke of grief work in which: "Each single one of the memories and situations of expectancy which demonstrate the libido's attachment to the lost object is met by the verdict of reality that the object no longer exists" (1961c/1917, p. 255).

The purpose of this mourning is to free the ego from the attachment to the deceased. "When the work of mourning is completed the ego becomes free and uninhibited again" (1961c/1917, p. 245). Freud contrasts this healthy mourning of a known lost object with depression, which appears to be mourning for an unconscious lost object. In that case, identification comes into play.

> The free libido was not displaced on to another object; it was withdrawn into the ego. There, however, it was not employed in any unspecified way, but served to establish an identification of the ego with the abandoned object. . . . The narcissistic identification with the object then becomes a substitute for the erotic cathexis, the result of which is that in spite of the conflict with the loved person the love relation need not be given up. (1961c/1917, p. 249)

But Freud was interested in a special loss, not loss in general. The unconscious object is the parent. In making that object part of the ego, the ego ideal is created—and thus was begun Freud's metapsychology. It is this use of identification in the metapsychology that Bowlby rejects in favor of attachment theory based on Lorenz's ethological instincts.

In the *New Introductory Lectures* (1961b/1933) Freud returns to mourning, saying, "If one has lost an object or has been obliged to give it up, one often compensates oneself by identifying oneself with it and by setting it up once more in one's ego, so that here object-choice regresses, as it were, to identification" (p. 63). But his interest is in the lost objects of primary attachments with the parents when the superego is formed from the introjection into the ego of that lost object. He does not deal with other lost objects, so the issue of identification as a resolution to grief is not carried further. There is an intriguing hint of a fuller treatment in *The Ego and the Id* (1961a/1923), where he says, "The ego is formed to a great extent out of identifications which take the place of abandoned cathexes by the id" (p. 48). But he does not pursue the idea.

The psychoanalytic group soon expanded Freud's concept of grief work and internalization. As early as 1924 Karl Abraham (1927) had developed Freud's basic idea, saying that the mourner in-trojected the lost object in order to retain it. Otto Fenichel (1945) thought of mourning in terms of an introjection to be made before the object could be given up. Roy Schafer's work on internalization (1968, 1976), which provides the basis for much current discussion in psy-choanalysis, distinguishes between two kinds of internalization: identification and introjection.

Vamik D. Volkan's book *Linking Objects and Linking Phenomena* (1981) provides the most complete development of a theory of grief using identification. Volkan is from the object relations group in psychoanalysis. The theory of grief begins with a theory of in-ternalized objects.

> The theory of internalized object relations views intra-psychic conflict in terms of an individual's self-and object-representations. . . . Those conflicts may. . . be seen in persons with cohesive self-representations and inte-grated object worlds when the death of a loved one precipitates the hyper-cathexis of the representation of the dead, reviving old conflicts among self-and object-relationships and demanding new inner adjustments to restore the previously established, newly disturbed balance among them. (p. 15)

Volkan sees mourning as a paradoxical process, for:

> the work of mourning comes to a practical end when the mourner no longer has a compulsive need to cling to the representation of the dead person. Meanwhile, however, paradoxically, the mourner identifies with certain aspects of the dead and comes to resemble him in these particulars. Thus, when such mourning is concluded the ego will often have been enriched. (p. 67)

Volkan uses Schafer's distinction between identification and in-trojection to distinguish between normal and pathological grieving. Identification is the healthy result of mourning, in that "the self-representations resemble the object representation"; and although such a similarity may be seen as an effort to maintain the relationship with the object, in fact it may be opening the way for independence from the object, for "when the self and model are perceived as one, relative independence from the original model is achieved" (Volkan, 1981, p. 70).

Introjection, on the other hand, is the direct incorporation of the object into the self without modifying the object representation in such a way as to make it compatible with the rest of the self. Thus, the ego is split in a harmful way, for the internalized object is felt to be other than the self and is maintained in such a way that the bond with the dead person is maintained in the same manner as it was when the person was living.

> When the act of introjection does not eventuate in the kind of melding of object representation into self-representation that characterized identification, the object representation is felt as existing within the patient himself, and is perceived by some patients an an ongoing and persistent phenomenon. (Volkan, 1981, p. 70)

The introject does not manifest itself directly, rather it takes the form of symptoms, internal regulations, ideation, and so forth. That which is internalized can also be externalized and the introject can be projected onto persons or objects in the environment. Of special interest to Volkan is the externalization onto *linking objects*, which can be used to call forth the presence of the deceased. A wide range is covered in Volkan's use of the word *object*. His examples include simple physical objects like a robe, a rock picked up at an accident site, or a picture of the dead person. But also included are ritual acts, a diary of notations on psychotic states, and dietary observances.

In Chapter 3 we found introjection objects common in parental bereavement. As we noted in Chapter 8, if introjection be pathology, then much of parental bereavement is pathological. Therefore, in this study, we have accepted Volkan's description of internalization, but have rejected his opinion on pathology.

IDENTIFICATION IN THE BOWLBY MODEL OF GRIEF

Bowlby's Own Work

Bowlby excluded identification from the themes that he would investigate in his 1961 paper on mourning. "To some a discussion of mourning that omits identification will seem like Hamlet without the Prince," Bowlby said, but his data "do not seem to lend themselves readily to the study of identificatory process and their deviations," though "I am inclined to the view that the role of identification amongst processes of mourning may become easier to discern after some of the problems to be tackled here have been clarified" (p. 319). Rewriting that paper in the third volume of *Attachment and Loss*, he added identification to the list of themes (1969–1980, Vol. 3, p. 25) but:

In the upshot, the role given to identificatory processes in the theory advanced here is a subordinate one: they are regarded as occurring only sporadically and, when prominent, to be indicative of pathology. (1969–1980, Vol. 3, p. 30)

Bowlby limits the place of identification by a limitation of its definition. The pathology of identification is a mislocation of the lost object within the self. Thus, it might be a strong sense of the deceased's presence, a fighter pilot's loss of concern about his life after friends were shot down, or experience of the symptoms of the deceased (1969–1980, Vol. 3, pp. 166–169). Each of those would have been called introjection by the psychoanalytic group.

Bowlby recognizes the continuing sense of the dead person's presence as compatible with healthy mourning but does not call it identification. Rather than seeing himself in agreement with the later psychoanalytic group, Bowlby uses this observation to refute Freud's concept of griefwork, even though that refutation is shared by psychoanalytic theorists who early on recognized internalization of the lost object as the resolution of grief.

> Failure to recognize that a continuing sense of the dead person's presence, either as a constant companion or in some specific and appropriate location, is a common feature of healthy mourning which has led to much confused theorizing. Very frequently the concept of identification, instead of being limited to cases in which the dead person is located within the self, is extended to cover also every case in which there is a continuing sense of the dead person's presence, irrespective of location. . . . Indeed, findings in regard both to the high prevalence of a continuing sense of the presence of the dead person and to its compatiblity with a favourable outcome give no support to Freud's well-known and already quoted passage: "Mourning has a quite precise psychical task to perform: its function is to detach the survivor's memories and hopes from the dead." (Bowlby, 1969–1980, Vol. 3, p. 100)

Bowlby does not say how the continuing sense of presence is accounted for in his own model of grief. Moss and Moss (1984) have expanded on the observation of this phenomenon in the study of widows.

One way to deal with the continuing relationship with the lost object is to use the concept from object relations theory of inner representation. We have an inner representation of a person; when the person dies, we have to change the inner representation, though the representation may continue to play a role in our psychic life.

Although Bowlby uses the language of inner representations, he cannot seem to use it to expand his model to include grief as a disequilibrium in the relationship of the griever to the inner representation of the lost object.

Bowlby introduced the concept of internalized models, that is, object relations theory. Attachments are maintained, he says, by internalized models of the external world, especially of the mother. He seems to have recognized that in using the idea of internal models to explain attachment, he has opened the door to other issues of internalization of relationships after mourning. In the first volume of *Attachment and Loss* Bowlby simply notes that the questions concerning inner models "raise too many problems (and giant controversies) for it to be sensible to attempt to deal with them here" (1969–1980, Vol. 1, p. 354). By the second volume, Bowlby seemed to be hoping that the metapsychology could be replaced as he earlier had claimed. He says:

> the concepts of working models and forecasts derived from working models. . . is no more than a way of describing, in terms compatible with systems theory, ideas traditionally described in such terms as 'introjection of an object' (good or bad) and 'self-image.' (1969–1980, Vol. 2, p. 204)

In the second volume, the model has become complex. There can be multiple models that may be conscious to varying degrees. But he does not connect the multiple models to the resolution of grief.

> Whereas common sense might suggest that a person would operate with only single models of each of his attachment figures and of himself, psychoanalysis from Freud onwards has presented a great deal of evidence that can best be explained by supposing that it is not uncommon for an individual to operate, simultaneously, with two (or more) working models of himself. When multiple models of a single figure are operative they are likely to differ in regard to their origin, their dominance, and the extent to which the subject is aware of them. (1969–1980, Vol. 2, p. 205)

In the third volume, which focuses on loss, Bowlby drops the idea of a complex inner model in favor of computer analogy. The organism is basically an information processing system and the models only operate to facilitate or retard the adequate processing of information (1969–1980, Vol. 3, pp. 44–73). Thus the concept of model in the third volume is brought into line with the reestablishment of equilibrium by reorganization of the relationship to the environment. The sense of the continuing presence is not accounted for within the inner model and internalization is relegated to pathology.

Because it is necessary to discard old patterns of thinking, feeling and acting before new ones can be fashioned, it is almost inevitable that a bereaved person should at times despair that anything can be salvaged. . . . Nevertheless . . . this phase may soon begin to alternate with a phase during which he starts to examine the new situation in which he finds himself and to consider ways of meeting it. This entails a redefinition of himself as well as of his situation. . . . It is a process of 'realization', of reshaping internal representational models so as to align them with the changes that have occurred in the bereaved's life situation. (1969–1980, Vol. 3, p. 94)

Colin Murray Parkes

Colin Murray Parkes, colleague and sometime collaborator of Bowlby, defines grief as the reaction to a severed "love tie" (1972, p. 1), a definition that seems to rely on some broader assumptions than does Bowlby's attachment behavior. But for Parkes, the end of bereavement is reattachment to new objects rather than settlement of old attachments. Like Bowlby, he understands the resolution of grief in a social equilibrium.

Parkes begins with an essentially social self, though the problems with the phenomona of identification do not allow him to maintain a consistent definition of the self. He begins with a self that consists of roles and interaction patterns. The roles that a person performs in life are made up of a complex series of focal action patterns that constitute a repertoire of problem solutions. This repertoire, because it is based on experience, assumes that reasonable expectations of the environment will be fulfilled. In time, after bereavement, the individual's stock of "solutions for all eventualities" grows greater, and novel situations requiring novel solutions become rarer (1972, p. 93). Of the widows in his study, he says:

The adoption of roles or attitudes of the dead person is seldom permanent and never complete. . . . The London widows seemed, rather, to find their new identity emerging from the altered life situations which they had to face. (1972, p. 105)

Parkes introduces identification as part of the discussion of phenomena often founded in bereavement. He says there is a double sense in which we see identity in grief: (1) the sense that the lost one is now part of the self and that the self is changed after the death, so that the self is more like the dead person; and (2) the sense in which the loss is felt to be a part of the self now missing (1972, pp. 88–105).

Parkes uses a theory of the boundaries of the self to explain those instances of identification, though he does not incorporate the idea of boundaries into his earlier concept of a social self in bereavement, nor does he use the theory of the boundaries of the self in later discussion of the possible pathologies of grief.

> At once it is apparent that although I think I know myself there is a hinterland between 'self' and 'other' which is not clear cut and which may change. If my little finger is cut off it ceases to be a part of me; if I lose my job I cease to be a psychiatrist; if I lose my temper I cease to be even-tempered; if my wife dies I cease to be her husband and she ceases to be my wife. . . . If I have relied on another person to predict and act in many ways as an extension of myself then the loss of that person can be expected to have the same effect upon my view of the world and my view of myself as if I had lost a part of myself. (1972, p. 96–97)

The theory of self-boundaries and social identity leads Parkes to some conceptual difficulties in his discussion of grief over the loss of a limb. He lists "identification phenomena" as one of the characteristics of grief for which he will look in amputees (1972, p. 183). But using boundaries between the self and other, he cannot say that the lost limb is within the self. So he settles on the "phantom limb" as identification phenomena, in that it is analogous to the widow who has symptoms of her husband's final illness. But clearly the inability to draw a better relationship between amputation and bereavement shows that interiorized relationships are not central to his understanding of widows' grief. In the study of bereaved parents, we find that they often used the amputation metaphor—as grieving for a part of themselves—and that they found the metaphor useful.

Parkes discusses Freud's concept of cathexis in griefwork, saying that it is a cybernetic model that is "useful in so far as it fits the observed data but it should not be taken too far. In recent years energy models of this type have come under scrutiny . . . and it seems to me that they add little to our understanding of bereavement" (1972, p. 76). Some of his data, however, might better be explained by the ideas of transference and countertransference within the cybernetic model. He gives an extended account of a widow who, shortly after her husband died, established a dependent relationship with an older man. The man denied there was any romantic element to the relationship, but he got angry and terminated the relationship when he found her drinking with another man. In another case, Parkes himself seems to have entered into a relationship that must have involved countertransference. Of one widow, he says:

As a thoroughly partial investigator I found myself persuading landlords, jogging the Assistance Board, and consulting doctors on her behalf, and it was in this capacity that I discovered that she was far from helpless, and indeed talented in the arts of persuasion. (1972, p. 144)

In *Recovery from Bereavement* (1983) Parkes and Weiss find some data that seem to be best accounted for with a theory of interiorized relationships, as opposed to predictive models. In discussing the fact that those in conflicted marriages seem at first less devastated and later more devastated by the loss, Parkes and Weiss cite Freud on the relationship of mourning to depression as the incorporation of the lost object in depression. We have noted that that distinction was not maintained in psychoanalysis. "But there is something glib about the thesis," they say, for how can one person "be said to incorporate and contain another?" (1983, p. 121). The question is answered in a non-Freudian way, but in order to do so, Parkes and Weiss abandon the earlier theory of boundaries of the self without substituting a theory that would cover the issues the earlier theory sought to explain.

> Those to whom we have established attachments may not stop affecting us when we are no longer in touch with them. They may continue to engage us as partners in our interior dialogues. . . . Those in our internal community who are seen as loving to us may be easily accepted, easily made a part of our own thinking and feeling. But those who are seen as hostile, who seem to use the privileged position of membership in our internal world to criticize our motives and disparage our worth, require our constant defense. (1983, pp. 121–122)

Inner dialogue and internal community would seem to qualify as internalizing the object as a part of the self, but the explanation Parkes and Weiss prefer is based in the trauma of bad early attachment.

> Some among those who form and remain in troubled marriages are individuals who because of earlier experiences in their lives, have difficulty establishing more satisfactory attachments and, furthermore, that these same earlier experiences make them less capable than others of successfully recovering from loss. (1983, p. 124)

The explanation, of course, refers directly back to Bowlby's childhood trauma of maternal deprivation. But no data is given to support the claim that these bad marriages had roots in childhood trauma. Nor are any data presented to show that those who continue defending themselves against the hostile inner representation of the deceased have childhood attachment trauma in their history more than do the general population. Thus we see that when identification appears as a possible explanation, Bowlby's followers insist on an explanation using attachment trauma in early life. But without data supporting a correlation of trauma to the phenomena reported, there is no reason for the rejection of identification as a part of normal grief.

Beverly Raphael

Beverly Raphael's (1983) model for bereavement, she says, is largely from Bowlby and to a lesser extent from Freud and Melanie Klein (1948, 1952). In fact, she has developed the Kleinian aspects of Bowlby's thought on inner models in a way that appears to hold great promise, but she has not accounted for the ongoing relationship to the inner representation of the deceased in the model of grief she uses. She introduces the concept of identification but does not give a reason for rejecting it as useful in understanding normal bereavement, except to cite Bowlby's rejection of the idea (Raphael, 1983, pp.66–69). For Raphael, attachment is understood in terms of *inner images*:

> The past of the relationship experience and other related relationship experiences are stored as symbols, which may be conceptualized as the "inner image" that is held of the relationship at any one time. That image is composed of the present symbols and the many other symbols that can be called from the past memory stores. (1983, p. 6)

Raphael finds a movement in forming attachments from inner reality to a more reciprocal reality. For example, in the process of "falling in love," the other person at first seems "to fit in every way the subjects's inner image" (p. 9). Later, however, the bond "must be increasingly adapted to the real qualities and real interactions of the individuals in it" (p. 10).

It would seem that the movement from individual reality to reciprocal reality in bonding would be mirrored by a movement from reciprocal reality to individual reality in mourning. This would be identification in a positive sense, as Lopata (1979) depicts it in her idea of sanctification of the memory of the spouse. But Raphael does not draw this conclusion. Rather, mourning proceeds along the same path and in the same direction as bonding.

This work, the psychological mourning process, may be seen as a reversing or undoing of the various processes that have gone into building the relationship. . . . The bereaved's preoccupation with the deceased's image is no longer external, expecting and hoping for interaction with him, but internal, whereby the interactions of the past are reviewed and the emotion they carry relived. . . . In the earliest phases of his review the image and memories are often idealized, the deceased and the relationship remembered in perfection. Then, if mourning is progressing satisfactorily, more of the real memories, the positive and negative aspects representing ambivalences inevitable in human relationships are recalled. (Raphael, 1983, p. 44)

The action moves along the same path and in the same direction as in the bonding process because Raphael posits a return to the narcissistic inner image as a temporary compensation and refuge from reality when the external relationship is no longer available. She paraphrases Bowlby and Parkes in understanding the emergence of hallucinations and the idealization of the deceased as a compensatory reaction to loss.

Thus the bereaved may believe he hears the return at a familiar time, sees the face in a familiar place, feels the touch of a body, smells a familiar perfume, or hears a familiar sound. These perceptual misinterpretations reflect the intense longing and, like dreams are a source of a wish fulfillment. (Raphael, 1983, p. 40)

Because in these early stages of grief the inner image is functioning as a shield between the survivor and reality, the inner image cannot be interiorized as a way of enhancing the self. Raphael understands mourning as a coming to terms with reality, not as any essential change in the self.

We are left with some difficulty in understanding why Raphael should develop Bowlby's idea of interiorized images in the direction of Klein's view of object relations in the formation of the ego but not use those images in the ongoing reformation of the ego after loss. In Raphael's view, it seems to be only bond making, not bond breaking, that brings about essential changes in the self. All identificatory phenomena are, following Bowlby, assigned to pathology and the talk of inner images is dropped in favor of behavioral description. She says, "Eventually these behaviors become extinguished, and new attachment bonds are formed, or it may be that in some instances the relationship persists in altered form in fantasy" (Raphael, 1983, p. 69; also see pp. 103-104). Raphael also omits her concept of inner images in the completion of mourning, and instead she uses Parkes' concept of social identity.

The identity of the bereaved may have been defined by mutual roles, by the satisfaction of mutually gratifying interactions, or by the reinforcement of competence. The definition of self may rely strongly on the other so that when he is lost, the self must find a new identity without him. (p. 57)

The new identity without the deceased is found in new attachments, not in an integration of old ones. For Freud, mourning is freeing the ego from the lost object. His followers find the incorporation of lost objects in all mourning. Bowlby uses the continuing sense of presence to refute Freud's concept of mourning. Raphael thinks Freud got it right the first time.

The psychological mourning process involves the review of these and many other aspects of the lost relationship in order that the bonds binding the bereaved to the dead partner may gradually be relinquished, freeing the emotional investment for ongoing life and further relationships. . . . The process is inevitably painful, yet must progress. S. Freud (1917) describes this clearly in dynamic terms. (Raphael, 1983, p. 187)

There is an interaction noted by Raphael that seems to point to a more complex relationship between identification and mourning than she allows. She cites a study of parents of stillborn children. The pattern was for parents to examine their baby closely, often noting familial resemblances. It was the same process of identification that follows live births. It seemed that seeing the baby often enabled the parents to enact two processes necessary for grief: to incorporate the baby as a tangible love object, a part of themselves, as well as to separate from it (1983, p. 244). But Raphael does not follow the theoretical implications of this unique case where bonding and loss are coextensive.

William Worden

William Worden's *Grief Counseling and Grief Therapy* (1982) is an intervention program that grows out of the Bowlby model. He divides grief work and thus grief therapy into four tasks. His first three tasks are clearly within the ethological model: (1) To accept the reality of the loss is to fight denial by searching and not finding. (2) To experience the pain of grief is a kind of acceptance that the object is not there. (3) To adjust to the environment in which the deceased is missing is to learn new patterns of relationship.

Worden's last task shows most clearly the avoidance of any continuing relationship with the inner representation of the deceased as part of grief. The fourth task is to withdraw emotional energy and reinvest it in another relationship. The financial metaphor seems to imply that the individual has a given quantity of "emotional energy [which] can be invested in another relationship" (Worden, 1982, p. 15). For Worden the energy does not have its own quality. Like money, it only takes on the character of the investment in which it is put at a particular time. In his discussion of reinvestment, Worden cites the Harvard study of widows (Parkes, 1972) on remarriage, as if any marriage is an investment of emotional energy. That remarriage may be an investment of different energy or a different part of the self is not considered. Thus Worden cannot suggest an additional task of renegotiating the old relationship even as the self is entering into new relationships.

SOME ALTERNATIVE DEVELOPMENTS OF BOWLBY'S MODEL

We have seen that the model of grief that Bowlby developed based on his attachment theory does not easily account for the aspects of grief that come from the disequilibrium in the relationship between the bereaved and the lost object. We have seen that the problems of the model grow out of Bowlby's rejection of Freud's concept of identification and his refusal to admit into normal grief anything associated with the concept of identification. Yet it does not seem that to adopt the model of grief based only on identification would be any better. A critique of Volkan's model could be developed showing it as deficient in dealing with the disequilibrium in the bereaved's relationship to the social environment. In this book I have rejected Volkan's understanding of pathology as excessive introjection. And I have added solace as a positive aspect of the internalized lost object. What we need is a model of grief that can read attachment theory in a wider way, or that can expand the idea of the social self to be more inclusive of inner representations. Rubin (1984) has incorporated continuing memories into a Bowlby-like model, but he has not developed his idea. Three potential directions in which to develop Bowlby's model are outlined by examining three nonpsychoanalytic scholars who develop Bowlby's social self and attachment theory in three quite different ways. The point is that we have more options than the ones exercised by those who have heretofore adopted the Bowlby model.

Philosopher Thomas Attig (1982) substitutes a more interactive metaphor of the self:

> A delicately woven web, much like a spider's web, attached to its sur-roundings at points beyond counting. . . . Each radiating thread represents an attachment or involvement of the person in the world. . . . it would be best to imagine a wedge, or an array of radiating threads, as representing the multidimensional attachments with any single other person. (p. 63)

This metaphor of the self, he says, "captures the manner in which persons are who they are by virtue of the many threads of care and involvement. . . . [and] insists that personal relationships and attach-ments are not accidents of but rather essential components of per-sonal integrity" (p. 64).

With this metaphor, Attig says he can explain the symptoms of grief. Yearning and searching are "responses of the self to those loose ends of caring, dangling in the void where once there was a connec-tion" (Attig, 1982, p. 67). Disorientation, he says, is "distortion throughout the pattern of involvement in the world, and new ten-sions are added on lines of connection established to sustain pre-viously experienced demands" (pp. 67–68). The metaphor accounts for the great variation in the way grief is expressed and in the way grief is resolved, because "the process of reintegration is largely one of reweaving a pattern of caring and involvement in the world" and there are countless possible patterns that can emerge (p. 68). Presum-ably Attig would not object to the idea that the leftovers of the broken attachment could enhance the self as the reweaving of the web puts those elements in new relationships with other elements within the self.

Helena Znaniecka Lopata's (1973, 1979) study of widows in-corporates a good deal of identification in grief. As a sociologist, she is interested in the "social integration and support systems involving . . . the woman who has become a widow" (1979, p. 3). A support is for her "an action or object which the society generally defines as necessary or helpful in maintaining a style of life," and a support network is the "people with whom a person is involved in supportive interaction" (1979, p. 4). The stated model, thus, would seem to be focused on the disequilibrium in the relationship to the social en-vironment. But apparently the sociological concept of *support system* is elastic enough to move beyond the Bowlby model.

The concept of *emotional support* allows Lopata to ask about "re-lational sentiments" and "feeling states" (1979, pp. 85–86). She asks where in the network did the widow feel closeness, enjoyment, shared problems, comfort, important, angry, safe in crisis, respected, useful, independent, accepted, self-sufficient, and secure. Presumably the woman had felt those things primarily with her now-dead husband. She finds that widows tend to increase dramatically their reliance on their children. Yet, clearly there is not a simple replacement of one attachment with another, for she says:

> The present emotional support system is more dispersed, although children pretty much take over for the late husband. In the few cases of remarriage the current husband often plays a different role in the system than does the remembered late husband. (1979, p. 89)

A healthy ongoing presence of the deceased is central to Lopata's model. She develops the concept of *husband sanctification*, that is, the tendency of the widow to idealize her late husband. She says this is not a temporary phenonenon, a compensation for the loss, but rather it seems to be a permanent change for many of her subjects, even as they resolve the disequilibrium in the social environment.

> The sanctification process is an effective means by which the widow can continue her obligation to the husband to remember him, yet break her ties and re-create herself into a person without a partner. Over time, with the help of mourning rituals and associates, she purifies the husband of mortal jealousies and demands for continued attention. He becomes saintly, safely out of the way in daily life and noninterfering as she goes about rebuilding her support network. Sanctification moves the late husband into an other-worldly position as an understanding, but safely distant, observer. (1979, pp. 126–127)

Sanctification appears to be a return to the time when the inner image was more real than was social experience, that time Raphael finds early in bonding, but not at the end of mourning. In short, from a psychoanalytic point of view, sanctification is introjection. In Lopata, the widows' social self includes a reworked inner representation of her dead husband.

Bowlby occasionally cites sociologist Peter Marris's (1975) work with widows, but does not adopt the modification Marris made in the attachment theory. Marris' central concept of the self is a gestaltlike theory of attachment. In place of Bowlby's behavior and instinct, Marris has a self made up of "structures of meaning," which are "the organized structures of understanding and emotional attachments by which grown people interact and assimilate their environment" (p. 4). Different attachments participate in differing structures of meaning. The challenge bereavement presents to structures of meaning is to assimilate a reality that is essentially unassimilatable within the present structures. That is, if the relationship with the husband is the ground of the structure of meaning, then the death of the husband erradicates the very structure by which the reality should be assimiliated. The response to such an impasse, he says, is very much like Piagetian stage transition. The structure is reorganized at a more abstract level to accomodate the new reality (Marris, 1975, p. 11). Grief is the working out of the new structure of meaning. The resolution of grief is a compromise between two impulses, to return to the time before the death and to reach forward to time when the past is forgotten.

But grief is not an easy transition, for the nature of structures of meaning is that they are cumulative and they are founded in specific relationships and circumstances that may not be readily translated (Marris, 1975, p. 13). Our ability to live effectively in the changed environment relies on conserving fundamental structure of meaning. In resolution of grief, the viability of the new structure is dependent on whether we can abstract the principles from the relationship to apply in other contexts (pp. 19–20). Thus attachments of the new structure of meaning are continuous with attachments of the former structure of meaning.

The sense of continuity allows us to see the identification in Marris' work. He says that "the sense of continuity [can] only be restored by detaching familiar meanings of life from the relationship in which they are embodied, and reestablishing them independently of it" (1975, p. 37). That reestablishment is a gradual integration of the old structure into the new self.

> At first, a widow cannot separate her purposes and understanding from the husband who figured so centrally in them: she has to revive the relationship, to continue it by symbols and make-believe, in order to feel alive. But as time goes by, she begins to reformulate life in terms which assimilate the fact of his death. She makes a gradual transition from talking to him 'as if he were sitting in the chair beside me', to thinking what he would have said and done, and from there to planning her own and her children's future in terms of what he would have wished. Until finally the wishes become her own, and she no longer consciously refers them to him. (Marris, 1975, pp. 37–38)

Grief is thus resolved for Marris in the process that Freud called identification, for it is "mastered, not by ceasing to care for the dead, but by abstracting what is fundamentally important in the relationship and rehabilitating it" (Marris, 1975, p.30).

CONCLUSION

John Bowlby's work is the foundation of a great deal of what we know about grief. His model of grief is based on an instinctual response in the paradigmatic human experience of the child separated from the mother. That model does not account for phenomena in grief that are associated with the disequilibrium bereavement brings in the relationship between the bereaved and the lost object. That disequilibrium is accounted for in psychoanalytic grief theory by identification. This shortcoming can be traced to Bowlby's rejection of Freud's use of identification in the metapsychology. Bowlby rejected the metapsychology and thereafter guarded against any element that might bring any of the metapsychology back. That guarding, as I have tried to show, creates many inconsistencies in the work of those who use the Bowlby model.

In the study of grief resolution in bereaved parents, however, data on internalizing the dead child are too central to work within the Bowlby model. The centrality of the amputation metaphor in parents' descriptions of their grief and the central role the internalized dead child plays in their ongoing life after the resolution of bereavement shows that there is more to the resolution of parental bereavement than adjusting to a changed social environment. For this reason, I have written in Chapter 3 that gaining solace by internalizing the dead child is of equal importance to the resolution Bowlby has outlined. It may be that the detailed study of bereaved parents will lead to a larger examination of the models we have of grief. That project, however, would call for a book of its own and move us afield from the unique grief that is experienced at the death of a child.

References

Abraham, K. (1927). A short study of the development of the libido, viewed in the light of mental disorders (pp. 248–279). In D. Brian & A. Strachey (Eds.), *Selected Papers*. London: Hogarth Press.

Ainsworth, M.D.S., & Bell, S.M. (1970). Attachment, exploration and separation: Illustrated by the behavior of one-year-olds in a strange situation. *Child Development, 41*, 49–67.

Alexy, W.D. (1982). Dimensions of psychological counseling that facilitate the grieving process of bereaved parents. *Journal of Counseling Psychology, 29*, 498–507.

Anisfeld, E., & Lipper, E. (1983). Early contact, social support, and mother–infant bonding. *Pediatrics, 72*(1), 79–83.

Antze, P. (1979). Role of ideologies in peer psychotherapy groups. In M. A. Lieberman & L. D. Borman (Eds.), *Self-help groups for coping with crisis: Origins, members, processes, and impact*. San Francisco: Jossey-Bass.

Arling, G. (1976). The elderly widow and her family, neighbors and friends. *Journal of Marriage and the Family, 38*(4), 757–767.

Attig, T. (1982). Grief and personal integrity. In Richard A. Pacholski & Charles A. Corr (Eds.), *Priorities in death education and counseling* (pp. 61–70). Arlington, VA: Forum for Death Education and Counseling.

Becker, H.S. (1970). *Sociological work: Method and substance*. Chicago: Aldine.

Benedek, T. (1959). Parenthood as a developmental phase. *American Psychoanalytic Association Journal, 7*, 389–417.

Benedek, T. (1970). The family as a psychologic field. In E. J. Anthony & T. Benedek (Eds.), *Parenthood: Its psychology and psychopathology*. Boston: Little, Brown.

Benedek, T. (1975). Discussion of parenthood as a developmental phase. *Journal of the American Psychoanalytic Association. 23*, 154–165.

Berger, P.L., & Luckman, T.L. (1966). *The social construction of reality: A treatise in the sociology of knowledge*. Garden City, NY: Doubleday.

Bollas, C. (1978). The transformational object. *International Journal of Psychoanalysis, 60*, 97–107.

Borkman, T. (1976). Experiential knowledge: A new concept for the analysis of self-help groups. *Social Service Review, 50*(3), 445–456.

Bourne, S. (1968). The psychological effects of stillbirth on women and their doctors. *Journal of the Royal College of General Practice, 16,* 103–112.

Bowers, F. (1940). *Elizabethan revenge tragedy, 1587–1642.* Princeton, NJ: Princeton University Press.

Bowlby, J. (1961). Processes of mourning. *International Journal of Psychoanalysis, 42,* 317–340.

Bowlby, J. (1969-1980). *Attachment and Loss Vols. 1–3: Attachment,* Vol. 1, 1969; *Separation: Anxiety and anger,* Vol. 2, 1973; *Loss: Sadness and depression,* Vol 3, 1980. New York: Basic Books.

Bowlby, J. (1979). Psychoanalysis as art and science. *International Review of Psychoanalysis, 6*(3), 3–14.

Bowlby, J. (1981a). Perspective. *Bulletin of the Royal College of Psychiatry, 5,* 2–4.

Bowlby, J. (1981b). Psychoanalysis as a natural science. *International Review of Psychoanalysis, 8*(2), 243–256.

Bowlby, J. (1982). Attachment and loss: Retrospect and prospect. *American Journal of Orthopsychiatry, 52*(4), 664–678.

Bowling, A., & Cartwright, A. (1982). *Life after death: A study of the elderly widowed.* London: Tavistock.

Bugan, L. (1979). Human grief: A model for prediction and intervention. In L. Bugan (Ed.), *Death and dying: Theory, research, and practice.* Dubuque, IA: William C. Brown.

Cain, A.C., & Cain, B.S. (1964). On replacing a child. *Journal of the American Academy of Child Psychiatry, 3,* 443–456.

Cantor, R.J. (1978). *And a time to live.* New York: Harper & Row.

Carr, D., & Knupp, S.F. (1985). Grief and perinatal loss. *Journal of Obstetric, Gynecologic, and Neonatal Nursing, 14*(2), 130–139.

Cary, R.G. (1979–1980). Weathering widowhood; Problems and adjustment of the widowed during the first year. *Omega, Journal of Death and Dying, 10*(2), 163–174.

Chess, S., & Thomas, A. (1982). Infant bonding: Mystique and reality. *American Journal of Orthopsychiatry, 52*(2), 213–222.

Clayton, P. J., Desmarais, L., & Winokur, G. (1968). A study of normal bereavement. *American Journal of Psychiatry, 125,* 168–178.

The Compassionate Friends. (1983). *Grieving, healing, growing.* Oak Brook, IL: Author.

Cook, J.A. (1983a). A death in the family: Parental bereavement in the first year. *Suicide and Life-Threatening Behavior, 13*(1), 43–61.

Cook, J.A., (1983b). If I should die before I wake: Religious commitment and adjustment to the death of a child. *Journal for the Scientific Study of Religion, 22*(3), 222–238.

Danto, B. L. (1982). Survivors of homicide. In B. L. Danto, J. Bruhns, & A. H. Kutscher (Eds.), *The human side of homicide.* New York: Columbia University Press.

Demi, A.S., & Miles, M.S. (1987). Parameters of normal grief: A delphi study. *Death Studies, 11*(6), 397–412.

deMause, L. (1974). The evolution of childhood. *History of Childhood Quarterly, 1*(4), 504–575.

Dickoff, H., & Lakin, M. (1963). Patients' views of group psychotherapy: Retrospections and interpretations. *International Journal of Group Psychotherapy, 13*, 61–73.

Edelstein, L. (1984). *Maternal bereavement: Coping with the unexpected death of a child.* New York: Praeger.

Eigen, M. (1981). The area of faith in Winnicott, Lacan, and Bion. *International Journal of Psychoanalysis, 62*, 413–433.

Elson, M. (1984). Parenthood and the transformations of narcissism. In R. S. Cohen, B. J. Cohler, & S. H. Weissman (Eds.), *Parenthood: A psychodynamic perspective* (pp. 297–314). New York: Guilford.

Erikson, E. (1964). *Insight and responsibility.* New York: Norton.

Fairbairn, W.D. (1952). *An object-relations theory of the personality.* New York: Basic Books.

Fenichel, O. (1945). *The psychoanaltyic theory of neurosis.* New York: Norton.

Feigenberg, L. (1980). *Terminal care: Friendship contracts with dying cancer patients* (P. Hort, Trans.). New York: Brunner/Mazel.

Fish, W.C. (1986). Differences of grief intensity in bereaved parents. In T.S. Rando (Ed.), *Parental loss of a child* (pp. 415–428). Champaign, IL: Research Press.

Forrest, G.C., Standish, E., & Baum, J.D. (1982). Support after perinatal death: A study of support and counseling after perinatal bereavement. *British Medical Journal, 285*, 1475–1479.

Frank, L. (1961). *Persuasion and healing.* New York: Schocken.

Freud, S. (1960). Group psychology and the analysis of the ego. In J. Strachey (Ed. and Trans.), *The standard edition of the complete psychological works of Sigmund Freud* (Vol. 18, pp. 69–143). London: Hogarth Press. (Original work published 1923)

Freud, S. (1961a). The ego and the id. In J. Strachey (Ed. and Trans.), *The standard edition of the complete psychological works of Sigmund Freud* (Vol. 19, pp. 12–66). London: Hogarth Press. (Original work published 1923)

Freud, S. (1961b). New introductory lectures. In J. Strachey (Ed. and Trans.), *The standard edition of the complete psychological works of Sigmund Freud* (Vol. 22, pp. 5–182). London: Hogarth Press. (Original work published 1933)

Freud, S. (1961c). Mourning and melancholia. In J. Strachey (Ed. and Trans.), *The standard edition of the complete psychological works of Sigmund Freud* (Vol. 14, pp. 243–258). London: Hogarth Press. (Original work published 1923)

Fulmer, R.H. (1983). A structural approach to unresolved mourning in single parent family systems. *Journal of Marital and Family Therapy, 9*(3), 259–269.

Gartner, A., & Riessman, F. (1977). *Self-help in human services.* San Francisco: Jossey-Bass.

Gates of prayer: The new union prayer book. (1975). New York: Central Conference of American Rabbis; London: Union of Liberal and Progressive Synagogues.

Gay, V.P. (1983). Winnicott's contribution to religious studies: The resurrection of the cultural hero. *Journal of the American Academy of Religion, 51*(3), 371–395.

Geertz, C. (1973). *The interpretation of cultures.* New York: Basic Books.

Glaser, B.G., & Strauss, A.L. (1965). *Awareness of dying.* Chicago: Aldine.

Glaser, B.G., & Strauss, A.L. (1967). *The discovery of grounded theory: Strategies for qualitative research.* Chicago: Aldine.

Glick, I.O., Weiss, R.S., & Parkes, C.M. (1974). *The first year of bereavement.* New York: Wiley.

Goldberg, S. (1979). Premature birth: Consequences in the parent–infant relationship. *American Scientist, 67*(2), 214–220.

Gordon, A.K., & Klass, D. (1979). *They need to know: How to teach children about death.* Englewood Cliffs, NJ: Prentice Hall.

Harlow, H. F., & Harlow, M. K. (1963). A study of animal affection. In C. H. Southwick (Ed.), *Primate social behavior: An enduring problem: Selected readings* (pp. 174–184). Princeton, NJ: Van Nostrand.

Herz, F. (1980). The impact of death and serious illness on the family life cycles. In E. A. Carter & M. McGoldrick (Eds.), *The family life cycle: A framework for family therapy* (pp. 223–240). New York: Gardner.

Hoeppner, M., & Klass, D. (1982). Factors in affiliation with a self-help group for bereaved parents. In R. Pacholski & C. A. Corr (Eds.), *Priorities in death education and counseling* (pp. 131–138). Arlington VA: Forum for Death Education and Counseling.

Hofer, M. A. (1984). Relationships as regulators: A psychobiologic perspective on bereavement. *Psychosomatic Medicine, 46,* 183–197.

Hood, R. (1977). Eliciting mystical states of consciousness in semistructured nature experiences. *Journal for the Scientific Study of Religion, 16*(2), 155–163.

Horton, P. C. (1981). *Solace, the missing dimension in psychiatry.* Chicago: University of Chicago Press.

Hrdy, S. B. (1981). *The woman that never evolved.* Cambridge: Harvard University Press.

Jacoby, S. (1983). *Wild justice, the evolution of revenge.* New York: Harper & Row.

Johnson, S. (1984). Sexual intimacy and replacement children after the death of a child. *Omega, Journal of Death and Dying, 15*(2), 109–118.

Jones, E. (1957). *The life and work of Sigmund Freud.* New York: Basic Books, 1957.

Kahn, A. S. (Ed.). (1984). *Victims of crime and violence* (final report). American Psychological Association Task Force on the Victims of Crime and Violence.

Kaplan, D. M., Grobstein, R., & Smith, A. (1976). Predicting the impact of severe illness in families. *Health and Social Work, 1*(3), 71–82.

Katz, A.H. (1970). Self-help organization and volunteer participation in social welfare. *Social Work, 15*(1), 51–60.

Kernberg, O. F. (1976). *Object-relations theory and clinical psychoanalysis.* New York: Aronson.

Kierkegaard, S. (1938). *The journals of Soren Kierkegaard* (A. Dru, Ed. and Trans.). London: Oxford University Press.

Kirkley-Best, E., & Kellner K. R. (1982). The forgotten grief: A review of the psychology of stillbirth. *American Journal of Orthopsychiatry, 52*(3), 420–429.

Klass, D. (1982). Self-help groups for the bereaved: Theory, theology and practice. *Journal of Religion and Health, 21*(4), 307–324.

Klass, D. (1984). Bereaved parents and The Compassionate Friends: Affiliation and healing. *Omega, Journal of Death and Dying, 15*(4), 353–373.

Klass, D. (1985). Self-help groups: Grieving parents and community resources. In C. A. Corr & D. M. Corr (Eds.), *Hospice approaches to pediatric care* (pp. 241–260). New York: Springer Publishing Company.

Klass, D. (1987). John Bowlby's model of grief and the problem of identification. *Omega, Journal of Death and Dying, 18*(1), 13–32.

Klass, D., & Gordon, A. (1978). Varieties of transcending experience at death: A videotape based study. *Omega, Journal of Death and Dying, 9*(1), 19–36.

Klass, D., & Shinners, B. (1983). Professional roles in a self-help group for the bereaved. *Omega, Journal of Death and Dying, 13*(4), 361–374.

Klein, M. (1948). Mourning and its relation to manic-depressive states. In *Contributions to Psycho-Analysis, 1921–1945* (pp. 311–338). London: Hogarth Press. (Originally published 1940)

Klein, M. (1952). Discussion of the mutual influences in the development of ego and id. *Psychoanalytic Study of the Child, 7*, 51–53.

Knapp, R. (1986). *Beyond endurance: When a child dies.* New York: Schocken.

Kowalski, K.E.M. (1984). *Perinatal death: An ethnomethodological study of factors influencing parental bereavement.* Unpublished doctoral dissertation, University of Colorado at Boulder.

Krell, R., & Rabkin, L. (1979). The effects of sibling death on the surviving child: A family perspective. *Family Process, 18*, 471–477.

Kuhn, T. (1970). *The structure of scientific revolution.* Chicago: University of Chicago Press.

Kushner, H. (1981). *When bad things happen to good people.* New York: Schocken.

Laing, R.D., Phillipson, H., & Lee, A.R. (1966). *Interpersonal perception, a theory and a method of research.* New York: Harper & Row.

Legg, C., & Sherick, I. (1976). The replacement child—A developmental tragedy: Some preliminary comments. *Child Psychiatry and Human Development, 70*, 113–126.

Lehman, R.L., Ellard, J.H., & Wortman, B.W. (1986). Social support for the bereaved: Recipients' and providers' perspectives on what is helpful. *Journal of Consulting and Clinical Psychology, 54*(4), 438–446.

Lieberman, M., & Borman, L. (1979). *Self-help groups for coping with crisis.* San Francisco: Jossey-Bass.

Lindemann, E. (1979). Symptomatology and management of acute grief. In E. Lindemann & E. Lindemann (Eds.), *Beyond grief: Studies in crisis intervention.* New York: Aronson.

Lindemann, E., & Cobb, S. (1979). Neuropsychiatric observations after the Coconut Grove fire. In E. Lindemann & E. Lindemann (Eds.), *Beyond grief: Studies in crisis intervention*. New York: Aronson.

Lopata, H. Z. (1973). *Widowhood in an American city*. Cambridge, MA: Schenkman.

Lopata, H. Z. (1979). *Women as widows, support systems*. New York: Elsevier.

Lorenz, K. (1966). *On aggression*. New York: Harcourt, Brace, & World.

Maddison, D., & Walker, W. L. (1967). Factors affecting the outcome of conjugal bereavement. *British Journal of Psychiatry, 113*, 1057–1067.

Main, M., & Weston, D. R. (1981). The quality of the toddler's relationship to mother and to father: Related to conflict behavior and readiness to establish new relationships. *Child Development, 52*(3), 932–940.

Mannheim, K. (1936). *Ideology and utopia, an introduction to the sociology of knowledge*. New York: Harcourt, Brace & World.

Marris, P. (1975). *Loss and change*. Garden City, NY: Anchor.

Masson, J. M. (1985). *The assault on truth: Freud's suppression of the seduction theory*. New York: Penguin.

Mawson, D., Marks, I. M., Ramm, L., & Stern, R. S. (1981). Guided mourning for morbid grief: A controlled study. *British Journal of Psychiatry, 138*, 185–193.

Melges, F. T., & DeMaso, D. R. (1980). Grief-resolution therapy: Reliving, revising, and revisiting. *American Journal of Psychotherapy, 34*, 51–61.

Miles, M. S. (1985). Emotional symptoms and physical health in bereaved parents. *Nursing Research, 34*(2), 76–81.

Miles, M. S., & Demi, A. S. (1986). Guilt in bereaved parents. In T.S. Rando (Ed.), *Parental loss of a child* (pp. 97–118). Champaign, IL: Research Press.

Miller, A. (1981). *The drama of the gifted child* (R. Ward, Trans.). New York: Basic Books.

Miller, A. (1983). *For your own good: Hidden cruelty in child-rearing and the roots of violence* (Hildegarde Hannum & Hunter Hannum, Trans.). New York: Farrar, Straus, & Giroux.

Miller, A. A., Pollock, G. A., & Bernstein, H. E. (1968). An approach to the concept of identification. *Bulletin of the Menninger Clinic, 32*(4), 239–252.

Moss, M. S., & Moss, S. Z. (1984). Some aspects of the elderly widow(er)'s persistent tie with the deceased spouse. *Omega, Journal of Death and Dying, 15*(3), 195–206.

Mulhern, R. K., Lauer, M. E., & Hoffmann, R. G. (1983). Death of a child at home or in the hospital: Subsequent psychological adjustment of the family. *Pediatrics, 71*(5), 743–747.

Nietzsche, F. (1967). *On the genealogy of morals* (Walter Kaufmann, Trans.). New York: Vintage.

Orbach, C. E. (1959). The multiple meanings of the loss of a child. *American Journal of Psychotherapy, 13*, 906–915.

Osterweis, M., Solomon, F., & Green, M. (Eds.). (1984). *Bereavement: Reactions, consequences, and care*. Washington, DC: National Academy Press.

Owen, G., Fulton, R., & Markusen, E. (1982–1983). Death at a distance: A study of family survivors. *Omega, Journal of Death and Dying,* 13(3), 191–225.

Parkes, C. M. (1972). *Bereavement: Studies of grief in adult life.* New York: International Universities Press.

Parkes, C. M. (1975a). Determinants of outcome following bereavement. *Omega, Journal of Death and Dying,* 6(4), 303–323.

Parkes, C. M. (1975b). Psycho-social transitions: Comparison between reactions to loss of a limb and loss of a spouse. *British Journal of Psychiatry,* 127, 204–210.

Parkes, C. M., & Brown, R. J. (1972). Health after bereavement: A controlled study of young Boston widows and widowers. *Psychosomatic Medicine,* 34(5), 449–461.

Parkes, C. M. & Weiss, R. (1983). *Recovery from bereavement.* New York: Basic Books.

Passman, R. H. (1976). Arousal reducing properties of attachment objects: Testing the functional limits of the security blanket relative to the mother. *Developmental Psychology,* 12, 468–469.

Passman, R. H., & Weisberg, P. (1975). Mothers and blankets as agents for promoting play and exploration by young children in a novel environment: The effects of social and nonsocial attachment objects. *Developmental Psychology,* 11, 170–177.

Peppers, L. G., & Knapp, R. J. (1980). *Motherhood and mourning.* New York: Praeger.

Piaget, J. (1965). *The moral judgment of the child.* New York: Free Press.

Powdermaker, H. (1966). *Stranger and friend: The way of an anthropologist.* New York: Norton.

Powell, T. J. (1975). The use of self-help groups as supportive reference communities. *American Journal of Orthopsychiatry,* 45, 756–764.

Poznanski, E. O. (1972). The 'replacement child': A saga of unresolved parental grief. *Journal of Pediatrics,* 81(6), 1190–1193.

President's Task Force on Victims of Crime (Final Report). (1982, December).

Rando, T. S. (Ed.). (1986). *Parental loss of a child.* Champaign, IL: Research Press.

Raphael, B. (1983). *The anatomy of bereavement.* New York: Basic Books.

Rieff, P. (1959). *Freud: The mind of the moralist.* New York: Viking.

Rosenblum, L. A. (1984). Monkey's responses to separation and loss. In M. Osterweis, F. Solomon, & M. Green (Eds.), *Bereavement: Reactions, consequences, and care* (pp. 179–196). Washington, DC: National Academy Press.

Rosenblum, L. A., & Alpert, S. (1974). Fear of strangers and the specificity of attachment in monkeys. In M. Lewis & L. A. Rosenblum (Eds.), *The origins of fear.* New York: Wiley.

Rosenblum, L. A., & Kaufman, I. C. (1968). Variations in infant development and response to maternal loss in monkeys. *American Journal of Orthopsychiatry,* 38(3), 418–426.

Rubin, S. S. (1984). Maternal attachment and child death: On adjustment, relationship, and resolution. *Omega, Journal of Death and Dying*, 15(4), 347–352.

Rutter, M. (1981). *Maternal deprivation reassessed*. Middlesex, England: Penguin.

Sanders, C. M. (1980). A comparison of adult bereavement in the death of a spouse, child, and parent. *Omega, Journal of Death and Dying*, 10(3), 303–322.

Sanders, C. M. (1980–1981). Comparison of younger and older spouses in bereavement outcome. *Omega, Journal of Death and Dying*, 11(3), 271–273.

Schafer, R. (1968). *Aspects of internalization*. New York: International Universities Press.

Schafer, R. (1976). *A new language for psychoanalysis*. New Haven: Yale University Press.

Schiff, H. (1977). *The bereaved parent*. New York: Crown.

Schreimer, R. L., Gresham, E. L., & Green, M. (1979). Physician's responsibility to parents after the death of an infant: Beneficial outcome of a telephone call. *American Journal of Diseases of Children*, 133(7), 723–726.

Schwartz, M. (1975). Situation/transition groups: A conceptualization and review. *American Journal of Orthopsychiatry*, 45, 744–755.

Shanfield, S. G., Benjamin, G. A., & Swain, B. J. (1984). Parent's reactions to the death of an adult child from cancer. *American Journal of Psychiatry*, 141(9), 1092–1094.

Shanfield, S. B., & Swain, B. J. (1984). Death of adult children in traffic accidents. *Journal of Nervous and Mental Disease*, 72(9), 533–538.

Silverman, P. R. (1986). *Widow-to-widow*. New York: Springer Publishing Company.

Spinetta, J. J., & Ringler, D. (1982). The child-abusing parent: A psychological review. In G. J. Williams & J. Money (Eds.), *Traumatic abuse and neglect of children at home*. Baltimore: Johns Hopkins University Press.

Spinetta, J. J., Swarner, J. A., & Sheposh, J. P. (1981). Effective parent coping following the death of a child from cancer. *Journal of Pediatric Psychology*, 6(3), 251–263.

Stayton, D. J., & Ainsworth, M. D. S. (1973). Individual differences in infant responses to brief, everyday separation as related to other infant and maternal behavior. *Developmental Psychology*, 9(2), 226–235.

Steele, B. (1980). Psychodynamic factors in child abuse. In C. H. Kempe & R. E. Helfer (Eds.), *The battered child* (3rd ed.). Chicago: University of Chicago Press.

Strauss, A. (1975). *Chronic illness and the quality of life*. St. Louis: Mosby.

Tillich, P. (1967). *Systematic theology*. Chicago: University of Chicago Press.

Turner, R. H. (1970). *Family interaction*. New York: Wiley.

Vachon, M. L. S., Sheldon, A. R., Lancee, W. J., Lyall, W. A. L., Rogers, J., & Freeman, S. J. J. (1982). Correlates of enduring distress patterns following bereavement: Social network, life situation and personality. *Psychological Medicine*, 12, 783–788.

van der Avort, A., & van Harberden, P. (1985). Helping self-help groups: A developing theory. *Psychotherapy*, 22, 269–272.

van Lawick-Goodall, J. (1971). *In the shadow of man*. Boston: Houghton Mifflin.

Videka-Sherman, L. (1982). Coping with the death of a child: A study over time. *American Journal of Orthopsychiatry, 52*(4), 688–698.

Vitano, A. (1972). Power to the people: Self-help groups. *Social Work, 17*(1), 7–15.

Volkan, V. (1971). A study of a patient's "re-grief work" through dreams, psychological tests and psychoanalysis. *Psychiatric Quarterly, 45,* 225–273.

Volkan, V. (1981). *Linking objects and linking phenomena: A study of the forms, symptoms, metapsychology, and therapy of complicated mourning*. New York: International Universities Press.

Volkan, V., & Showalter, C. (1968). Known object loss, disturbance in reality testing, and "re-grief" work as a method of brief psychotherapy. *Psychiatric Quarterly, 42,* 358–374.

Wax, R. (1971). *Doing fieldwork: Warnings and advice*. Chicago: University of Chicago Press.

Weizman, S. G., & Kamm, P. (1985). *About mourning: Support and guidance for the bereaved*. New York: Human Sciences Press.

Whyte, W. F. (1973). *Street corner society: The structure of an Italian slum*. Chicago: University of Chicago Press.

Winnicott, D. W. (1953). Transitional objects and transitional phenomena. *International Journal of Psychoanalysis, 34,* 89–97.

Winnicott, D. W. (1971). *Playing and reality*. New York: Basic Books.

Worden, J. W. (1982). *Grief counseling and grief therapy: A handbook for the mental health practitioner*. New York: Springer Publishing Company.

Yalom, Y. D. (1975). *The theory and practice of group psychotherapy* (2nd ed.). New York: Basic Books.

Index